The Wall

Fragmenting the Palestinian

Fabric in Jerusalem

Robert D. Brooks, Editor

Contributors:

Rami Nasrallah	Rassem Khamaisi
Robert Brooks	Abdalla Owais
Sari Hanafi	Michael Younan
Shahd Wa'ary	Amer Hidmi

A Publication of the International Peace and Cooperation Center
Jerusalem

International Peace and Cooperation Center: Publication XIV

Language Editing: Robert Brooks

Proof Reading: Joan Williams

Preparation for the Print: Shahd Wa'ary

Photos: Ammar Awad, Shahd Wa'ary, Abdalla Owais

Layout: Rania Mufarreh

Cover Design: George Kajjo

Printed and Bound in Jerusalem by: The Golden Press

ISBN 965-7283-11-6

First Edition, 2007

The International Peace and Cooperation Center
21 Sheikh Jarrah, Ard Assamaar, 'Issawiya Road, Jerusalem
P.O. Box: 24162

E-mail address: info@ipcc-jerusalem.org
Website: www.ipcc-jerusalem.org

Tel: + 972 (0) 2 5811992 or + 972 (0)2 5812032
Fax: + 972 (0) 2 5400522

Table of Contents

Page

Acknowledgements 5

Forward 6

Maps   1: The Israeli Separation Wall/ Barrier in the West Bank 9
           2: The Separation Wall in the Jerusalem Area 10
           3: The Wall Enclaves in the Jerusalem Area 11
           4: Settlement Annexation (Greater Jerusalem) 12

Chapter One   *Rami Nasrallah*

               The Jerusalem Separation Wall: Facts
               and Political Implications 13

Chapter Two   *Robert D. Brooks, Ph. D.*

               The Wall and the Economy of the
               Jerusalem Governorate 27

Chapter Three *Rassem Khamaisi, Ph. D.*

               Truncating the Right to the City 55

Chapter Four   *Abdalla Owais, Ph. D.*

               The Wall and the Enclaves: Case Studies
               in Disrupted Communities 75

Chapter Five   *Robert D. Brooks,   Rassem Khamaisi,*
               Sari Hanafi, Amer Hidmi,   and Shahd Wa'ary

               IPCC Survey of Jerusalemite Perceptions
               of the Impact of the Wall on Everyday Life 137

Chapter Six   *Rami Nasrallah*

               A Map of Palestinian Interests 151

List of Tables

                                                                                              Page

Table II: 1   Distribution of the Jerusalem Municipal Budget (NIS) 2003 32
Table II: 2   Selected Infrastructure Investments 32
Table II: 3   The Infrastructure Gap 33
Table II: 4   Percentage of Governorate Households Perceiving Difficulties from
              Impact of the Wall, 2005 34
Table II: 5   Annual GDP-pc, GNDI-pc and GNI-pc (2002) 37
Table II: 6   Sources of Personal Income: April-June 2005 38
Table II: 7   Selected Standard of Living Measures (2004) 38
Table II: 8   Governorate Employment, and Distribution of Work Force by Sectors
              (%) 2005 39
Table II: 9   Employment, Unemployment, Earnings, Spending, and Poverty Levels 40
Table II: 10 Hotel Activity in the Governorate for the Years 2000 and 2005 46
Table IV: 1   Transportation Costs between Ar Ram and Neighboring Areas 87
Table IV: 2   Schools and Enrollments in Ar Ram/Dahiyat Al Bareed 87
Table IV: 3   Medical Facilities in the Ar Ram Enclave 89
Table IV: 4   Area and Estimated Population of the Shu'fat Section of the Enclave 93
Table IV: 5   Social Centers Operating in Shu'fat Refugee Camp 94
Table IV: 6   Schools, Pupils and Teachers in Shu'fat Refugee Camp, Ras Khamis and
              Ras Shehadeh 96
Table IV: 7   Transportation Costs in Shu'fat Refugee Camp, Ras Khamis and Ras
              Shehadeh Prior to and After the Wall 97
Table IV: 8   Settlements Established on Anata Lands 99
Table IV: 9   Enterprises Damaged in Anata and Dahiyat As Salam 102
Table IV: 10 Schools, Pupils and Teachers in Anata 104
Table IV: 11 Transportation Costs in Anata before and after the Wall 106
Table IV: 12 Abu Dis Schools 111
Table IV: 13 Transportation Costs in Abu Dis 113
Table IV: 14 Al Eizariya Schools 117
Table IV: 15 Transportation Costs in Al Eizariya 118
Table IV: 16 As Sawahira Ash Sharqiya Schools 121
Table IV: 17 Transportation Costs before and after Construction of the Wall 122
Table IV: 18 Schools and Teachers in Bir Nabala, Al Jib, Al Judeira and Beit Hanina Al Balad 124
Table IV: 19 Governmental and Public Schools in Bir Nabala 126
Table IV: 20 Transportation Costs from Bir Nabala prior to and after Construction of
              the Wall 128
Table IV: 21 Transportation Costs in Al Judeira 129
Table IV: 22 Al Jib Schools 132
Table IV: 23 Transportation Costs in Al Jib 133
Table IV: 24 Selected Transportation Costs from Beit Hanina Al Balad 135
Table IV: 25 Beit Hanina Al Balad Schools 136

Acknowledgements

The International Peace and Cooperation Center (IPCC) gratefully acknowledges the generous support the Friedrich Ebert Stiftung (FES) Germany has provided for the research and publication of this book, IPCC's second work on the Israeli barrier wall around Jerusalem. FES has steadfastly supported IPCC's publications on Jerusalem, of which this book is the 14th volume.

Through its support FES has significantly aided IPCC to fulfill its mission as a center that focuses on Jerusalem issues that relate to the city's problems, its future as the capital of the Palestinian culture, and as a city that in many ways is the kernel of the Middle East crisis.

We would especially like to thank Mr. Knut Dethlefsen, the FES Resident Representative in East Jerusalem.

Forward

This study of the Israeli separation wall in and around Jerusalem is the 13th volume in IPCC's Jerusalem Strategic Planning Series. The overarching goals of the series is to provide an expert factual data base about conditions in the city, to offer analyses of the urban, political, economic, geographic and social issues which emerge from the data, to provide a statistic and analytical backdrop for those who will have the task of resolving the issues, and to offer concepts about the image and future of the city.

In a previous IPCC study on the wall in the Jerusalem area, we noted with obvious disappointment that "…the world watches as Israel builds a 600 kilometer barrier." Best estimates now place the projected length of the wall at over 700 kilometers and our despair only grows. Events in Palestine and Israel—the Israeli withdrawal from Gaza, Olmert's controversial "convergence/realignment plan" now proffered, now withdrawn, the surprise election victory of Hamas, a siege of Gaza, and the Israeli/Lebanese war—have all combined to distract the international community's attention. But construction of the wall, most especially the Jerusalem segments, has continued. And the effects that were predicted or documented in the earlier study have, by and large, materialized or worsened.

It was hoped, perhaps naively, that the advisory opinion of the International Court of Justice—the UN's highest judicial body—would impact on international opinion, even if the United States chose to ignore it. The court held, in a 14-1 decision, inter alia, that:

1. The wall is being built on occupied territory and is therefore a violation of international law.

2. The wall construction should cease and it and the legal, administrative and military regime that supports it, should be dismantled.

3. Reparations should be paid to those who have suffered damages.

The UN General Assembly voted overwhelmingly to accept the advisory. But the effect of the ICJ's opinion has since withered on the vine. Only legal scholars now discuss it. It has virtually disappeared from political discourse.

Clearly, however, the wall has not disappeared. The finished Jerusalem sections have increased by 50% since our first report on its progress. And in the Jerusalem area it is no mere "barrier." It is an ugly 10-meter concrete scar that follows a political path through Jerusalem and its suburbs, a route that has less to do with security than it has with incorporating outlying Israeli settlements into West Jerusalem and expanding Israel's area of control. And while ethnic separation is one of its goals, it seems to have less to do with separating Israelis from Palestinians than with separating Palestinians from Palestinians. In the process of unifying the Israelis the wall fragments the Palestinians.

The content of this second IPCC treatment of the wall is almost entirely new, presenting updated data or data not previously available and analyses from new perspectives. Of the many books that are available on the wall, we believe that this study is the only one that not merely gives the facts but also offers arguments and discussions on the wall's immediate effects and long term consequences. Further, we believe the study is unique in that it reveals the dynamics of the Palestinian Jerusalem area: at the micro level, how the city works with respect to the movement of people, standards of living, access to services, interactions between communities, and within family structures; and at the macro level, East Jerusalem's connections with its hinterland and the Occupied Palestinian Territories, including its historical role as the heart of the Palestinian culture. Much of the discussion takes place in the context of a local, national, and international *Right to the City*.

In Chapter One, Rami Nasrallah establishes the basic facts concerning the wall and examines in depth the political consequences of the barrier for the Palestinians, the Israelis, and the region. His review of the wall places it in the context of a separatist campaign that confiscates vast land areas and fragments the Palestinian society. He warns that the wall seriously marginalizes East Jerusalem and limits the city's capacity to fulfill its historical role as the heart city of the Palestinian culture. Mr. Nasrallah is the author, co-author, or editor of over a dozen books on Jerusalem and other divided cities. He has given invited lectures at American, British, and Canadian universities and is a research associate at the University of Cambridge. He is the Head, International Peace and Cooperation Center (IPCC) in Jerusalem.

In Chapter Two, Robert Brooks examines the economic fallout of the wall. His analysis places the wall in the context of a long term effort of Israel to control, subordinate, and ultimately separate from the Palestinian economy. Treatment of this topic has been significantly enhanced by data from IPCC surveys and case studies of impacted communities. Dr. Brooks is IPCC's Senior Consultant on Research and Publications and the Principal Editor of IPCC's *Jerusalem Strategic Planning Series*.

In Chapter Three, Rassem Khamaisi explores the impact the wall has on the basic human Right to the City. In a very innovative treatment of the wall, Dr. Khamaisi views the barrier through the lens of the French sociologist Lefebvre. In its fullest form, the Right to the City subsumes such ancillary basic rights as equality of opportunity, especially before the law, freedom of movement without impediments, the right to participate in the life of the community, and to share in the allocation of its resources. With this chapter, Khamaisi raises the discussion of the wall issues to the level of philosophical and ethical concerns basic to our idea of a just society. Dr. Khamaisi is Senior Lecturer in Geography at Haifa University and is the Head of IPCC's Academic Committee; he has published extensively on land issues in Jerusalem, and he has prepared the master plan for Ramallah and other localities in the West Bank and Israel.

In Chapter Four, Abdalla Owais examines in detail through case studies one of the wall's most erosive effects: the creation of ethnic and demographic ghettos that separate Palestinians from Palestinians. The wall, as presently projected, will create many enclaves within and without East Jerusalem. Dr. Owais received his doctorate in Urban Planning from the Frei Universitaet in Berlin and is a Project Manager at IPCC. He examines four of these enclaves which are composed of twelve major Jerusalem communities and a number of suburban neighborhoods. He spent months in these besieged enclaves interviewing local council officials, residents, education leaders and representatives of medical and health centers. His discussion illuminates the effect of the wall on the communities of the enclaved citizenry.

The visual materials in the chapter were provided by two IPCC project coordinators; Arch. Mona Al Qutob who received her Bachelor Degree of Architectural Science majoring in Building Science from Ryerson University, Toronto, Canada; and Arch. Shahd Wa'ary, who received her Bachelor Degree of Architecture and Urban Planning from Birzeit University.

Chapter Five presents the results of a major IPCC survey taken of 1,200 Jerusalemites and households on both sides of the wall. It is the product of an IPCC expert team and a group of energetic field workers. The results document in detail the effect the barrier has on the daily activities of those who live in the shadow of the wall.

In Chapter Six, Rami Nasrallah offers a geopolitical analysis of the wall's impact. He offers a thoughtful response to the Israeli rationales underlying the construction of the wall, including a prognosis of the wall's effects. He extends the *Right to the City* concept to Jerusalem's national and international constituencies and, in examining how best to protect that right, Mr. Nasrallah proposes several criteria and a number of guidelines that could instruct future negotiations on the status of Jerusalem and the future of the Occupied Palestinian Territories.

The maps which appear in this volume were produced by Michael Younan. He is an internationally recognized authority on Geographic Information Systems (GIS), mapping cartography, and remote sensing. He is the Director of engineering and computing at the Palestinian Mapping Center.

RDB
Jerusalem, January 2007

MAP 1: THE ISRAELI SEPARATION WALL/ BARRIER IN THE WEST BANK

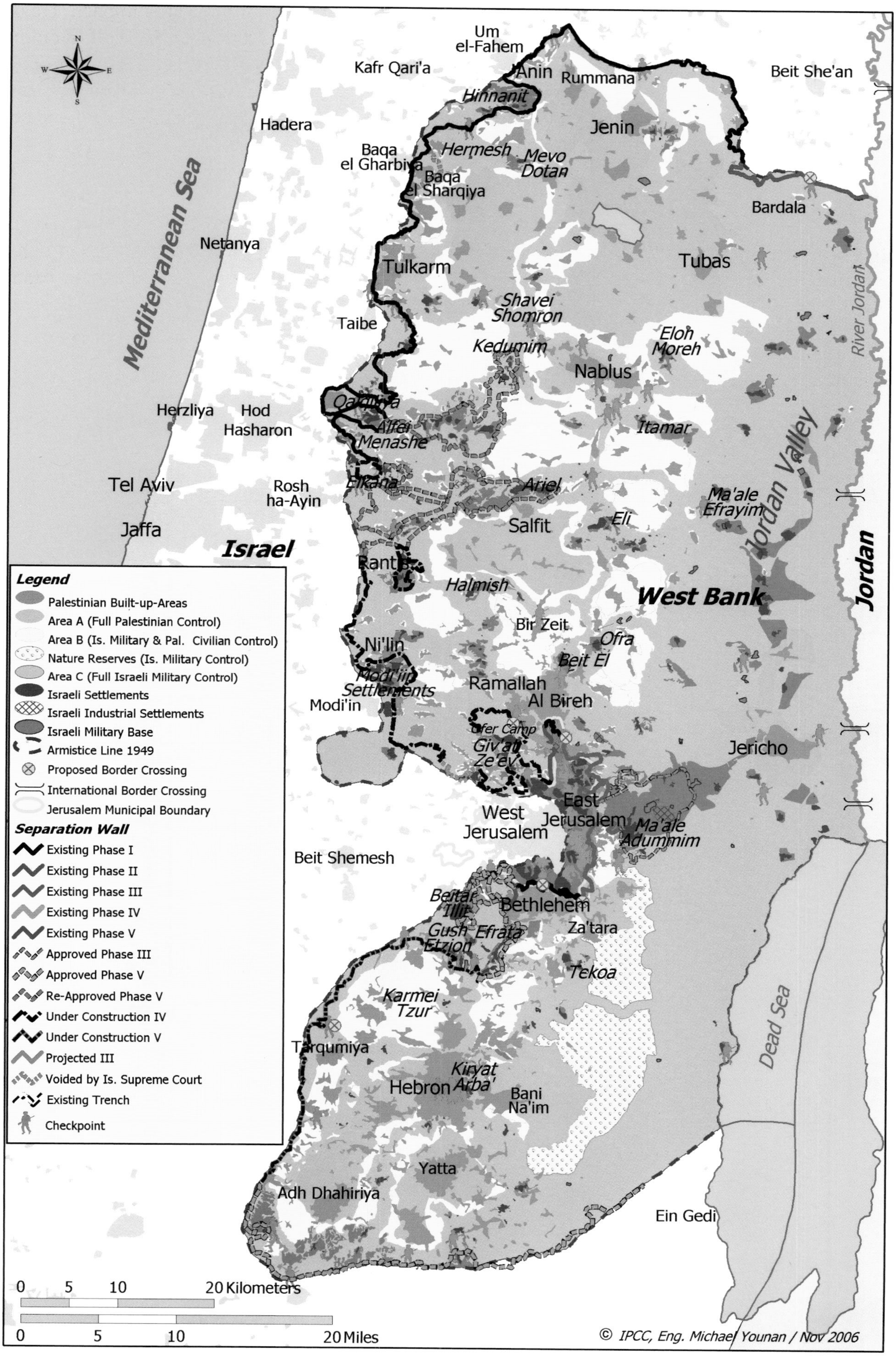

Mediterranean Sea

Israel

Jordan

West Bank

Jordan Valley

River Jordan

Dead Sea

Um el-Fahem
Kafr Qari'a
'Anin
Rummana
Beit She'an
Hinnanit
Hadera
Jenin
Baqa el Gharbiya
Hermesh
Mevo Dotan
Baqa el Sharqiya
Bardala
Tubas
Tulkarm
Shavei Shomron
Eloh Moreh
Taibe
Kedumim
Nablus
Herzliya
Hod Hasharon
Qalqilya
Alfei Menashe
Itamar
Tel Aviv
Elkana
Ariel
Ma'ale Efrayim
Rosh ha-Ayin
Salfit
Eli
Jaffa
Rantis
Halmish
Ni'lin
Bir Zeit
Ofra
Beit El
Modi'in Settlements
Ramallah
Modi'in
Al Bireh
Jericho
Ofer Camp
Giv'at Ze'ev
West Jerusalem
East Jerusalem
Ma'ale Adummim
Beit Shemesh
Beitar Illit
Bethlehem
Za'tara
Gush Etzion
Efrata
Tekoa
Karmei Tzur
Tarqumiya
Kiryat Arba'
Hebron
Bani Na'im
Yatta
Adh Dhahiriya
Ein Gedi

Legend

- Palestinian Built-up-Areas
- Area A (Full Palestinian Control)
- Area B (Is. Military & Pal. Civilian Control)
- Nature Reserves (Is. Military Control)
- Area C (Full Israeli Military Control)
- Israeli Settlements
- Israeli Industrial Settlements
- Israeli Military Base
- Armistice Line 1949
- Proposed Border Crossing
- International Border Crossing
- Jerusalem Municipal Boundary

Separation Wall

- Existing Phase I
- Existing Phase II
- Existing Phase III
- Existing Phase IV
- Existing Phase V
- Approved Phase III
- Approved Phase V
- Re-Approved Phase V
- Under Construction IV
- Under Construction V
- Projected III
- Voided by Is. Supreme Court
- Existing Trench
- Checkpoint

0 5 10 20 Kilometers

0 5 10 20 Miles

© IPCC, Eng. Michael Younan / Nov 2006

MAP2: THE SEPARATION WALL IN THE JERUSALEM AREA

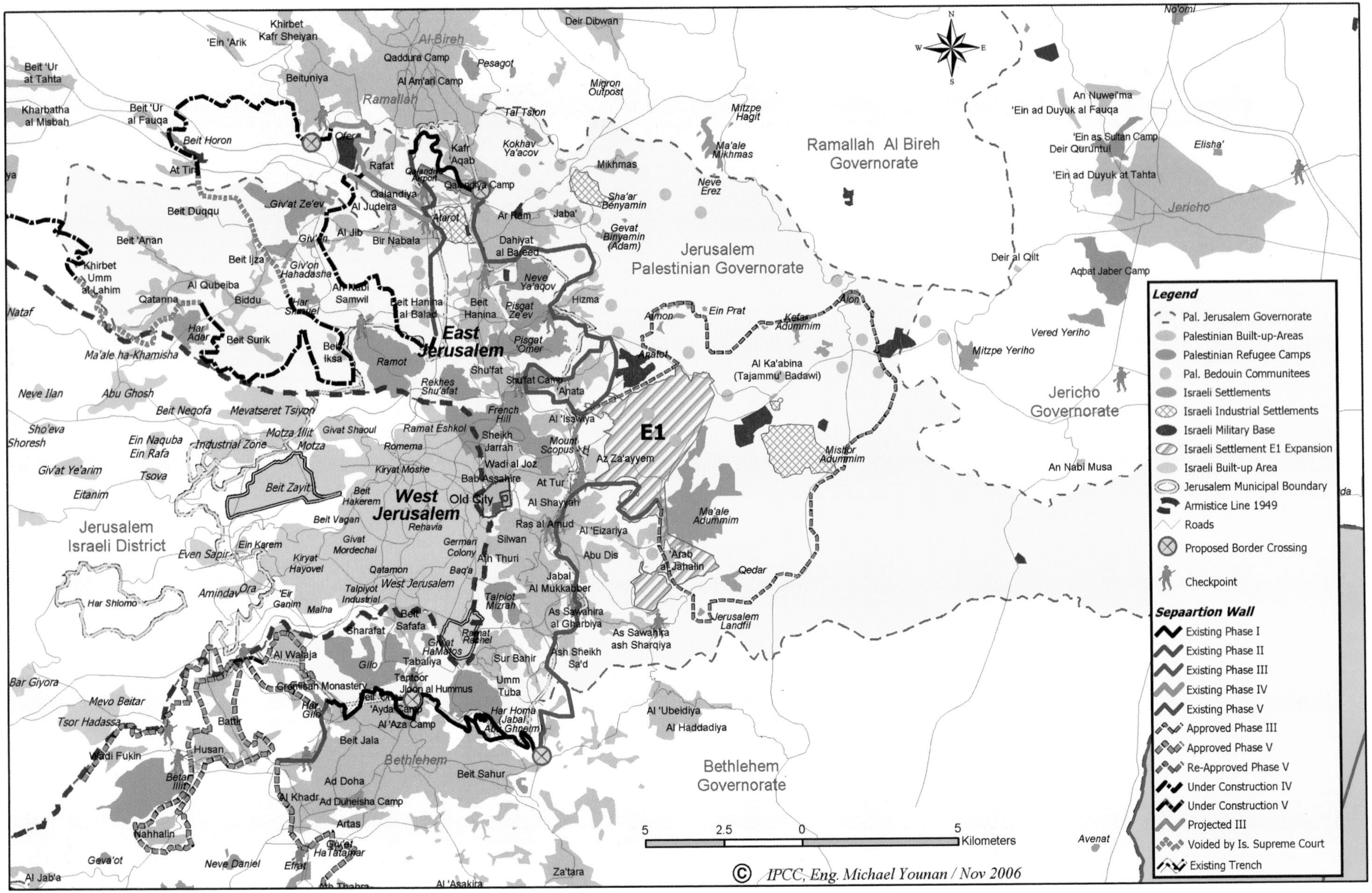

Legend

- Pal. Jerusalem Governorate
- Palestinian Built-up-Areas
- Palestinian Refugee Camps
- Pal. Bedouin Communities
- Israeli Settlements
- Israeli Industrial Settlements
- Israeli Military Base
- Israeli Settlement E1 Expansion
- Israeli Built-up Area
- Jerusalem Municipal Boundary
- Armistice Line 1949
- Roads
- Proposed Border Crossing
- Checkpoint

Separtion Wall

- Existing Phase I
- Existing Phase II
- Existing Phase III
- Existing Phase IV
- Existing Phase V
- Approved Phase III
- Approved Phase V
- Re-Approved Phase V
- Under Construction IV
- Under Construction V
- Projected III
- Voided by Is. Supreme Court
- Existing Trench

© IPCC, Eng. Michael Younan / Nov 2006

5   2.5   0   5   Kilometers

MAP3: THE WALL ENCLAVES IN THE JERUSALEM AREA

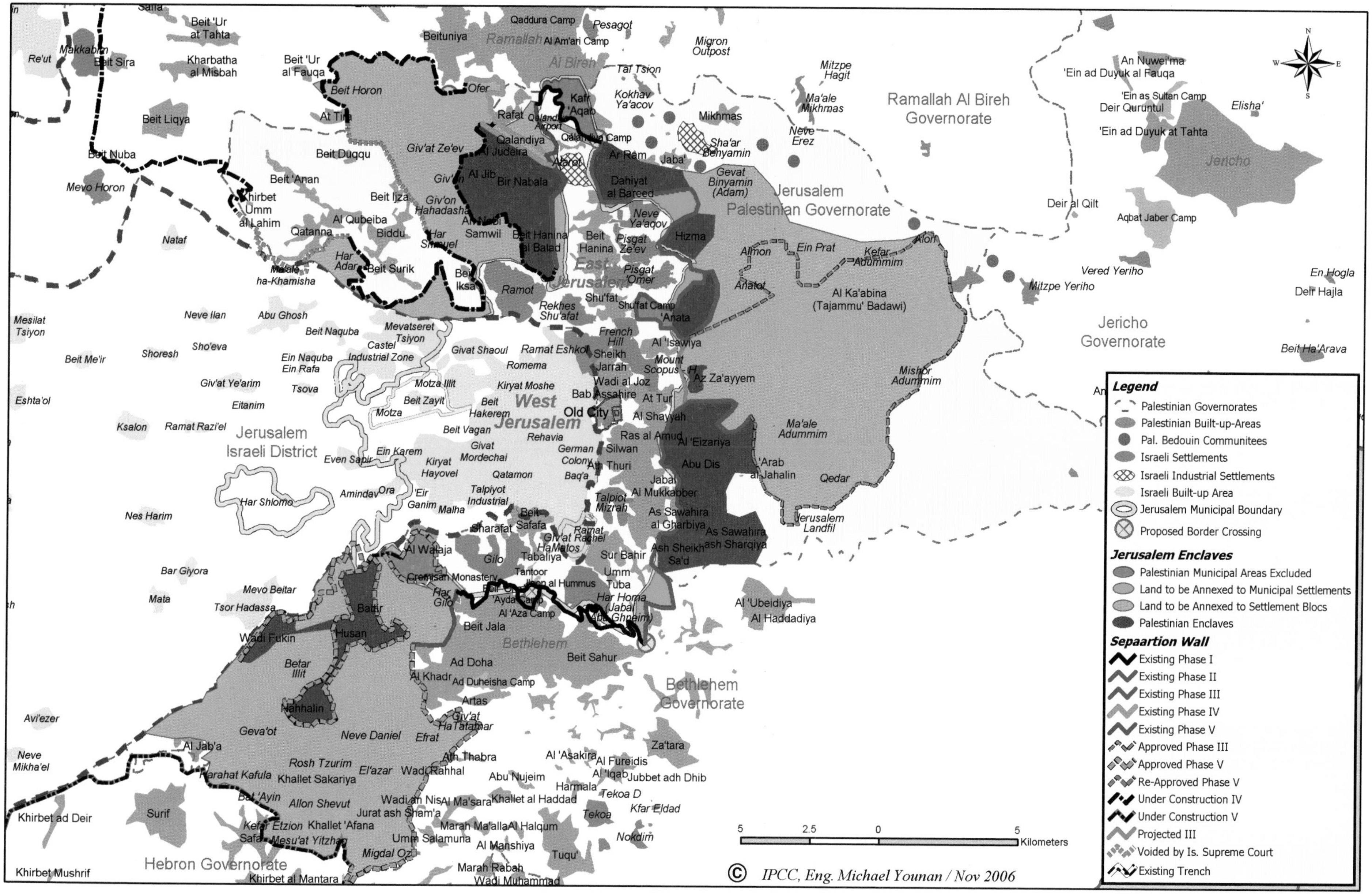

Legend
Palestinian Governorates
Palestinian Built-up-Areas
Pal. Bedouin Communitees
Israeli Settlements
Israeli Industrial Settlements
Israeli Built-up Area
Jerusalem Municipal Boundary
Proposed Border Crossing
Jerusalem Enclaves
Palestinian Municipal Areas Excluded
Land to be Annexed to Municipal Settlements
Land to be Annexed to Settlement Blocs
Palestinian Enclaves
Sepaartion Wall
Existing Phase I
Existing Phase II
Existing Phase III
Existing Phase IV
Existing Phase V
Approved Phase III
Approved Phase V
Re-Approved Phase V
Under Construction IV
Under Construction V
Projected III
Voided by Is. Supreme Court
Existing Trench
5 2.5 0 5 Kilometers
Ramallah Al Bireh Governorate
Jerusalem Palestinian Governorate
Jericho Governorate
Bethlehem Governorate
Hebron Governorate
Jerusalem Israeli District
West Jerusalem
East Jerusalem
Old City
Ramallah
Al Bireh
Jericho
Bethlehem
Ma'ale Adummim
Al Ka'abina (Tajammu' Badawi)
Bir Nabala
Al Jib
Qalandiya
Ar Ram
Dahiyat al Bareed
Hizma
'Anata
Shu'fat Camp
Al 'Eizariya
Abu Dis
As Sawahira ash Sharqiya
Ash Sheikh Sa'd
Beit Sahur
Beit Jala
Battir
Husan
Nahhalin
Wadi Fukin
Betar Illit
Giv'at Ze'ev
Beit Surik
Biddu
Gilo
Har Homa (Jabal Abu Ghneim)
© IPCC, Eng. Michael Younan / Nov 2006

MAP4: SETTLEMENT ANNEXATION (GREATER JERUSALEM)

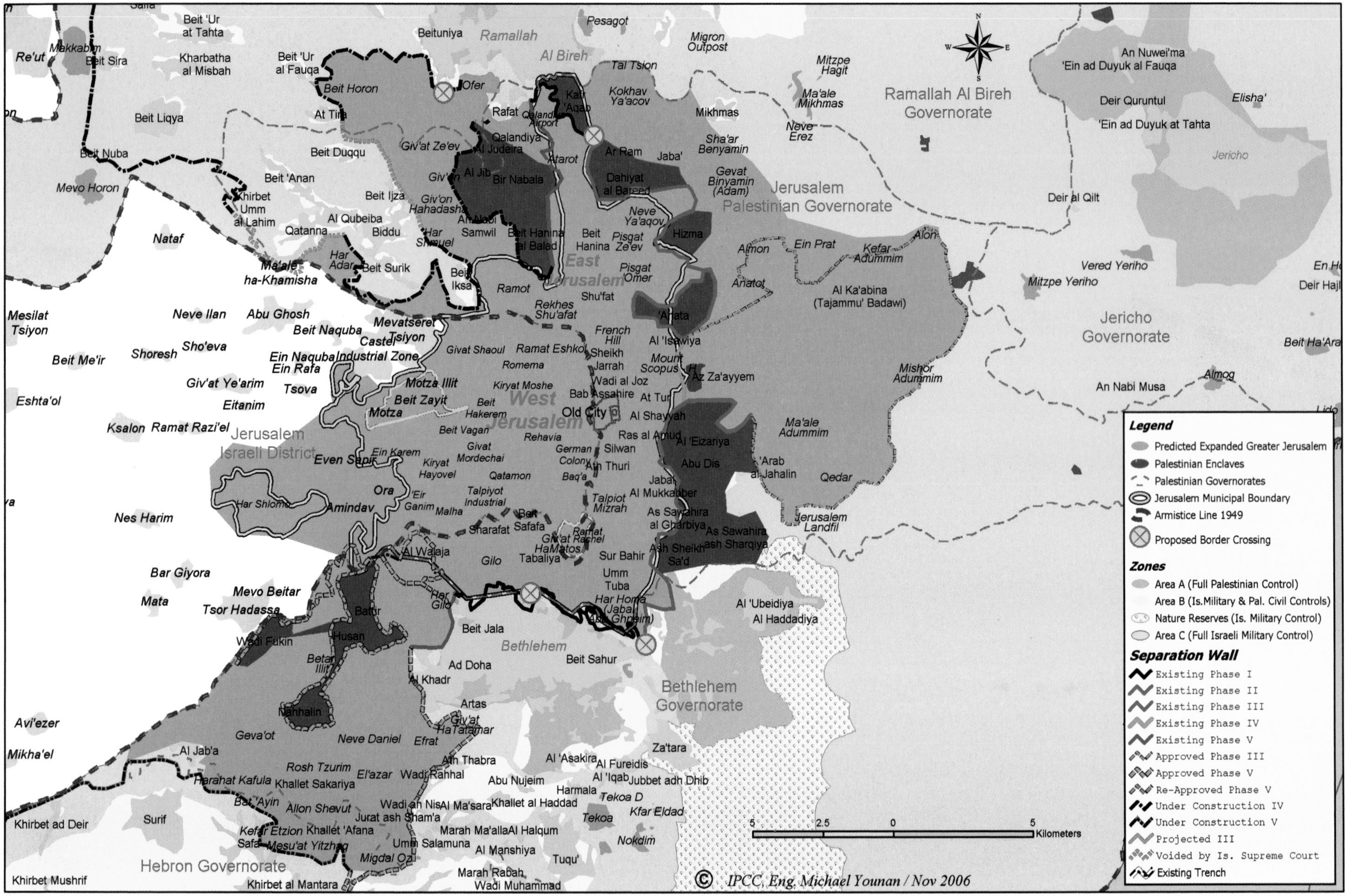

Legend

- Predicted Expanded Greater Jerusalem
- Palestinian Enclaves
- Palestinian Governorates
- Jerusalem Municipal Boundary
- Armistice Line 1949
- ⊗ Proposed Border Crossing

Zones

- Area A (Full Palestinian Control)
- Area B (Is.Military & Pal. Civil Controls)
- Nature Reserves (Is. Military Control)
- Area C (Full Israeli Military Control)

Separation Wall

- Existing Phase I
- Existing Phase II
- Existing Phase III
- Existing Phase IV
- Existing Phase V
- Approved Phase III
- Approved Phase V
- Re-Approved Phase V
- Under Construction IV
- Under Construction V
- Projected III
- Voided by Is. Supreme Court
- Existing Trench

© IPCC, Eng. Michael Younan / Nov 2006

Kilometers 5 2.5 0 5

Ramallah Al Bireh Governorate

Jericho Governorate

Jerusalem Palestinian Governorate

East Jerusalem

West Jerusalem

Israeli District Jerusalem

Bethlehem Governorate

Hebron Governorate

CHAPTER ONE

The Jerusalem Separation Wall:
Facts and Political Implication

Rami Nasrallah

The Separatist Imperative

Israel occupied the West Bank, East Jerusalem and the Gaza Strip in June 1967 and immediately began planning for territorial domination and for imposing a Jewish settlement presence and Jewish demographic superiority in the Occupied Palestinian Territories(OPT). Initially, this strategy was implemented in the Jerusalem area and in the Jordan Valley, areas which Israel wanted to keep under its control in any future scenario for the Palestinian territories. While these actions fragmented Palestinian territory and scattered Israelis and Palestinians alike, the underlying goal was to de facto annex vast Palestinian areas to Israel. A fundamental imperative within Israeli nationalist ideology, left or right, is to preserve the Jewish nature of the state and to maintain a Jewish majority in it. It is feared that in an unseparated demography, or in an ethnically integrated state, Palestinian growth rates would eventually create a Palestinian majority—an unacceptable situation in a country which defines itself as Jewish and sees itself as democratic. While there is considerable debate within Israel on the religious and political meaning of a "Jewish state," there is nevertheless a general Israeli consensus supporting the separatist concept as a basic national goal. In its most extreme form, separatism may include the removal or elimination of Palestinians from the State of Israel and areas of "strategic interest".

But the most conclusive and widespread Israeli support for "separation" from Palestinians came in May 1993, a few months before the Oslo peace process. Indeed, a unilateral separation from the Palestinians was introduced by Israeli politicians even prior to the Palestinian suicide bombings which Israel later used as the issue which called for a physical separation from the Palestinians as one of the major means of achieving Israeli security, controlling Palestinian movement, minimizing the demographic threat of a bi-national state and maintaining a Jewish demographic majority in the areas to be annexed under the Israeli law. By 2002, the physical components of separation had been drafted by a group of center -left former military leaders. The original plan included substantial withdrawals from Israeli settlements in Gaza and the West Bank, and that drew the ire of the right wing, which saw any formal division of the broad religious concept of the ancient Land of Israel as a concession to the Palestinian side. Eventually, however, right wing Prime Minister Ariel Sharon was convinced of the need for drastic measures to halt the demographic threat represented by a rapidly growing Palestinian population; he also recognized that a physical separation could be used to achieve further West Bank annexation, and to impose the 1967 Allon Plan which would keep approximately fifty percent of the West Bank under Israeli control.

"We are here, and they are there": Oslo and Pre-wall Efforts toward Separation

The Oslo Accords of 1993-95, with a vision of two ethnic domains, and with an emphasis on creating security for Israel, underscored the separatist goal and implemented the slogan of the day, "We are here, and they are there". At the same time, the accords secured Israel's strategic interests and strengthened the state of Israel by eliminating the perceived "Palestinian demographic danger". The Oslo agreement, however, was preceded by the introduction of practical steps toward implementing a separation plan: in the early 1990's Israeli employers began laying off Palestinian workers who commuted daily to jobs in Israel and replacing them with imported foreign workers on the pretext of addressing Israeli security needs, even though the number of Palestinian workers involved in anti-Israel activities was minimal. The policy was a tactic to reduce even a transitory Palestinian presence in Israel.

Moreover, in 1993, just a few months before the first Oslo signing, Israel implemented a separatist closure policy by erecting checkpoints between the West Bank and Israel and between Jerusalem and the West Bank. East Jerusalem was thus isolated from its direct surroundings and the rest of the West Bank. The closure policy applied to all Palestinians. Only persons carrying special permits were allowed to enter Israel and Jerusalem, and permits were normally issued to only a very small number of Palestinians, and then only after a complicated and drawn out bureaucratic process designed to discourage the Palestinians from even submitting an application. Closure checkpoints were placed along the borders between the West Bank and Israel as well as at the entrances to Jerusalem. They constituted an integrated system linked to the Jewish settlements and the by-pass roads leading to them. In practice, those checkpoints represented the beginning of employing physical barriers to bar Palestinians from approaching Israeli areas inside the Green Line (i.e. the armistice line of 1949) and from entering Israeli settlements built on the Occupied PalestinianTerritories.

A "Temporary" Barrier

On the eve of the outbreak of the Second Intifada (September 2000), Israeli voices demanding acceleration of the unilateral separation plan became louder, especially within Labor Party circles. In October 2000, Labor leader Ehud Barak, Israeli Prime Minister at the time, approved a decision to establish a systematic array of barriers and other hindrances to control the entry of vehicles from the West Bank to Israel. The barrier network extended through the border areas from the far northwest West Bank to the central region of Latrun, which lies between Jerusalem and Tel Aviv. In June 2001, newly elected Likud Prime Minister Ariel Sharon, under pressure from separatist advocates within the military and political leaderships, formed a committee chaired by Uzi Dayan, Head of the National Security Council at the time, to study various means of barring Palestinians from entering Israel. Sharon was initially opposed to the construction of a wall and even to the whole idea of separation for ideological reasons. He was accused repeatedly of procrastinating in constructing the wall. But he eventually changed his position and incorporated the idea of the wall within his geopolitical proposals. He elected to personally oversee the routing and construction of the wall. The Israeli government approved recommendations of the appointed committee to establish "a temporary barrier" east of Um El-Fahm, around Tulkarem and a section around and through East Jerusalem. The barrier was designed to hinder motorized as well as pedestrian movement.

The Wall in Jerusalem

The Wall is the saddest chapter in the continuing saga of the Israeli land grab. The wall impacts Palestinians most directly, it is important to point out, because it is being built on Palestinian land. Approximately 536,200 dunums (109,050 acres; 1 dunum=one-quarter acre or 1000 square meters) of previously confiscated settlement land lie to the west of the wall. Another 160,500 dunums (80,125 acres) of West Bank village land is partially or completely surrounded, on one side by the wall and on the other by a secondary barrier, and usually not made accessible to its landowners. These areas alone total 12.4% of the entire area of the West Bank. Moreover, at publication time, another 205,350 dunums (51,087 acres) west of the wall were slated for confiscation with the approval of the Israeli government.

Inspection of the implemented and planned path of the wall in and near Jerusalem shows that the criteria guiding the establishment of the separation wall in Jerusalem are different from those generally applied in the West Bank. In Jerusalem the wall's path in most areas follows the municipal annexed line that was created after the 1967 occupation and has not been guided by the Green Line which is the UN-administered armistice line between Israel and Jordan created in 1949;

to the contrary, it penetrates deep into the Occupied Palestinian Territories. This results in a de facto annexation of all Greater Jerusalem Israeli settlement blocs, spanning an area of 10 to 16% of the West Bank. In essence, the wall concretizes the 1970s planning concept of a metropolitan Jerusalem, a plan which established roadways and services for highly populated Israeli settlements on the periphery of the Jerusalem Municipality. National and regional traffic arteries are included on the Israeli side of the wall, facilitating travel between Israeli East Jerusalem settlements and outlying settlements in suburban Jerusalem, and linking them with West Jerusalem and central Israel. The gaps of land that lie between the Jerusalem-area settlements have been annexed to those settlements: Ma'aleh Adumim, for one, has been expanded so that its borders span over 53,000 dunums (13,250 acres); its area now rivals that of Tel Aviv and merges with the municipal borders of Jerusalem. The East 1(E-1) Plan, for which land has been prepared, will establish a settlement neighborhood north of Ma'aleh Adumim comprised of 3,500 residential units. A new Border Police base (Muzudat Edomim) on a built-up area of 3,300 square meters was completed there in November 2003. It serves two units of the border police. A military base is also located in E-1. It includes the headquarters of the Israeli police responsible of the West Bank settlements. A building of 5,400 square meters is under construction financed indirectly by an extreme settler group, which will occupy the current building of the police headquarters in Ras al Amoud. This building will be annexed to the settlement compound in that area which is in the heart of a Palestinian neighborhood.

Phases of the West Bank Wall/ Barrier

In June 2002 the Israeli cabinet approved construction of the first section of the wall, a 175-kilometer northwest stretch, which extends from the West Bank area near Salem Village (inside the Green Line) to the Elkana settlement (southeast of Qalqiliya). Construction of this section was completed in August 2003. This phase included the initial stage of the wall in Jerusalem, a 22-kilometer segment in the north and south of the city.

The second phase of wall construction extends from Salem Village eastwards toward Tayaseer Village, a stretch of 60 kilometers. This phase was approved in December 2002 and construction of most of it was completed by April 2004. This segment is considered the beginning of the isolation of the Jordan Valley from the rest of the West Bank. This segment is the most eastern one; it lies close to the Jordanian border. Some Palestinian experts consider this segment as the initial stage for Israel to guarantee its control over the Jordan Valley and the settlements there. There has been no official decision regarding this plan, but the reality of Israel's control over the Jordan Valley and the isolation of the Palestinian areas from it, and the barriers to prevent the Palestinians from reaching it (including the prohibited use of Road No. 90) is a clear indication of a separation scheme in the Jordan Valley as an Israeli security zone.

The third phase of the wall in the West Bank was officially approved in August 2003, the so-called "Jerusalem Envelope," with a length of 70 kilometers around Municipal Jerusalem. In October 2003, a 107 kilometer segment was approved, which extends southwards from the Elkana Israeli settlement to the Ofer militarily base. In February 2005, the Israeli cabinet approved the entire route of the wall, as it was then projected; its path was to be based in accord with the Supreme Court ruling that required a route that had a "proportionate" balance between security and the inhabitants' needs. The court decision had been made on the 30th of June 2004 in connection with the Beit Surik case. The length of the newly approved segment was 187 kilometers. However, in April 2006, a new map was approved that added an additional 141 kilometers to the length of the wall/ barrier. (see **Map 1**)

The Separation Wall in Jerusalem and its Environs: Seven Segments

While approval of the first phase of the wall primarily concerned the northwestern West Bank barrier, it also included approval of construction of what Israeli spokespersons have come to call "the Jerusalem Envelope." The plans initially included a 22-kilometer wall around East Jerusalem comprised of two segments: the first, north of the city in the area extending from the Ofer military Base (southwest of Ramallah) to the Qalandiya Checkpoint; the second, south of the city in the area extending from Ras Beit Jala to Deir Salah Village southeast of Jerusalem. Construction of the two segments was completed in July 2003, thereby isolating Palestinian East Jerusalem from Ramallah in the north and from Bethlehem in the south and excluding from the city the Samiramis and Kafr Aqab neighborhoods which lie within the northern borders of East Jerusalem. (The population of the two Palestinian neighborhoods is approximately twelve thousand.)

In August 2003 the Israeli security cabinet approved all the segments of the wall in and around Jerusalem, excluding the Ma`aleh Adumim settlement segment. These segments were approved as part of phase 3 and 4 of the overall wall/barrier plan of the entire West Bank and they include a segment from Deir Salah Village southeast of East Jerusalem running toward the north to Abu Dis and then eastwards toward Al Eizariya. The length of this component is 17 kilometers. The fourth segment of 14 kilometers extends from the south of Anata Village toward the northwest and excludes from East Jerusalem the Shu'fat Refugee Camp and the Ras Khamis and Dahiyat As Salam neighborhoods, all of which are located within the municipal borders of the city. This stretch continues northbound and toward the northwest and separates the Jerusalem Palestinian suburb of Ar Ram from East Jerusalem before ending at the Qalandiya Checkpoint.

This fourth segment will isolate the refugee camp and eastern neighborhoods of approximately twenty-two thousand Palestinians from East Jerusalem; and it will also separate the nine thousand residents of Anata Village from the city. Moreover, the villages of Hizma (population approximately 6,500) and Az Za'ayyem (2,495) will be completely isolated from their entire surroundings. The same fate will befall the residents of Ar Ram and Dahiyat Al Bareed (with a combined population of 50,000). These latter communities will be "enclaved" by a wall that extends along the east, south and northern area perimeters, converting these suburbs into an isolated island. Previously they were a vital commercial and service center serving East Jerusalem and its relationship with the West Bank.

A fifth segment (18 kilometers) of the scheme for isolating East Jerusalem consists in consolidating the city's suburban villages of Bir Nabala, Al Judeira, Al Jib and Beit Hanina into an isolated enclave area linked not to East Jerusalem but to Ramallah by a tunnel. The total population of these villages is approximately 28,000 residents, about half of whom carry West Bank identity cards and the remaining half are holders of East Jerusalem identity cards. The Bir Nabala area grew during the period from 1985-2001 to become an important commercial and industrial axis linked to East Jerusalem. This area began losing its importance at the beginning of the Second Intifada (September 2000) when Israel sealed its western entrance leading to the Atarot industrial zone and constructed an alternative road for the use of Israelis (Road No. 45). The total area of this enclave is 10,500 dunums. Moreover, the wall around the Biddu area on the northwest part of the Jerusalem Governorate (five villages are within the Ramallah Governorate) will include a segment (the sixth) of about 56 kilometers. The area of the enclave is 54,000 dunums and it includes 14 Palestinian localities: Beit Sira, Kharbatha Al Misbah, At Tira, Beit Liqia, Beit Nuba, Beit Duqqu, Beit Anan, Al Qubeiba, Kharayeb Um Al Lahim, Biddu, Qatanna, Beit Surik, Beit Iksa and Beit Ijza. This area is surrounded by a barrier from all directions and by Road No. 443 which will isolate this enclave from Ramallah in the north. The population of the enclave is 49,681 Palestinians. A seventh segment will create an enclave around Al Walaja village southwest of Jerusalem; the village will be transformed into an isolated area. Part of this village is located within the borders of East Jerusalem, the total area of this enclave will be 2,300 dunums, with a population of 1,818. (see **Map 2**)

Figure I: 1 shows the territorial and demographic affect of the wall in the Jerusalem Area. In the areas of the east and northwest of Jerusalem and in the southwest in the Bethlehem area, a total of at least 163,000 dunums of Israeli settlements built in Palestinian lands were annexed to Jerusalem negatively changing the lives of 412,000 Palestinian in Jerusalem and its hinterland and suburbs. A total of at least 5,000 dunums of Palestinian built up areas that lie within the municipal boundary were excluded from the city changing the demographic balance in the city by at least 55,000 Palestinians in favor of the Jews. At least 43,000 Palestinians were enclaved in their 9 villages and towns of a total area of 24,000 dunums. (see also **Maps 3 and 4**)

Figure I: 1 The Area of Jerusalem: Annexation and Exclusion

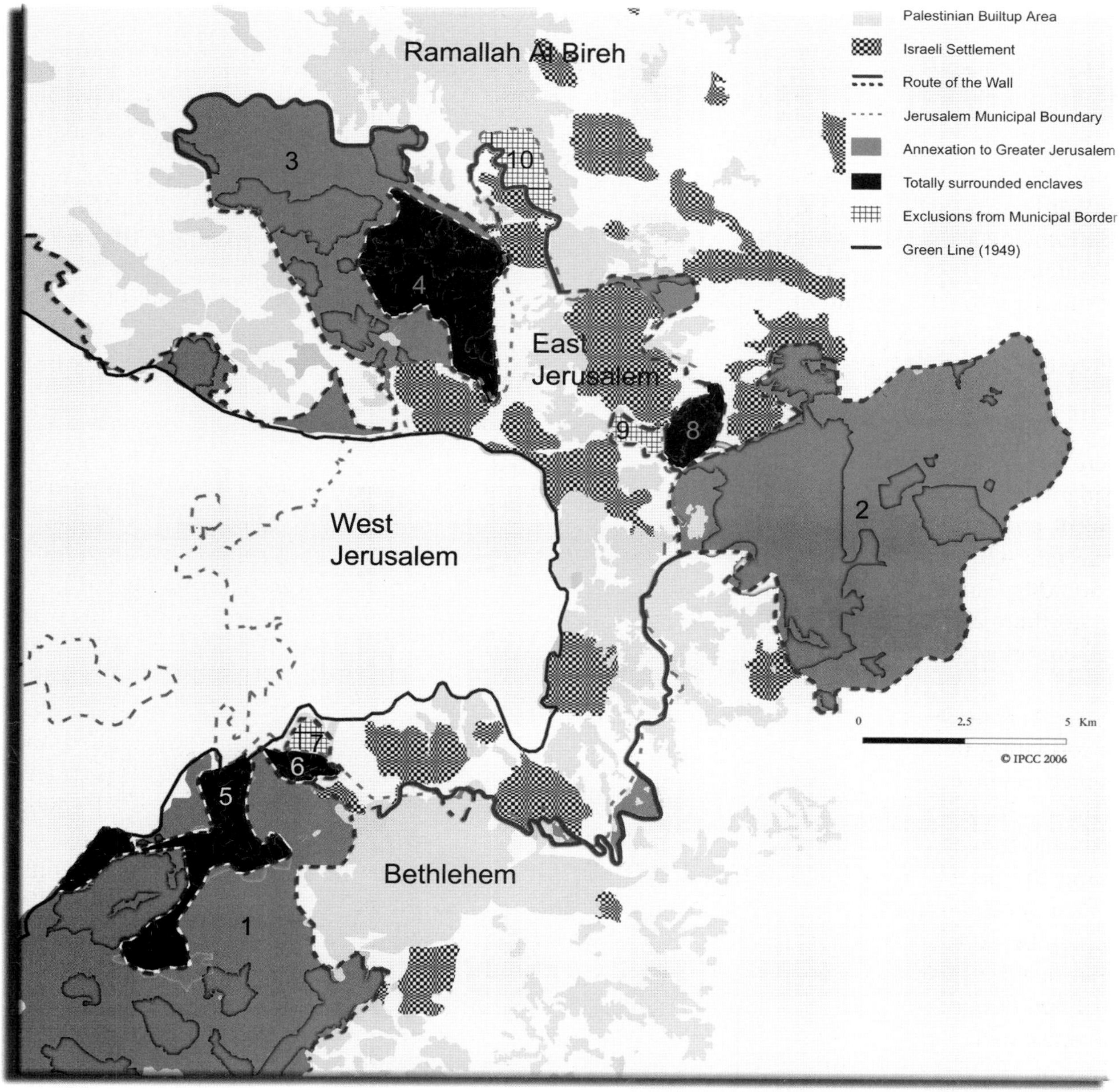

Estimated Area and Population Data for Annexed, Excluded and Enclaved areas

Number	Area	Surface Area (dun)	Number of Palestinians
1	Gush Etzion Bloc	70,300	600
2	Ma'aleh Adumim Bloc	60,400	3,683
3	Giv'at Ze'ev Bloc	32,000	222
4	Bir Nabala enclave	10,500	15,272
5	Battir enclave	8,000	18,000
6 +7	Al Walaja enclave	2,300	1,818
8	Anata enclave	5,076	9,700
9	Shu'fat RC	347	22,000
10	Kafr Aqab and Samiramis	2,441	12,000

The Key Statistics

The total length of the West Bank Barrier /Wall will be 703 kilometers, as approved by the Israeli government on 30 April 2006. This contrasts with the 670 kilometer route previously approved on 20 February 2005. The length of the new route is more than twice the length of the 315 kilometer Green Line. Only 25 percent of the barrier in the West Bank is on the Green Line and the rest stretches deep into the heart of the West Bank, especially in the Ariel settlement group area where it extends 22 kilometers across the width of the West Bank. Construction of 362 kilometers have been completed (approximately 51 percent of the projected total); 88 kilometers are under construction; and the remaining 235 kilometers are planned and approved but not under construction as this goes to press. Of the completed sections, 42 kilometers are concrete segments slabs and 320 kilometers of the barrier consists of an area approximately 50 meters wide that includes fences, patrol roads, barbed wire, tracking sands and electronic observation systems. The wall and barriers will have a direct impact on the lives of 500,000 Palestinians, or nearly 21 percent of the Palestinian population of the West Bank who will live inside or adjacent to the barriers or wall. The total area of West Bank lands affected by the wall will reach 671,000 dunums (167,750 acres) or approximately 12 percent of the total area of the West Bank (including East Jerusalem). Further, the wall effectively allows Israel to annex sixty-six Jewish settlements to its west, inhabited by 182,400 settlers in the West Bank and 183,300 in East Jerusalem, or about 80% of the entire settler population in the West Bank, including the settlements built on East Jerusalem lands.

The Construction Components of the Wall

The Jerusalem Barrier will be mainly composed of the most offensive wall elements, enormous concrete sections 6 to 9 meters high. The segments southeast and northeast of the city will be multi-layered obstacle structures whose combined width will extend to 50 meters.

Typically, the following elements are included in the barrier:

Barbed wire (six coils)   Ditch (5.5m wide)
Patrol road (5m wide)   Intrusion-detection fence (3m. high)
First dirt tracking road (to detect footprints)   Paved patrol road
Sophisticated observation system   Second dirt tracking road
Barbed wire

A cross section view of the barrier. Source: www.securityfence.mod.gov.il

The nine meter wall cutting the suburb of Abu Dis from Jerusalem. Nov 2006.

The Primary Effects of the Wall

The wall will have a dramatic impact on the future of Jerusalem and its surroundings; it is the most significant change to the city since its occupation in 1967. It will radically impact the boundaries of East Jerusalem, the movement and placement of the Palestinian population, and it is considered to be the final step to eliminate the central status of Jerusalem as a political and metropolitan center for all Palestinians.

Territorial and Demographic Effects of the Wall on Jerusalem and its Environs

* The process of building the wall represents a redrawing of the borders of the Israeli Jerusalem Municipality and the areas under its direct jurisdiction. The wall will annex to the Israeli settlements within the municipal boundaries more than 4,000 dunums (1,000 acres). The benefiting settlements are Neve Ya'akov, Pisgat Ze'ev, Pisgat 'Omer and Har Homa (Jabal Abu Ghneim). Moreover, 3,200 dunums (800 acres) of established Palestinian neighborhoods presently within the boundaries of East Jerusalem will be excluded from the city as areas east of the wall (Shu'fat Refugee Camp, Dahiyat As Salam and Anata) or north of the wall (Kafr Aqab and Samiramis).

* Construction of the wall will lead to the annexation of vast areas of occupied Palestinian lands on which Israeli settlements have been built outside Jerusalem's municipal borders. Such Ma'aleh Adumim (an area which, when one includes its plan for development, exceeds 70 km and its population of 30,162); Giv'at Ze'ev (population 11,000); Bet Horon, Giv'on Hadasha and Har Shmuel settlements (a combined population of 1800 settlers and an area of 42 km^2); and an area of the Bethlehem Governorate that is located southwest of Jerusalem, which includes Betar Elite (28,600), and Efrat (7,700). The total area of these Bethlehem settlements is approximately 80 km.

* The wall will allow Jewish West Jerusalem to annex to itself several outlying Israeli settlements. Such settlements represent parts of neighborhoods originally established within the Green Line

borders of 1967 but, over time, development in them spread to Occupied Palestinian Territory. They include the Har Adar settlement (population 2,459) and parts of Mivasert Tzion, a suburb of West Jerusalem.

* The wall will place outside the city borders 55,000 Palestinian Jerusalemites who presently live within municipal Jerusalem, separating them from the city and from the crucial public and personal services it provides. In addition, 40,000 to 60,000 Palestinian Jerusalemites presently living in the suburbs of Jerusalem adjacent to the municipal border surrounding East Jerusalem (Ar Ram, Bir Nabala, Al Eizariya and Abu Dis) will be isolated from the city. This will effectively reduce the percentage of the Palestinians in the total population of the Jerusalem Municipality (East and West), which reached 34% in 2005. These actions also arise as an attempt to address Israel's inability to implement a 1973 decision to keep the percentage of the Palestinian population of the Jerusalem Municipality below 25.5%. Taking the number of Jerusalemites cut from the city-- both those who live within municipal Jerusalem and the West Bank suburbs of Jerusalem-- the remaining Palestinian areas that lie within the city will be inhabited by no more than 60% of the actual Palestinian Jerusalemite population, and their percentage in the total municipal population will shrink to a mere 21%.

* Migration back to East Jerusalem from the suburban Palestinian neighborhoods outside the wall is expected to increase among suburbanites who still hold the blue ID card which gives them the right to reside in the city. Indeed, already entire suburban neighborhoods have become empty with the loss of such migrants. For example, blue card residents of the suburban Al Eizariya Housing Project, initiated and built by the Israeli government outside of the municipal bounders in the early seventies for Palestinians whose original homes in the Al Maghariba quarter of the Old City were confiscated and demolished to allow expansion of the Wailing Wall and the Jewish quarter, have been returning in droves since 2004 to East Jerusalem. As a result of roadblocks, checkpoints, and closures, entry to the city has become increasingly difficult for them, even though formally they had retained their East Jerusalemite status. Moreover, they fear that, with the wall, entry may be barred entirely and they will risk losing their legal status and their social entitlements as official Jerusalem residents. Further, some neighborhoods which expanded outside city borders, such as the Az Za'ayyem neighborhood, which developed as an extension of the East Jerusalem At Tur neighborhood, have witnessed in recent months the migration of most of its Jerusalem identity card holders; they are returning to live with their families in At Tur. Another example depicting the size of the phenomenon of the return to East Jerusalem is the Ar Ram and Dahiyat Al Bareed neighborhoods, whose population was more than 60% Jerusalemite during the 1990's. With the advent of the wall this segment decreased to 40% in 2003, and by November 2006, it is estimated to be at less than 25%. Their number is dwindling every day.

* These returnees impact seriously on the already troubling housing shortage and unhealthy population density of East Jerusalem. Many families are forced to live in shops or stores inside the Old City or in the neighborhoods of Wadi Al Joz and Silwan; they can neither find nor afford to rent houses inside East Jerusalem. Rents have increased in some areas by more than 50% since the end of 2003.

The Effects of the Wall on the Functioning of East Jerusalem as a Metropolitan Center and on Its Potential to Serve as the Capital of the Palestinian State

* *The city's relationship to the West Bank.* For decades Jerusalem functioned as the central Palestinian city for all of the West Bank. The city stands astride the major north/south and

east/west territorial corridors. Many of Palestine's most holy shrines are here, as well as a broad array of professional, social and personal services. In short, the city has functioned as a major intersection and as a destination in itself for hundreds of thousands of West Bankers. That role has been dealt a huge blow by Israeli decisions in the 1990's to bar entry to the city to holders of West Bank identity cards. The policy, which began by the creation of entry checkpoints, special permits requirements, and periodic closures, culminates with the erection of the Jerusalem wall. Collectively, these measures have marginalized East Jerusalem's influence as a Palestinian metropolis: residents of the territory are no longer allowed to enter East Jerusalem to shop, pray, and receive such basic services as healthcare and education. Indeed, East Jerusalem and its cultural and economic standing have been so diminished that it is no longer the institutional, commercial, service, religious and functional center for the West Bank.

Several years ago, Jerusalem's economy represented one-fourth to one-third of the entire West Bank economy. Today, however, East Jerusalem is being transformed into a few fragmented neighborhoods artificially affiliated with West Jerusalem and Israel. Simultaneously, the urban center and political heart that has developed unintentionally in Ramallah and al-Bireh competes with Jerusalem. The continuation of Jerusalem's isolation from its surroundings threatens any possibility that Jerusalem could become the capital of the Palestinian state. Moreover, the wall will undermine contiguity between the northern and southern Palestinian West Bank. Israel is planning to replace geographic contiguity with a transportation route: it plans to link the north and south West Bank with a road passing through the Ma`aleh Adumim settlement block, thereby by-passing Jerusalem. No longer will West Bankers be allowed to visit Jerusalem for medical treatment, pilgrimage, or even as a way-stop on to other West Bank sites. As such, the wall constitutes a geopolitical fait accompli preventing Jerusalem's development as a Palestinian economic and administrative center, weakening the city, and impoverishing its citizens [Brooks et. al., 2005]. The city's urban elite may well choose to leave the city, further isolating Jerusalem's poor. Ultimately security and social instability, increased poverty and crime can be expected in Jerusalem.

* *The city's relationship to its suburbs.* The process of building the wall has severed East Jerusalem's linkage with its suburbs and hinterland and weakened the city by ending its role as the area's service center. In fact, it has become isolated from its contiguous hinterland and suburban Palestinian communities and functions nowadays primarily as a local center for residents of internal East Jerusalem neighborhoods cut off from the West Bank by the wall.

* *The fragmentation and decline of the city.* The wall will create new "facts on the ground" that will increase the fragmentation of Jerusalem neighborhoods. It will fracture East Jerusalem's functional integrity and sever the urban continuity with its natural expansion and potential development areas. All lands that can be allocated for Palestinian development and construction in Jerusalem and its hinterland will be cut off from the city by the wall. This means East Jerusalem must struggle to absorb suburban blue card returnees to the inner city neighborhoods; the city cannot build new neighborhoods to accommodate them. In fact, the wall will accelerate the transformation of the city's neighborhoods into high-density poverty slums which will lead to the sociological and economic degradation of large groups of city residents. That fate is especially likely in neighborhoods which until recently were characterized as elite or middle class, such as Ath Thuri, Ras Al Amud, Wadi Al Joz and As Suwana.

* *The enhancement of Israeli West Jerusalem.* In stark contrast to East Jerusalem's demise as the primary Palestinian center, the wall will significantly enhance West Jerusalem as an Israeli metropolis. That process began to evolve in 1973 and developed with the establishment

of Jewish settlements around Jerusalem inside the Palestinian territory. In order to assure the role of West Jerusalem as a Jewish metropolitan center, since the end of the 1990's Israel has intensified this process by establishing an infrastructure of roads, tunnels, bridges and settlement by-pass routes that reduce distances between the settlements and West Jerusalem and strengthen the linkage of the settlements with the Jewish capital. These physical facts on the ground have created two road networks: the first is a modern and developed system that has contributed to the strengthening and development of Jerusalem's Jewish settlements, and the second is an old network that the winding wall has transformed into a disjointed collection of dead end roads which are used only by the Palestinian side. Whereas the road system was once a regional network composed of main roads that linked East Jerusalem with the north and south West Bank and eastward to Jericho and Amman, its function is now limited essentially to travel between Palestinian neighborhoods within East Jerusalem.

* *Wither the Palestinian capital?* The wall in and around Jerusalem may well have an irreversible negative impact on East Jerusalem as a cultural and service center capable of serving as a political capital. The stature lost by Jerusalem since Oslo due to the closures and isolation of East Jerusalem from the West Bank, the development of alternative administrative centers in Gaza and Ramallah, and the departure of institutions from East Jerusalem have made it almost impossible for the city to recapture its standing. The situation is only exacerbated by the wall: the exclusion of its neighborhoods and suburbs will further shrink the city; the blocking of its natural paths of expansion will curtail its growth; and lands previously available for development are isolated by the wall. These trends and new facts on the ground appear irreversible if the wall remains.

The new reality imposed by the wall and the disruptive Israeli infrastructure undermine the possibility of ever restoring Palestinian centrality to East Jerusalem and significantly, if not entirely, deny its potential to serve in the future as the capital of a Palestinian state. Further, the wall will end the role of the secondary centers linked with Jerusalem, especially Ar Ram and Bir Nabala to the north and Al Eizariya to the east. These communities, which were essentially extensions of East Jerusalem, served the city and also functioned as "interaction meeting zones" that allowed contact between Jerusalemites and residents of West Bank areas and thus abetted a sense of Palestinian unity and identity. These secondary centers now will be isolated from East Jerusalem and artificially oriented toward Ramallah and Bethlehem, even though they do not have a strong functional relationship with those cities. Transformation of these areas into enclaves will not only strip them of their relational role to Jerusalem but will also cause these centers to lose commercial and institutional bodies that are the lifeblood of these communities. They will become peripheral or frontier towns.

A Political Prognosis

The constructed and planned segments of the wall in the Jerusalem area are intended to realize demographic objectives (ensuring a Jewish demographic majority in Jerusalem and the area annexed to it within the wall), territorial objectives (annexation of additional Palestinian lands for the free movement of Israelis and expansion of their interests), and "soft" ethnic cleansing (ensuring and consolidating Israelis' life fabric, while fragmenting Palestinian life and ultimately forcing Palestinians to emigrate).The wall has been built in accordance with the specifications required for a formal border. It includes a wall, electric and barbed-wire fences, border patrol roads, and crossings that cannot be traversed without permits issued from the Israeli side. Israel has presented this wall as a temporary security barrier that can be dismantled in case of a political settlement with Palestinians. But the reality is very different. A number of factors are at work to make the structure a permanent part of the geographical and political landscape: it will allow Israel to create security zones to control the entire West Bank; it will be easily construed by Israeli politicians and strategists to be a border; the immense investment in the wall can hardly be justified for something "temporary"; the territorial/security/demographic considerations made in determining its path, and the settlement schemes accompanying it all suggest that the wall is an imposed permanent border fulfilling Israel's interests and contradicting the most basic human rights. Ignored is the Palestinian national right to establish a capital in Jerusalem in accordance with a peaceful two state solution.

The historical road previously connecting Bethlehem to Jerusalem is now interrupted be the wall.

The wall is a geopolitical settlement imposed by Israel. It is the final phase of the separation process that began on the eve of the Oslo Accords with the erection of checkpoints isolating Jerusalem from its Palestinian environment. The wall will render it nearly impossible to conduct geopolitical talks concerning Jerusalem, or to make the city an open city with two capitals for two states-West Jerusalem as the capital of the State of Israel, and East Jerusalem in accordance with the 1967 borders as the capital of the future state of Palestine. In fact, it is possible to argue that, while the symbolic importance of Jerusalem formed an obstacle to reaching a bilateral solution in the past, the new reality imposed by Israel in the form of the wall and the annexation of Greater Jerusalem, is a new physical barrier to the peaceful existence of two states.

CHAPTER TWO

The Wall and the Economy of the Jerusalem Governorate

Robert D. Brooks, ph. D.

I. INTRODUCTION

The Economic Imperative: Israeli Control of the Palestinian Economy

Various UN and NGO organizations have recognized that decades of military occupation have made the Palestinian economy essentially if not totally dependent on Israel.* Indeed, with the onset of the occupation in 1967 the Palestinian economy has functioned at the sufferance of Israeli economic policy. The goal of that policy originally was to integrate the West Bank, East Jerusalem and Gaza economies with the Israeli economy, and, at the same time, to keep the Palestinian economy underdeveloped and dependent upon the Israeli economy.

Five features of the policy have accounted for most of its effect:**

The creation of bureaucratic obstacles by civil administrations, military authorities and Israeli laws, that discouraged, delayed, or prevented investment in the Palestinian economy. The best known tactics were banking restrictions affecting loans and development; land-use prohibitions; delayed and exorbitant permitting fees; multi-layered red-tape and unpredictable cycles of road and border closures.

Inflicting de jure and de facto Israeli trade monopolies on Palestinian markets by blocking imports on selected products from other countries, resulting in non-competitive pricing and controlled availability. Unfortunately, after Oslo, in some product areas the Palestinian government not only accepted Israeli organizations as "sole supplier" but also aggravated the effect of the Israeli monopoly problem by creating exclusive Palestinian distributing organizations for those imported products. The matching Israeli and Palestinian gas and oil monopolies come to mind immediately but there are many others.

Encouraging large numbers of Palestinians to enter the Israeli labor market in fields not attractive to Israeli nationals: agriculture, construction, and low-end service sector positions. This doubtless had some positive impact initially, but Palestinian dependence on this source of income has come back to haunt the economies of the Occupied Palestinian Territories (OPT). Palestinian laborers are now being rapidly replaced by Israelis effectively moved back into the workforce by an American-styled Welfare-to-Work program and by illegal immigrants from developing countries***.

---

*See for example the UNCTAD report, " Palestinian Economy Has Deteriorated," August 27, 2005; L. Mair and R. Long, "Israel's Stranglehold on the Palestinian Economy is Consolidated by a Massive Wall," in *Dollars and Sense,* November 2003; B'Tselem and HaMoked, *One Big Prison: Freedom of Movement to and From the Gaza Strip on the Eve of the Disengagement Plan, Jerusalem:* March 2005; E. Young, "The Palestinian Economic Dependence on Israel," *Policy Watch Report No. 1088,* The Washington Institute for Near East Policy, March 23, 2006 and, for Jerusalem in particular, see M. Margalit, "Part 2: Municipal Budgets," in *Discrimination in the Heart of the Holy City,* IPCC: Jerusalem, 2006.

**The framework for the analysis which follows draws from the work of two Israeli organizations, B'Tselem and HaMoked cited in the footnote above.

***R. Auit and S. Hever, "Breaking the Labor Market: The Welfare to Work Plan in Israel," in *Economy of the Occupation,* Alternative Information Center, Jerusalem, 2006, pp. 34-49.

The World Bank has estimated that the dilapidated Palestinian infrastructure in urban areas alone requires an investment of five billion USD. A deteriorated infrastructure has not only driven down potential Palestinian production and severely handicapped the transport and the movement of goods, it has discouraged both internal and external investment in new enterprises, especially those dependent upon export trade. Israel has essentially ignored the obligation of an occupying power to maintain the OPT infrastructure.* Indeed, it has done much to destroy it.

An assault on the Palestinian agricultural sector by expropriating land, limiting water supply, and restricting export by policy and, later, by controlling access to fields and restricting the movement of goods. Most recently in the area of the northwestern stretch of the wall that is now completed, Israel has expropriated 25,000 acres of Palestinian farm land in an area that accounts for 42% of the West Bank agriculture sector and 80% of the West Bank wells. And while the Israelis have provided twenty gates in the wall so that farmers can have access to their lands and water, most gates are permanently closed and the others open only sporadically.**

Palestinian dependence was not significantly alleviated by the 1993 Oslo Agreements and the 1994 Paris Protocols that developed from them. The Palestinian Authority (PA) and Israel formed a customs union which facilitated trade and, importantly, provided a significant revenue flow to the PA. The protocols obligated the Israelis to pass on to the PA import duties Israel collected on goods shipped to the occupied territories and the VAT tax collected by Israel on goods and services intended for consumption in Palestine. The gross for these revenues is about 75 million USD per month, which, after certain Israeli charges, nets the PA approximately 60 million USD per month.*** On the other hand, these Israeli actions and the revenues that flowed from them have made Palestine even more dependent on Israel and effectively have sustained Israeli control of the Palestinian economy.

The devil was in the details.

While the Palestinian economy was very dependent upon Palestinian employment in Israel, there was nothing in the Paris Protocols that ensured the free movement of labor. Israel has repeatedly imposed restrictions on the number of workers allowed in daily and, on many occasions, has stopped the labor flow completely.**** In 1993 nearly one-third of all Palestinian employment was in Israel or in its settlements: 73,000 from the West Bank and 43,000 from Gaza. By the year 2000, the Jerusalem and West Bank flow alone had increased to 116,000. However, over recent years, Israel has gradually sought to replace Palestinians by foreign workers and by incentives to attract Israeli workers to the low-end jobs Palestinians have filled. The labor flow from the Jerusalem Governorate to Israel, for example, has slowed substantially from 43,000 in 2003 to 28,000 in Q2-2005. While this still represents 25.7% of the employed governorate workers (and 32% in J1) and accounts for over 25% of personal income in the governorate, Israeli policy now calls for the Palestinian labor flow to stop completely by the end of 2007. Historically this source of income for Palestine has been second only to the wages paid to the 165,000 PA employees. Thus, to control the labor market, is to have a fundamental grip on the governorate and national economy, and to close this source of income for the OPT is to strike a near fatal blow to the economy of a state-in-the-making.

*See **Table II: 3** below for data on the neglect of the East Jerusalem infrastructure which Margalit estimates as "...at least one billion NIS" [p. 136-137].
**L. Mair and R. Long, 2003.
***E. Young, 2006.
****The common Israeli army explanation for closure has been the anticipation of a "security" problem, usually rumors of a pending attempt to infiltrate a suicide bomber. But in the four decades of the occupation only a very few acts of violence or terror that have occurred can be attributed to legal or illegal Palestinians working in Israel.

Following Oslo, a closure regime was imposed on the OPT. Virtually all Palestinian trade with Israel and other countries had to be handled via Israeli seaports or across borders which Israel controlled. The Israeli imposed closures, long delays at crossings and the embargoing of loaded incoming containers at ports for months on end are legendary. Israel controls these shipping points and has used the control to the absolute detriment of the Palestinian economy. Most recently in Gaza, after agreeing to keep the border for trade to and via Egypt open, the Israelis in fact closed the crossing for "security reasons" for frequent and lengthy periods. Most of the vegetable export crop of Gaza rotted in trucks and had to be dumped in the fields. In the Kafkaesque border regime, Israel at times has allowed Palestinian trucks to exit but not permitted them a return entry. The internal movement of goods is also frequently stymied by bazaar bureaucratic closure policies. Ir Amim reports on the situation in the Shu'fat Refugee Camp, a large East Jerusalem J1 community with many small trade a gate in the wall there for auto and pedestrian traffic, but goods from the Refugee Camp shops cannot transit here even though the camp is in East Jerusalem. Shippers must take their goods many kilometers north to the Betunia West Bank Terminal near Ramallah which West Bankers use to import goods into Israel. They must use the back-to-back method of transferring their goods by off-loading them onto another vehicle on the Israeli side of the terminal. And their goods are taxed as imports. Thus, a mile or so local delivery from one East Jerusalem community to another has been turned into a 30-mile international shipment. [October 31, 2006.]

Israeli control over collected VAT and customs revenue intended for the PA has been used as a means to pressure or punish Palestinians. The current withholding of these funds to the Hamas government is several hundred million USD; this has caused a crisis for 165,000 government employees (and their 800,000 dependents) who cannot receive their salaries, the vast majority of whom were hired by the Fatah government and thus owe no special loyalty to Hamas per se. The income from this revenue accounts for nearly one-half of the salary and wage income in the West Bank and Gaza. The expressed Israeli desire to "Hurt the Palestinian Government but not the Palestinian people" rings hollow. This economic weapon--withholding Palestinian revenues--has been used brutally by several Israeli regimes, most recently by Messrs. Sharon and Olmert. Many international organizations view the withholding actions as further instances of collective punishment.

In a real sense, Israel has controlled not only the movement of trade goods via the customs union and by border controls, but also by setting taxes and quotas on other country imports. This has kept non-Israeli goods out of Palestine or has inflated the prices for non-Israeli products and thus allowed Israeli goods to be marketed in Palestine at higher prices than what a free market would have permitted, all to the benefit of Israeli producers and at the expense of Palestinian consumers.

Small economies are especially dependent on trade. They often lack natural resources and almost always lack the ability to manufacture the goods they require. These have to be imported. But a serious economic problem arises: Palestine imports much more than it exports. This results in an annual trade deficit of 2 billion USD, a seemingly small number for the developed economies of the world, but in Palestine it represents approximately 50% of the total GNP. The deficit cannot be sustained at that rate. But with Israel's ability to restrain Palestinian production, to limit the movement of goods, and to discourage investment, there is no "jump start" in exports on the horizon.

We will postpone a detailed examination of the Jerusalem economy until the next section of this chapter, but we would be remiss in this overview of Israeli economic policy if we did not briefly observe the Jerusalem Municipal Budget at work. The data will show that Israel systematically under-funds Arab East Jerusalem even though it claims sovereignty over the area, collects property taxes, and social security payments, among many other levies, and asserts its responsibility for the public services and infrastructure of the community. Chronic under-funding abets the process of economic underdevelopment and leads to *de-development*.

Our analysis is drawn from Meir Margalit's [2006] pioneering research, *Discrimination in the Heart of the Holy City*. Margalit worked for the Jerusalem Municipal Government for twenty years and writes as an insider. The basic premise of his work is that the Arabs of Jerusalem represent 34% of the municipal population; expenditures of the municipal budget for Arab East Jerusalem should, in general approximate that percentage as a ratio to West Jerusalem funding. **Tables II: 1, 2, and 3** demonstrate that the budgets do not approach this criterion level; the levels of under-funding keep the Palestinian areas of the city depressed and ill-served.

Table II: 1 Distribution of the Jerusalem Municipal Budget (NIS) 2003

	Municipal Budget	E. Jerus. %	W. Jerus. %
Aggregate Budget	3,547,261,000	8.48	91.3
Less Adm&Debt Expense.	2,566,052,204	11.72	88.8
Development Funding	768,563,000	13.00	87.0

Source: Margalit, 2006, pp. 106-112. These are audited data which are approved at the conclusion of the budget year.

When Margalit examined line items for investment in infrastructure, the disparity between the two urban areas was evident **(Table II: 2).**

Table II: 2 Selected Infrastructure Investments

	W. Jerus.	E. Jerus.	Residents per unit of Service W. Jerus	Residents per unit of Service E. Jerus.
(Streets (km	680	87	780	2,448
(Sidewalks (km	650	76	690	2,917
(Sewage network (km	650	76	743	2,809
Garbage containers	11,040	655	39	5,641
Garbage trucks	2,371	49	185	4,489

Source: Margalit, 2006, pp. 115 and 126.

A similar pattern of disparity occurs for other infrastructure service departments such as Engineering Services, City Planning, Health, and Education. **Table II: 3** shows the accumulated effect of neglecting the East Jerusalem infrastructure in terms of the expenditures that would be necessary to close the gap between the two areas.

Table II: 3 The Infrastructure Gap

Year	Sum Needed to Equalize East and West Infrastructures (NIS)
1994	520,000,000
1999	776,000,000
2001	980,000,000
2005	1,000,000,000*

Source: Margalit, 2006, pp. 136-137: "At least one billion."

This systematic short-changing of East Jerusalem is not a new development associated with the Intifada. It is enduring Israeli policy. Consider these remarks from a 1990 interview with the longtime mayor of Jerusalem, Teddy Kollek:

> We said things without meaning them, and we didn't carry them out. We said over and over that we would equalize [the treatment of the two urban areas, West and East Jerusalem]. Empty talk...For Jewish Jerusalem I did something in the past twenty-five years. For East Jerusalem? Nothing! What did I do? Nothing?...Yes we installed a sewerage system for them and improved the water supply. Do you know why? Do you think it was for their good...Forget it! There were some cases of cholera there, and the Jews were afraid they would catch it, so we installed sewerage and a water system against cholera. [B'Tselem, 1995, p. 38]

In summary, we would stress three ideas. Firstly, while Israeli economic policy has evolved away from integration and toward separation from the Palestinians, it remains an economic policy of dominance and control tempered only by indifference and malign neglect. Second, we would emphasize the obvious: the ability to control the flow of goods, labor, and investment capital is clearly the ability to destroy. To date these powers have been used to de-develop the Palestinian economy. Thirdly, in the instance of Jerusalem, biased Israeli budgeting—which is policy in action--has operated to depress the economy. In the following sections we shall see how the wall will be a critical element in tightening the Israeli economic stranglehold on Jerusalem.

The Jerusalem Social Fabric

In considering the economy of the Jerusalem Governorate*, and the serpentine containment wall that will wind through and around it, we must take a geographic and sociological perspective that complex metropolitan fabric whose functionality extends from Salfit in the northwest area of the West Bank, south to the city of Hebron, eastward to Jericho, and westward to the Latrun villages. At the center of this broad metropolitan area lies the Jerusalem Governorate, itself a sprawling megalopolis

---

*The Jerusalem Governorate, as opposed to the Israeli defined Jerusalem Municipality, has been defined by the PA as 51 communities with a total estimated end-of-2006 population of 412,000 (rounded). The urban J1 area (20 communities) has a population of 256,000; the suburban J2 area (31 communities), 156,000 [Palestinian Central Bureau of Statistics (hereafter, PCBS), *Jerusalem Statistical Yearbook*, No. 8, June 2006, p.157.] We will be working within this governorate frame except where otherwise specified. The PCBS *Yearbooks* report data in J1, J2 or combined governorate format in most reports. However, not all *Yearbook* data are updated annually. Thus, while most of the data used in this chapter are drawn from the most recent edition (No. 8, 2006), they may reflect, variously, 2000, 2001, 2002, 2003, 2004, 2005 or estimated end-of-2006 measures. While the Israeli Central Bureau of Statistics reports are also available, they generally have not been consulted since the Israeli definitions of Jerusalem's boundaries differ from the Palestinian definitions, and the Israeli reports commonly merge and do not segregate East (Palestinian) and West (Israeli) Jerusalem data.

made up of the J1 area (the area forcefully annexed by Israel in 1967 which includes Palestinian East Jerusalem and its immediate neighborhoods) and the J2 area (a scattered belt of outlying suburban and hinterland centers, towns, and villages). The core of the governorate lies in J1 East Jerusalem and from there the governorate stretches through J2, north to Ramallah and south to Bethlehem. This is a geography with broad sociological and economic implications. Many members of the Palestinian society encompassed within this metropolitan/megalopolis frame reside in one location, attend mosque or church at another governorate town, have family in one or more of the other 50-plus governorate communities, pay their bills and visit medical facilities in other communities, and send their children (often by necessity) to school or university in still another town and have their place of work in yet some other center, town, or village. In short, on any given day, a typical Jerusalemite will—by necessity-- travel to and navigate through several communities. Introducing a serpentine wall into this commuting culture produces more than mere inconvenience. It effectively nullifies a way of life. **Table II: 4** illustrates the complexity of daily life and the impact the wall has on mobility.

Table II: 4 Percentage of Governorate Households Perceiving Difficulties from Impact of Wall,2005

Perceived Impact Area	J1	J2	Gov
Difficulties in Visiting Relatives	69.1	65.1	67.6
Difficulties in Enjoying Social Activities	71.1	69.9	70.7
Difficulties in Accessing Culture/Entertain	66.7	87.3	74.2
Difficulties in Accessing Education	39.7	44.2	41.4
Difficulties Conducting Personal Business	33.0	79.0	49.6
Change in Employment	31.5	49.8	38.1
Difficulties in Economic Relations	34.4	67.0	46.2
Difficulties in Health Care	27.4	96.7	52.5
Increase in Transportation Time or Cost	68.1	98.0	78.9
Changed Place of Residence	30.6	22.8	27.8
Decrease in Income	47.2	81.7	59.7

Source, PCBS, "Main Findings" in *Social Survey of Jerusalem Governorate*, Jerusalem: November, 2005, p. 87 and unpublished IPCC Survey of 1200 Households, 2005.

The number of Palestinians who reside in the Jerusalem Governorate and who will be trapped outside the wall or contained within an enclave will exceed 180,000.* However, this solitary datum, chilling as it is, ignores the plight of all East Jerusalemites and that of residents of other parts of the governorate. They will no longer be able to transit to the walled-off and enclaved areas without either long delays at checkpoints or significantly longer routes to their destinations. In short, the total Palestinian Jerusalemite population affected by the so-called Jerusalem Envelope is 412,000.

_____

*We have determined this number based on the population statistics of nine enclaves; each enclave includes one or more J1 or J2 communities that have either been placed on the Israeli side of the wall, cut off from East Jerusalem or are essentially surrounded by the wall. The enclaves are: Enclave One, Bir Nabala, Al Judeira, Al Jib, Beit Hanina Al Balad, (14,450); Enclave Two, Qalandiya (1,171); Enclave Three, Kafr Aqab (10,565); Enclave Four, Ar Ram, Dahiyat Al Bareed (55,000 est.); Enclave Five, Hizma (6,187); Enclave Six, Shu'fat Refugee Camp, Anata , Al Fheidat (28,064); Enclave Seven, Abu Dis,Al Eizariya, As Sawahira ash Sharqiya, Ash Sheikh Sa'ad (37,675); Enclave Eight, Beit Anan, Beit Duqqu, Beit Surik, Al Qubeiba, Beit Ijza, Biddu, Qatanna, Kharayeb Umm al Lahim (27,052); Enclave Nine, Rafat (2155). Total: 182,319. While most Israeli sources consistently grossly understate the number of communities and the population affected by the wall, Eldar recently put the figure at "some 200,000)" [2006, p. 9]. Four of the enclaves are examined in detail in Chapter 4.

The ID Card and the Center of Life

Unlike most democracies, whose citizens may be issued a single ID document or none at all, Israel imposes upon the occupied Palestinian population an array of ID cards, residency permits, mobility, and "overnight" stay passes. Central to an understanding of the economic effects of the wall is the blue Israeli identity card issued to Palestinians who are entitled to reside in J1-East Jerusalem. Since 1996, in order to obtain this card, East Jerusalem (J1) must be one's "Center of Life," the place where one resides, pays taxes, works, and sends his or her children to school.

The bearer of this card is entitled to participate in a wide range of social and welfare benefits supported in large by the Israeli government, including child support, unemployment and family health insurance. However, during the 1980's, before the "Center of Life" residency policy came into effect, thousands of "Blue Carders" migrated outside the city limits to J2 and West Bank communities; still more migrated after 1996.* In the intervening years, the East Jerusalem transplants to J2/WB have multiplied significantly, obeying the Palestinian high birthrate pattern. Indeed, prior to the beginning of construction of the wall, PASSIA [2006, p. 325] estimates that as many as one-third of all Blue Carders, or 90,000, resided outside the J1 area in J2 or in the West Bank hinterland of the governorate. Many, if not most, of the migrants have not informed the Israeli government of their new domicile. Most continue to work within J1 and continue to pay their taxes and social security charges to Israel, seemingly proving that Jerusalem is still their "center of life." Upon completion of the wall, these blue card J2/WB-migrants will probably be cut off from their employment in East Jerusalem and from access to the city's culture and services; more importantly for a poverty-stricken population, they will be cut off from the Israeli entitlement and welfare programs.

Our research has uncovered no informed Palestinian or Israeli source who predicts that J1 blue card migrants to J2/WB, or J1 Blue Carders now living in the wall-recreated enclaves, will be able to retain their East Jerusalem J1 status. Most, such as Klein, believe that Israel does not intend to grant them the rights of East Jerusalemites. [Klein, 2003, p. 1] Today, in anticipation of this unpleasant likelihood, wall victims have already begun returning to the city to protect their center of life status. The scale of the problem is revealed by examining data from just four of the enclaves: Kafr Aqab and Shu'fat Refugee Camp have over 30,000 Blue Carders now cut off from J1; of the 2300 residents of Shiekh Sa'ad, an estimated 1000 Blue Carders have already abandoned the enclave and moved to the Palestinian side of the J1 wall; in Ar Ram/Dahiyat Al Bareed, out of an estimated population in excess of 50,000, 60% are thought to be Blue Carders who will have to choose between moving back to East Jerusalem or re-orienting their life northward toward Ramallah. Klein [2003] and Shragai [2004] estimated that 300 blue card families (which extrapolate to 1200+ residents) have been returning weekly. Collectively, this movement wave, which PASSIA [2006, p. 32] places currently at tens of thousands, has generated a mass population transfer that is exacerbating population density, rental rates, slum creation and crime rates in the city and eventually will create in its wake further deterioration and moribund J2 and West Bank suburban neighborhoods. Given the general trend of the Israeli governments toward separatism, the probability of migrant Blue Carders losing their J1 status would appear to be strong, barring a basic change in Israeli policies.

The Population and the Land Area Affected by the Wall

The projected length of the Jerusalem wall is 130 kilometers, 33 of which have been completed as of May 2006; 13 kilometers are under construction and 42 are pending court decisions [Harel, pp.

---

* Many factors fueled the migration, not the least of which were economic considerations: the suburbs offered substantially more land for building, lower construction costs, lower tax rates, and lower rental expense.

1-3; Lynk, pp. 17 and note 65, p. 23]. In as much as the exact route of the barrier has not been officially decided, with significant stretches pending court decisions, and with some aspects of the wall contested internationally and by the US administration, it is difficult to predict with total accuracy how much land it will effectively consume, how much governorate territory will be affected, and the population most seriously impacted.* The PCBS 2006 estimates are: the wall construction project has led to the confiscation of 11,000 dunums (2773 acres) of land; it has isolated within the wall 41,000 dunums (10,200 acres); it has directly disrupted 27 localities; it has displaced 1,635 households and 9,609 residents. At least 180,000 Palestinian residents of enclaves will be affected. Indeed, PCBS calculates that 50% of the Palestinian Jerusalem population will be inside the wall and 50% outside of it.**

In some communities, such as Rafat, a town of 2300, which is surrounded on three sides by the wall, as much as 75% of the land has been appropriated. Moreover, the Israeli cabinet has approved routing the wall significantly eastward in the governorate to bring the Ma'aleh Abdumin and other outlying eastern settlements within Jerusalem's wall. Incorporating these communities into the city will involve implementing the so-called E-1 massive annexation plan. This annexation area, which until recently was viewed as the natural expansion zone for a number of Palestinian J1 villages, will add an additional 53,000 dunums (14,000 acres) to Israeli territory [Horowitz, 2005]. The absorption of E-1 is part of PM Olmert's Convergence/Realignment Plan that will enfold thousands of settlers (35,000 in Ma'aleh Abdumin alone) into Jewish Jerusalem, significantly thwarting the "demographic threat" posed by the higher Arab birthrate. At the same time, the eastward thrust of the wall to capture outlying settlements will extend West Jerusalem's borders 14 kilometers in the direction of Jericho and the Jordan, virtually bisecting the West Bank and rendering a meaningfully contiguous future state very improbable.***

Each day, approximately 65,000 commuters transit Israeli controlled crossing points each way. And while the Israeli planners envision a reported eleven "gates" and two cargo depots to service the Jerusalem wall traffic, they are also planning a regime of electronic cards that include biometric data. These may facilitate somewhat the movement of those commuters with Israeli ID cards, but that will not lubricate the passage of J2 residents, nor that of West Bankers, tourists, and the thousands of international civil servants and foreign NGO employees who work and move about in Jerusalem and the West Bank areas. Or, to take the most ubiquitous commuter: students. Over 15,000 students will pass through the barrier each way daily from Ar Ram alone. It is difficult to imagine, even with 21st Century technology, how this volume of traffic can be handled without serious delays. Indeed, just in the area of education, PCBS[2005] surveys indicate 3.2% of individuals who live in checkpoint

---

* As this is writing, The High Court of Justice (Israel's Supreme Court) has ruled in at least one instance that defense officials routed the wall on non-security grounds, acquiring additional Palestinian land for industrial development near an Israeli settlement. In short its route was based on substantially economic considerations. That stretch of the wall has been ordered dismantled and moved to a position closer to the settlement [Yoaz, 2006, p A-3]. Following this decision, Defense Minister Peretz has ordered a review of the route of the barrier, particularly in the Jerusalem area. It is reported that he is concerned about "the number of Palestinians left on the western side." [Eldar, 2006, p. 1] Minor changes in the route of the wall have been made in Beit Surik, Beit Liqia, Beit Iksa, Ar Ram and Dahiyat Al Bareed.

**_Yearbook_ No. 8, pp. 370 and 398. PCBS also reports that an astonishing 62% of the governorate population over the age of ten has moved or will move as a consequence of the wall (p. 400).

***The West Bank is only 56 km (35 miles) broad at its widest point. And the distance between the eastern border of the municipality and the Jordan River is a scant 25 km (15.5 miles). The wall around E-1 and its eastern settlements will consume 14 km (approximately 8.75 miles) of this, leaving a bottleneck corridor only 11 km (less than 7 miles) wide connecting the northern and southern West Bank, far to the east of East Jerusalem. This geographical pattern will make the would-be Palestinian capital a peripheral city and will break the West Bank into two barely contiguous north and south cantons. Moreover, settlements, walled enclaves and a network of "Israelis Only" highways will fragment the two cantons further into isolated and disconnected Bantustans.

and wall affected areas have abandoned their education because of the difficulties of movement; that 89% of the households in the affected localities which have university students and 48% of those with basic or secondary education students are currently forced to use long detour roads to reach thei schools; and 80% of the latter have had to be absent due to movement obstacles [PCBS, August 2006, pp. 6-7]. No one imagines that the completed wall will alleviate this problem.

While we may cite the total acreage or kilometers effectively fenced off and the size of the affected population, the reality of the situation is that all of the governorate and the rest of the West Bank are affected. East Jerusalem is the historic, economic, social and cultural center of the Palestinian people, and the wall will effectively deny access to J2/WB/G residents. Indeed, it is often said, and not in jest, that the so-called security wall around Jerusalem does not so much separate Palestinians from Israelis as much as Palestinians from Palestinians.

II. THE GOVERNORATE ECONOMY

While it is true that the economy of J1 and J2 is somewhat stronger than that of the rest of the West Bank and certainly that of the Gaza Strip, it remains a fact that the governorate economy has been in shambles for several years. Three generalizations provide the appropriate context for assessing the situation: 1) The levels of unemployment, poverty, dependency ratios, population density, and malnutrition among children are among the highest in the Middle East region; 2) The national incomes account data of its neighbor Israel are eight to ten times that of the governorate, which is among the highest differentials between any two neighboring states in the world; 3) Even from the Israeli perspective, the Jerusalem Municipality (which combines Palestinian East and Israeli West Jerusalem) is the poorest urban area in Israel.

Economic Indicators and Standard of Living in the Governorate

Tables II: 5, 6, 7, 8 and **9** present an overview of the East Jerusalem economy.

Table II: 5 Annual GDP-pc, GNDI-pc and GNI-pc (2002)

GDP per capita	J1	1365 USD
	J2/WB	1350 USD
GNI per capita	J1	2,004 USD
	J2/WB	1,431 USD
GNDI per capita	J1	2,194 USD
	J2/WB	1,779 USD

Source: *Yearbook* No. 8 (2006), p. 247. The World Bank reports GNI data for West Bank and Gaza at a mere USD 930. In stark contrast, Israeli GNI-pc data for 2004 was 17,380 USD.

Table II: 6 Sources of Personal Income: April-June 2005

Main Source of Income	J1	J2	Governorate
Agriculture and Fishing	0.4	2.2	1.1
Household business	14.4	19.0	16.0
Wages/Salaries from PA	5.3	15.0	8.8
Wages/Salaries from Private Sector	21.5	31.7	25.2
Income from Israeli Sectors	32.2	14.2	25.7
National Insurance	21.0	1.6	14.0
Transfers within Palestine Territories	0.1	4.5	1.7
Transfers from Abroad	0.5	3.0	1.4
Social Assistance	0.3	4.2	1.7
Other	3.9	2.9	3.5
No Source	0.4	1.7	0.9

Source: PCBS, "Main Findings," *Social Survey of Jerusalem Governorate* 2005, p. 104

Table II: 7 Selected Standard of Living Measures (2004)

Housing

Percent owning their own home:	J1	68.6
	J2	78.1
Average size of living unit:	J1	3.1 rooms
	J2	3.7 rooms
	Gov.	3.3
Average No. of persons per housing unit:	J1	4.9
	J2	6.0
	Gov	5.3
No. persons per room:	J1/J2	2.0
Percent in unit with 3 or more rooms:	J1	21.4
	J2	12.7
Percent units having bathrooms:		79.5
Percent units with more than one family:		15.6

Table II: 7 (countinued)

Services and Durable Goods	
Number of registered private automobiles (J1 2003):	18,519
Percent persons with health insurance:	75.5
Percent households with television:	98.7
Percent households with satellite:	80.9
Percent households using computer:	45.6
Percent households using internet:	20.1
Percent with land line telephones:	54.7
Percent with cell phones:	92.5

Source: *Yearbook* No. 8, pp. 44, 138, 163, 176, 342; *Yearbook* No. 5 and No. 6 (website); PCBS *Household Social Survey of Jerusalem*, 2004.

Table II: 8 Governorate Employment, and Distribution of Work Force by Sectors in 2005 (%)

Work Force Sector	J1	J2	Governorate
Construction	16.6	21.7	12.8
Manufacturing, Mining and Quarry	11.4	17.6	15.6
Services	29.3	29.9	31.5
Commerce, Hotels & Restaurants	32.3	21.3	28.9
Transport., Storage, Communication	9.8	6.9	9.7
Agriculture	3.6	2.6	1.5
Total			100%

Source: *Yearbook* No. 8, p. 217 and PCBS *Social Survey* 2005, p.81. The PCBS *Service Sector includes* data for Public Administration; Education; Health, Welfare and Social Work Services; Community, Social, and Personal Services (including cultural); and Private Households with Domestic Personnel. Note: the PA provides no government services in J1 but some in J2. *Commerce* here includes internal wholesale and retail trade and repairs and auto sales and repairs.

Table II: 9 Employment, Unemployment, Earnings, Spending, and Poverty Levels*

Labor Force Participation rate, ILO standard:	37.2 %
Labor Force Participation rate, relaxed definition**	40.8%
Employed in Israel or Settlements:	J1 32.2%; J2 14.2 %; Gov. 25.7%
Unemployment rate, relaxed definition**:	24.0 %
Unemployment by ILO standards:	16.8%
Average Daily Wages in Governorate:	96.2 NIS (22 USD)
Average Daily Wages in Israel and Settlements:	134.6 NIS (30 USD)
Average Monthly Wages in Governorate:	2,357 NIS (523 USD) ***
Average Monthly Wages in Israel and Settlements:	3,257 NIS (723 USD)***
Monthly Family Consumption:	970 JD (6,256 NIS or 1,390 USD)
Monthly Household Expenditures:	JD 870(5611 NIS or 1,247 USD)
Households below poverty level (Oct.-Dec. 2004):	60.6%****
Households losing more than 50% of income in most recent 6 months:	51.6%

*Data are for the governorate, year 2005, taken from *Yearbook* No. 8, 2006, pp. 186, 190, 194, 216, 218, 220-222, 385, and 405.

**Includes long-time unemployed who are no longer actively seeking work.

*** Most workers do not receive monthly pay. It is approximated here by calculating *average daily pay X average days worked per month*. An IPCC survey of 1200 households revealed the following monthly *family* incomes : 12% of the households surveyed had monthly incomes of less than 2,000 NIS (444 USD); 57% of the households reported a combined income of less than 4,000 NIS (888 USD) per month.

****PCBS defines the poverty line here (p. 405) as *household* income less than 2,000 NIS (444 USD) per month. The World Bank poverty rate (2.30 USD per person per day, for the average governorate household of 5.3 persons) would yield a monthly poverty criterion of 1,646 NIS (366 USD).

In the following section, we will track the likely effects of the wall on future employment in the governorate. We shall see that the wall will significantly increase unemployment.

Unemployment

Mobility and Access Effects

The initial major impact of the wall on unemployment will develop from mobility problems: the wall and its associated crossing points and gates will hinder access to places of employment throughout the governorate. Checkpoint delays, often hours long, and longer circuitous routes around them will mean that many workers will not be able to arrive at work reliably, if at all; their number of hours and number of days worked will be reduced, which will contribute significantly to underemployment and unemployment. The IPCC Survey of 1200 Governorate Households found that 84% of those surveyed report moderate-to-high levels of difficulty in commuting to the work place. A recent PCBS social survey (see **Table II: 4** above) indicates that 38.1% of workers in the governorate have experienced changes in employment as a consequence of the wall.

Mobility problems will surely impact unemployment. For workers already unemployed and who are seeking employment, the barrier and delays will increase frustrations and discouragement substantially; de-motivated, many of them will join the ranks of the no-longer-seeking-employment. Agricultural workers residing in the governorate will also be affected. We know from the experience of the northern West Bank completed stretch of the wall, that the barrier will separate governorate farmers and their workers from their fields and water resources and increase difficulties in getting products to the market. While the first effects of this will be a decrease in productivity, and an increase in underemployment and lower earnings, it will eventually lead some farmers to reduce their work force and some to give up farming entirely. Reportage on the wall abounds in family case studies of farmers who have laid down their plows and joined the ranks of the unemployed.* According to a 2005 PCBS survey for all of Palestine, the number of households in the wall areas who depend upon agriculture for the main source of their income has decreased from 61% to 53% after construction of the wall [PCBS, 2006].

Closure of Enterprises

The routing of the wall has vitiated the commercial life of the governorate principally by two mechanisms: by isolating a community from other communities that made up its market area and by physically disrupting the business district by running the wall through it and thereby cutting off all or part of the district from its client base. The effect has been the closure of hundreds of businesses. In a survey of five communities, IPCC has found that over 500 establishments have been closed: in Ar Ram/Dahiyat Al- Bareed, where the wall runs along the very center of the Jerusalem-Ramallah Road, 131 businesses out of a total of 321 in the area have closed; in Anata, where the wall cuts the community off from East Jerusalem, 100 out of 348 enterprises have been shuttered; and in the communities of As Sawahira, Al Eizariya, and Abu Dis respectively, 103, 106, and 63 businesses have closed.** Many more businesses are on the brink of shutting down. Suppliers complain of bad checks and are insisting on cash transactions. And business loans, which might help struggling enterprises survive, are expensive and increasingly difficult to obtain.*** As the situation deteriorates further, countless marginal operations will simply close, and this dismal trend will continue.

---

*According to Mair and Long [2003], the first phase of the wall in the northern West Bank effectively blocked communities there from 25,000 acres (100,000 dunums) of agricultural land. Unemployment in the 18 villages in the Qalqiliya area had averaged 18% before the wall; after the wall, 78%.

**See the IPCC case studies in Chapter Four.

***The Palestine Business Report states that banks had reduced their loans to the industrial sector by 25% well before the Intifada [2001, pp. 1-2 and p. 14]; the PCBS 2003a Household Social Survey of Jerusalem indicates 54% of West Bank business owners have financial difficulties and have difficulties in obtaining loans.

Mobility problems will also impact on business closures, and this is also well documented in the case studies. Here, let us consider the experience of the Intifada closures that began in 2000. The time required to bring products to an outlet tripled; the cost of transport rose by 110% in just one year (2000-2001); the average distance to market doubled.*The completed wall with limited crossing points and cargo depots, and the anticipated traffic jams at "gates" operated by a capricious IDF regime, all spell disaster for the businessman and an increase in firms going out of business. [Dolphin, 102-fn 10.]

Nor can we ignore those establishments that have been or will be simply demolished to make way for the wall. While the precise number of wall-related business demolitions in the governorate is unknown at this writing, Mair and Long [2003] report that 200 shops were demolished for the northern wall in the Nazlat Isa area.**

Movement of Enterprises

Some of the business closures are the result of moving enterprises to areas less impacted by the wall. For example, some businesses have moved their operations to East Jerusalem in order to access a reliable work force, to reduce their transaction costs, and to better serve a city clientele who seek to avoid the inconvenience of checkpoint delays or the time and expense of circuitous routes to J2 enterprises. As a result, these businesses have had to bear the opportunity costs of operating and living in East Jerusalem, such as higher commercial and residential rental rates, higher wages and generally higher costs of living. Other owners have moved because of difficulties in getting raw materials delivered to their enclave or in delivering their finished products or services to the market. The problems will of course only worsen with the completion of the wall and will motivate many more operators to move their businesses. The transfer of operations to J1 has left behind unemployed workers in J2, especially those who lack the blue card and who do not have the option to relocate or work in the city.

The Israeli Labor Market

As we noted earlier in this chapter, for several decades a substantial segment of the governorate work force has been employed in Israel and the settlements—28,000 J1 card holders worked in Israel as recently as Q2-2005. However, Israel's stated intention is to reduce that percentage to zero by the end of 2007 [World Bank, December 2005, p. 16 and fn. 70, p. 28]. There are two dimensions to this reduction: workers with legal permits and illegal or "silent" workers. The legal permit reductions will be phased in; the illegal workers will effectively end with the completion of the wall. Thus J1/WB Palestinian employment in Israel will have followed a steep path of decline: from 116,000 in Q3-2000 to 43,000 in Q1-2003 to zero at the end of 2007. As the wall moves toward completion and Israeli employment opportunities diminish, an unemployment crisis of major proportions will occur.

To conclude this discussion of the impact of the wall on employment, we make four observations.

1. First, and most obviously, the summary fact: the wall will dramatically increase unemployment. The experience of the "separation" in the West Bank districts of Qalqiliya

---

*PCBS, Press Conference, August 2006, p. 7

**The PCBS *Yearbook* (No. 8, pp. 360-361), citing B'tselem data, reports that 294 houses in J1 have been demolished during 2003-2005, and citing Arab Society Studies data for the same period, 461 were demolished in the governorate overall. One may assume that many of the J1 demolitions were for houses built without Israeli permits; the wall would seem a probable explanation for many in the J2 area of the governorate.

and Tulkarm is relevant here. The wall has effectively sealed 18 communities there and caused unemployment to rise from 18% in 2000 to an estimated 78% [PENGON, 43, 2003]. A fate so dire may not be in store for the Jerusalem Governorate, but no one doubts that the effect will be quite serious. Alone, the number of new Palestinians entering the labor market increases by over 4% annually. Even with substantial donor support—which is problematic—given the current Western governments stand-off with Hamas, the World Bank expects Palestinian unemployment to grow throughout 2006—2008.*

2.　　Second, unemployment data are the tip of the poverty iceberg. For many workers, there are a number of additional Jerusalemites (family and extended family members) who are dependent upon him or her for the basic necessities of life—food, clothing, shelter, and for the young, education. For example, the West Bank dependency ratio for Q3-2005 is 5.1 per worker. Alas, the dependency ratio is tied inextricably to the unemployment rate. As the latter increases, which it surely will, more and more people will be dependent upon fewer and fewer employed persons.

3.　　Given the depressed economic situation and the limited investment and development resources, it will be extremely difficult for the Bantuized economy to create new jobs, and as the labor force grows, this will translate into additional unemployment. Indeed, the World Bank projects that even with the return of donor aid, the transfer of VAT and customs revenues, and the easing of closures, the status quo ante will not support development and significant job creation and could not prevent the Palestinian economy from continuing to deteriorate.** As unemployment becomes long-term, hopelessness increases, and so too, its partners-- discontent, resistance, and violence.

4.　　While the long term solution to economic decline lies in increasing the export of goods and services and reducing dependence on labor flows to Israel and on remittances from the Diaspora, the World Bank stresses that in the interim period, "...a priority must be given to employment." According to the Bank, each additional 10,000 Palestinians working in Israel generates 120 million USD for the Palestinian economy and increases GNI by 2.5% [Young, 2006]. Conversely one can reckon that the pending loss of 28,000 J1 Blue Card workers in Israel will cost, when the wall is completed, approximately 316 million USD and 7% of the GNI, unless Israel reverses its labor market separation policy and allows the Palestinian labor flow to continue.

III. KEY ECONOMIC SECTORS

Below we present an analysis of selected key sectors with respect to the governorate economy under conditions of separation and containment.

---

*The World Bank reported that the up-tick in WB/G employment in Israel observed in late 2004 and early 2005 dropped sharply (25%) in the final two quarters of 2005 [World Bank, December 2005, p. 10]. See also the World Bank's economic scenarios for Palestine, under conditions of with/without donor aid or recovery, for years 2006 - 2008 [pp 26-28].

** The World Bank assessment is bleak. "At its core, the Palestinian financial predicament [is] the product of a suffocating economic crisis rooted in a deeply unfavorable political environment." Donor aid, the report continues, "... could only help Palestinians to survive but would have no tangible effect on the economy" [World Bank, March 2006].

*Construction**

In 1997, the Jerusalem Municipality was given an Israeli Government mandate to plan and provide the infrastructure for 3,000 living units in Arab East Jerusalem. The estimated cost of the project was 185 million NIS (41 million USD). Only 9 million NIS (2 million USD) was ever appropriated—en toto from the Israeli municipality and the national government-- and the project was allowed to die. [Margalit, p. 42]. The housing need has continued to grow. Khamaisi and Nasrallah projected in 2003 [p. 173] that the need had grown to six thousand new housing units in the J1 area alone, and it is important to note that estimate did not include the anticipated needs of the thousands of Blue Carders who are now returning to the city. Nevertheless, the need for new construction will remain essentially unaddressed and continue to increase with the population. High unemployment and attendant poverty rates are simply not a platform from which to launch a commercial or residential building boom to rescue the construction sector. Indeed, as Israel moves further along its planned path of disengagement in the construction sector, employment in the field will decline further, with concomitant increases in poverty levels.

There are, further, many regulatory obstacles in the financing of construction in the governorate. Arab banks are not allowed to operate or take real estate as loan collateral in J1. While they may operate in J2 and the West Bank, even here corporate loans require Israeli approval [Hasboun and Baboeram, 2003, p. 87]. Palestinians on the other hand are generally reluctant to take loans from Israeli banks: they naturally hesitate to offer up their real estate as collateral in the hands of institutions that are linked with an adversary that has been active in confiscating and demolishing Palestinian property [Khamaisi and Nasrallah, 63-64, 2003a]. While some international and Diaspora financial institutions have established representation in East Jerusalem, the focus of their activities appears to be on selected areas in the West Bank which are politically more stable. The Jerusalem barrier wall is properly seen as an additional de-stabilizing condition. Obviously, these obstacles and attitudes militate against construction activity and employment in the sector.

While some envision a construction sector revitalized by outside development funds from international donor organizations and investments from the Palestinian Diaspora, we must ask will donors and lenders be motivated to invest in residential or commercial construction if Palestine is not a viable state? While donor states and organizations have made promises of robust aid, in many cases their intentions are highly conditioned on the demise of Hamas or on the formation of a unity government that includes Fatah and other parties. Additionally, some donors await the settlement of the "final issues" between Palestinians and Israel (e.g. recognition of the Palestinian state, the status of Jerusalem, national borders, and the rights of refugees); such a settlement, in the present climate, seems quite unlikely. And, fenced-off from ports and from direct access to Jordan and the Arab countries beyond, global manufacturers who have built facilities in underdeveloped countries elsewhere are unlikely to spur industrial construction in the governorate since they will have significant obstacles in getting their goods to regional or world markets.

Last, hanging over the construction sector, most especially in East Jerusalem, there is a very severe land shortage for any envisioned Palestinian development. The shortage arises from several factors: a) nearly four decades of Israeli massive land appropriations to accommodate 180,000 Jewish settlers; b) thousands of acres confiscated for hundreds of kilometers of broad Israeli roadways linking the

---

* In many of the annual PCBS reports on the various economic sectors, the data column for the "Construction Sector" appears blank. This may in part be due to a PCBS confidentiality policy or it may reflect the fact that most residential construction activity in the governorate is conducted without Israeli permits (10 illegally for every 1 legally, according to Margalit) and thus escapes official PCBS statistics. Our most recent data (2004) record 49 permits for J1 and 95 in J2.[PCBS *Yearbook* No. 7, 2005, p. 244 and Margalit, 2006, pp. 27- 28]. PCBS *Yearbook* No. 8 (2006) records 170 permits for J2 (p. 251) and no data for J1.

Jewish settlements to each other and to Israeli West Jerusalem; c) Israeli demographic objectives to maintain a 70% percent majority Jewish population in the Municipality of Jerusalem; d) dubious zoning policies that designate Palestinian tracts as "open space" and as unplanted "green spaces"; e) the absence of infrastructure (water, sewage, roads) in vacant areas; f) expropriation of land on which to build the wall ; and, most recently, g) the so-called E-1 plan which will effectively grab most of the planned Palestinian expansion area east of Jerusalem. Of the 46,000 dunums (11,500 acres) that remain in Arab East Jerusalem for expansion, only 9,000 (2,250 acres or 19.6% of the total) are zoned for construction. [Margalit, p. 38]. To some, that may seem a reasonable allotment. But, under the yoke of occupation, utilization of this land requires negotiating an incredibly long, complex, and very expensive Israeli permitting policy whose underlying purpose is to discourage and limit Arab building in East Jerusalem. The permitting process takes years—if allowed to go forward—and the various Israeli fees associated with the permit will often exceed the cost of the building itself. In short, Israeli bureaucratic obstacles interact with the limited supply of land to severely limit the prospects of a construction boom, and any employment growth that might be expected in this sector is minimal.

Services

Two major problems currently afflict the OPT service sector: government employment and the tourism component of the sector. At this writing, Israel and the international community have refused to transmit revenues and donor funds to the PA in reaction to the Hamas election victory. Presently 165,000 government employees have not been paid salaries for months, and while donor nations appear to be prepared to resume some transfers, it is unclear under what conditions the transfers might resume and whether the funds will be allowed to find their way into PA salary accounts. The outcome of this problem will have major consequences for J2. Over 15% of personal income there is derived from PA employment. However, since the PA government essentially is not allowed to have offices or facilities in East Jerusalem, only 5% of the personal income in the J1 area is derived from that source.* The tourism area of the service sector is virtually in ruins, and we will discuss that industry separately later in the chapter.

With those two important exceptions--PA employees and employees in the tourism component— the service sector is relatively stable. It encompasses the large number of public and private workers in health, welfare, and social work services; community, social and personal services; and professionals and workers in public and private education. Nevertheless, the sector is not "recession proof." There is exposure, for example, due to dislocation and unemployment in the health and private education fields [Rubenstein, 2005].

Looking first at schools, many families already make enormous financial sacrifices to send their children to private schools. Tuition at these schools may be fairly considered as somewhat discretionary spending since a much less expensive education option is available at government schools. As unemployment, poverty and dependency rates have risen, discretionary family spending has shrunk and this has led to a decline in private school enrollments--and record increases in government schools. But a decrease in family income is not the only force at work here: mobility and access problems arising from the construction of the wall is a significant contributing factor. Private schools throughout the governorate have relied heavily upon students and faculty from outside their towns. Now, with the serpentine wall fracturing the governorate and creating more gates and crossings, longer routes, longer delays, and higher transport costs, more students are enrolling in their local government schools, and commuting faculty, who face those same obstacles and often have the additional problem of securing entry permits, are in danger of losing their positions. Several private schools, afflicted with revenue losses from decreases in enrollment and with faculty access problems,

---

*PCBS *Social Survey* 2005, p. 104 and see **Table II: 6** above.

have already begun to discharge some of their teachers. The 16 UNRWA schools are likely to follow suit: while their enrollments do not present a problem, one third of their faculty are J2/WB residents who experience difficulties accessing their schools reliably. One may expect discharges or re-location of employees in these schools as well. A similar mix of problems has befallen J1 hospitals. They, too, rely heavily upon J2/WB patients and as much as 75% of their staff commutes from homes in J2 and the WB. Declines in revenue and in staff reliability will have economic consequences for these segments of the sector.

Tourism

As a center for the three great monotheistic world religions, tourism has been the keystone of the Jerusalem area economy. The components of this sector include hotel staffing, overnight stays, restaurants, travel and tour agencies, tour guides, tour busses, and the ubiquitous retail shops purveying souvenirs and catering to the diverse needs of tourists. A walk along the Christian Road in the Old City will convince even the casual observer that this sector is in near ruin. Shop after shop stands empty of customers, especially foreigners; dignified owners stand in doorways, some almost frantically beckoning the occasional passing foreigner to come in the shop. Or a stroll in another direction in the "New Center" area will take one by shuttered major Palestinian hotels and numerous closed smaller inns, as well as past the hulls of several major hotel projects abandoned in mid-construction. While there was a clear up-tick in 2005 hotel activity figures which continued to mid-2006, any comparison to 2000 will demonstrate a catastrophic decline in this area (see **Table II: 10**). More recently, hotel bookings (person-nights)in West Jerusalem have increased by 60%*; much of the increase has been absorbed by new Israeli hotels built on the western side of the seam line between East and West Jerusalem, directly adjacent to large Palestinian lots which were planned for hotel construction but never permitted. Doubtless the improvement in the Israeli sector has had some trickle-down impact on commerce, mainly in the Old City of East Jerusalem, where the tourists are hustled through rapidly by their Israeli guides on the way to the Jewish Quarter. But clearly the 2006 situation for East Jerusalem tourism remains far below pre-Intifada levels.

Table II: 10 Hotel Activity in the Governorate for the Years 2000 and 2005

	2000	2005	Decline	%Decline
No. of hotels	43	18	25	58%
No. of rooms	1,997	869	1128	56%
No. of beds	4,345	1,967	2378	54%
Average of room occupancy	897	308	589	65%
Room occupancy rate (%)	44.4	36.5	7.9	17.8%
Average of bed occupancy	1,824	513	1311	72%
Bed occupancy rate	42%	26%	16	38%
No. of guests	206,583	64,784	141,799	69%
No. of guest nights	665,929	187,284	478,645	72%

Source: Yearbook No. 8, p. 281.

During the years of occupation, Israel has used its financial resources and power (political and military) to develop West Jerusalem as the staging area for tourism, clearly at the expense of East Jerusalem.

---

*Jerusalem Post, in "Jewish Population in Jerusalem Slips to 66 percent", May 24, 2006, p. 4.

In 1967, hotel capacity in East Jerusalem was 2,061 rooms, nearly double the West Jerusalem total of 1193 rooms. Today, nearly four decades later, East Jerusalem capacity has declined while the West Jerusalem segment has increased six-fold to 7,129. Similarly, in the associated area of travel agencies, 46 East Jerusalem firms were registered in 1967; by 2000 they had declined to 31, while West Jerusalem travel firms increased twelve-fold during this period from 35 to 436. The same pattern characterizes tour bus activities, but the most dramatic shift may be in the area of licensed tour guides. From a 1967 base of 202 guides and a virtual East Jerusalem monopoly on the profession, their number shrank to 31, while the Israeli base mushroomed from zero to an incredible 4,300. By 1999, East Jerusalem had only 18% of the tourist business, while West Jerusalem had 82%. Israeli firms in West Jerusalem reportedly now market East Jerusalem sites largely as a mere oriental side trip [Hazboun, 210; Hazboun and Baboeram, p. 84; Khamaisi and Nasrallah, 2003a, p. 61].

A number of factors have facilitated the Israeli takeover of this sector, some wholesome, some otherwise. While Jerusalem may be the natural and historical home of the Palestinian people, East Jerusalem is not now the groomed capital of a sovereign state. Under Israeli control East Jerusalem's aesthetics are utterly ignored. Street sanitation is meager, under-budgeted, and understaffed. The citizenry often resort to setting fire to the accumulated trash in the public dumpsters in order to make room for further trash. The miscellaneous street trash, except in the commercial district, is unattended and generates an overall image of a littered, scruffy environment and a people who ignore their community, despite a Palestinian culture that values household and personal cleanliness and pride in grooming and appearance. The Municipality budgetary response to this scene may be gleaned from the allocations detailed in **Table II: 2** (above) and in these data from Margalit [p. 109]: of the 206 million NIS budgeted for Jerusalem cleanliness, less than 17% is earmarked for East Jerusalem: of the 83 million NIS designated for beautification, less than 1% is for East Jerusalem. Similar under-funding in the range of less than 2% occurs in allocations for culture and art. The neglect of East Jerusalem's environment and aesthetics is clearly central to Israel's tourism policy.

Nor does Israel allow Palestinian national edifices and commercial dynamics that one associates with the status of a capital or national home. With PA governmental operations divided mainly between Ramallah, Abu Dis and Gaza City, East Jerusalem verges on becoming a peripheral city. In contrast to this, consider the Israeli capital, West Jerusalem. It has development challenges as well, but on a comparative basis it is the handsome seat of the national government, comparatively very well funded, with many attractive neighborhoods and a modern infrastructure. However, having addressed infrastructure, aesthetic and cultural inequities, let us recognize that much of the Palestinian political "instability" and decline as a tourist destination can be attributed to Israeli policies and actions: the massive annexation of East Jerusalem territory following 1967; the expulsions of the PLO during pre-Oslo years; the installation of a weak Palestinian Authority; the fragmentation of the East Jerusalem area; the repressive nature of the occupation and the disruptive intifadas in response; the periodic withholding of tax and custom revenues due the PA from the Israelis; and the economic colonialism that has stifled development--all of these have combined to create political instability and uncertainty. That is not a scenario for attracting tourists. The wall will obviously accelerate the decline of this sector by diminishing the tourist's experience. Imagine, he or she will see a landscape scared by an ugly structure. They will tour a fragmented city, and based on current projections, movement between many areas of the governorate will be via a very few gates and crossing points. The result will be delays and a disproportionate amount of time spent sitting in the bus.

In summary, the decline in the tourism sector is the greatest economic fall-out of the occupation, except for the general crises in unemployment and poverty. The wall will only exacerbate this situation.

Trade

While it is difficult to segregate Palestinian Jerusalem external trade data out of OPT statistics, it is instructive to look at the combined EJ/WB/G activity. The first datum to be noted is the serious decline Palestine has suffered in this area. In the period 1999-2002 trade declined by more than 50%, and currently the annual trade deficit is running at two billion USD, or the equivalent of 50% of the annual GNP. [MIFTA, 2004] There are many ironies underlying this dismal trade situation.

- Even with closures and construction of the wall, over 90% of Palestinian trade is with Israel.

- While the Arab Summit of 2001 passed a resolution urging members to remove barriers and tariffs on Palestinian trade, only Jordan, Saudi Arabia, and the UAE actually comply to some degree.

- Syria, Lebanon, and Kuwait prohibit imports from the OPT on the tortured reasoning that such trade implies recognition of, or peace with, Israel, since the goods are exported from Israeli ports or via Israeli controlled crossings.

- Libya and Egypt impose barriers to reduce the flow of Palestinian goods.

- In addition to Israel, Palestine has free trade agreements with the USA, Canada, the EU, Switzerland, Liechtenstein, Iceland, and Norway—but not with 20 Arab states. Indeed, only 5.7% of Palestine's 2004 trade was with Arab countries.

- Prior to 1948, "Palestine possessed the most vibrant port of the entire Middle East." [MIFTA, 2004].

Earlier we noted that the wall will discourage manufacturers from locating in the governorate because of difficulties in exporting their products to regional or international markets. Here we will look briefly at four broad key components of trade: production of goods, means of transport trade agreements, and investment. We shall see that the wall will operate to the economic detriment of Palestinian trade and to the benefit of Israel.

1. *Production:* labor policies and raw materials. As we noted in the earlier discussion of the Israeli labor market, Palestinian and East Jerusalemite employment in Israel and the settlements has been declining overall since 2002 and in some industries since 1996. The Palestinian worker has been replaced by new Jewish immigrants to Israel and by the importation of foreign workers from underdeveloped countries. An American-styled Welfare-to-Work program has moved additional Israelis into the labor market. The wall has accelerated this separatism trend and its completion will signal essentially the end of Israeli dependence on Palestinian labor.

   Further, the wall will also mean that Israel will substantially reduce or eliminate the importation of raw materials from the Palestinian territories. Substantial progress in that direction has already been made in the agricultural and construction sectors. In sum, Israel will approach a virtual vertical trade relationship with Palestine: *it will be able to produce and export goods without any Palestinian inputs.* Thus it will have evolved from the integration policies of the Paris Protocols to a condition of independence and further separation. Inasmuch as 94.3% of Palestinian trade is with Israel, unabated this trend promises an economic disaster for the colonized OPT.

2. *Transportation difficulties.* East Jerusalem's main exports are to Israel, the West Bank, and Jordan. The barrier wall will severely restrict this export market by sealing the borders of East Jerusalem from its West Bank hinterland and from Israel by controlling trade through gates, checkpoints and special permits that act as an economic choke-collar in the hands of the IDF and Israeli policy makers. The effect of these closures will be to shift regional trade away from East Jerusalem's main center into secondary J2 centers such as Ar Ram and Abu Dies. But

ultimately the wall will diminish the regional trade role of even those J2 secondary centers by transforming them into walled enclaves with severed arteries, isolated within the West Bank. Moreover, in addition to cutting the routes for overland transport for trade, the Qalandiya airport, which in the future would have been within the Palestinian state and an important factor for airborne trade, will be kept under Israeli control.

3. *Economic treaties.* The disruption of trade routes effectively creates an economic blockade around East Jerusalem and its governorate. This will deny East Jerusalem the ability to perform as a responsible partner in any trade agreements. On the other hand, it will give an overwhelming comparative advantage to Israeli West Jerusalem, which has unfettered access to land, air, and sea routes, allowing it to engage in regional and international trade.

4. *Predictability and investment in trade related fields.* While virtually all investments entail some measure of risk, investors quite naturally seek to minimize risk by selecting opportunities that yield somewhat predictable results. Capricious IDF actions on closures, disproportionate punitive actions, and security operations undertaken based on rumor all render access to foreign markets and the movement of goods to and through Israel unpredictable. Such conditions raise investment risk to very problematic if not intolerable levels. *Predictability* of the mobility of goods—the *sine qua non* of trade—is made impossible, a situation most investors will not accept.

This was a business destrict in Abu Dis. The wall divides the district and shops on both sides have had to close. August 2006.

The wall along the main Jerusalem-Ramallah Road has caused a significant decrease in commercial activities along the former strong economic strip. Jan 2007.

Palestinian experience at the Karni crossing–the only portal to Egypt and Europe--brings these actions and policies into focus. In November 2005, in an agreement brokered by the United States, Israel agreed to allow Palestine trade through the crossing unless there was an immediate security threat. Yet, as one Israeli critic has observed, the crossing "...is for all intents and purposes closed to Palestinian merchandise from the Gaza Strip despite pledges by Defense Minister Peretz to keep [it] open as much as possible" [Benn, 2006]. It would certainly appear that it has been closed as often as it has been open. For example, Greg Myre of the New York Times reports that it was closed most of September, August, and July 2006 [Myre 2006]. This followed its closure in parts of June and May and much of March, February and January, 2006. Indeed, during this latter period, most of Gaza's export vegetable crops rotted in trucks blocked at the crossing or remained unpicked in the fields. The value of the trade lost for this period alone exceeded 65 million USD. On the days it has been open, on average, only 23 trucks have been allowed out, despite the Israeli pledge to allow egress to 150 trucks per day. Imports fared no better: for weeks UNRWA—the main social and health net of Gaza and the UN World Food Program were unable to import medicines and humanitarian supplies. Shortages of grain, dairy, sugar, cooking oil and fruit products were severe. [Shaoul, 2006; Young, 2006].

IV. CONCLUSION

Throughout former PM Sharon's military and political career, he followed a realpolitk of creating immutable facts on the ground which preempted meaningful negotiations. PM Olmert's unilateral "Convergence/Realignment" plans are in the same mold, and President Bush has acknowledged that facts on the ground, such as the need to accommodate large settlement blocks, must be considered. The barrier and containment wall is an enormous and terrible fact on the ground. While one hopes, no one seriously believes that Israel will allow world opinion to take precedence over that of its own public who overwhelmingly support the wall. Some sections in the northern West Bank region may be altered, and relocating a thirty kilometer stretch of the Jerusalem wall has been ordered by the Israel Supreme Court, but few Palestinians who follow the land confiscation and court appeals processes assume that Israel will make major changes in the routing of the wall. Nor does anyone believe that the wall is a temporary scheme. Too many parties (liberal and conservative) have partnered in its origins; too many ministries and agencies have committed several years in coordinating its planning and implementation; and too many shekels (and dollars) have been allocated from Israel's own stressed economy for this to be a temporary edifice. The sages of the conflict have long recognized that nothing is so permanent as a temporary Israeli action. Moreover, the wall—as presently planned—guarantees a Jewish majority in Jerusalem, a demographic goal that resonates in all sections of the Israeli society. Several Jerusalem sections of the wall are currently under legal challenges and some minor re-routing has resulted, but it would be unrealistic to expect major changes, least of all changes that would significantly soften its impact on the governorate economy.

Nor is there hope on the economic horizon. Consider:

- Israel is unlikely to reverse its policy of social and economic disengagement from the Palestinians. The Jerusalem Governorate economy is now in the process of absorbing tens of thousands of unemployed workers who had found employment and higher wages in Israel. The job creation challenge from this source alone would exceed the capacity of most underdeveloped nations.

- Israel is unlikely, even with the West Bank and the governorate fragmented into Bantustans, to adopt policies that would facilitate mobility between and within J1 and J2 and between J2 and the rest of the West Bank. At some point this will force the blue card issue to a head, and without Israeli flexibility, the only questions will be which Palestinian area and which economic sectors will be damaged most.

- Without Israeli cooperation, peace, stability, and significant business infrastructure investment, the governorate has little prospect of regaining its role in the tourism sector. And without those same preconditions, it has little opportunity to develop an education and training base to create new competencies in other domains, such as information technology.

- Even following the Israeli withdrawal from the Gaza Strip, Gaza is not assured access to the sea and an active port; and even were a port to be developed there, the West Bank and the Jerusalem Governorate are not assured access to Gaza. And, looking to the Jordan Valley, a wall projected there will interdict trade between the governorate and the Arab states to the east, rendering regional and international trade via that route minimal and uncompetitive.

- As unemployment lingers and poverty festers, Palestinians, especially younger generations, will have less and less to hope for and less and less to lose. Unrest will become protest, protest will become resistance. Resistance will put the lie to a "security barrier."

At the conclusion of the first edition of this IPCC study on the effects of the wall we were able to report that world opinion against the barrier was running high and that the issue of the wall had just been addressed—in Palestine's favor-- by the International Court of Justice in the Hague. In an advisory opinion to the UN General Assembly, the court voted 14 to 1 that the construction of the wall in "...occupied territory violated international law, and it held that Israel was required to dismantle it immediately and pay reparations to those who had suffered damages."* Moreover, the court instructed Israel to dismantle the legal and military apparatus that related to the building of the wall. And, we believe for the first time, the court also officially declared the Palestinian territories as "occupied" and the settlements, including those in East Jerusalem, were deemed to be in breach of international law. The General Assembly voted 150 to 6 (with 10 abstentions) to accept the advisory opinion and to demand that Israel comply with its terms. For a time, the decision enjoyed some media attention. But the Supreme Court of Israel (and, perhaps as importantly, the Bush administration and the US House of Representatives in a 361 to 45 vote condemning the ICJ opinion) rejected the international court's authority in this matter. It soon became, in Michael Lynk's words, "...a ruling without consequences."[Lynk, 2005, p.15]. In the meantime, the issue of the wall has receded in the world's consciousness as the media have turned their attention first to the Sharon withdrawal from Gaza, then to PM Olmert's Convergence/Realignment Plan for the West Bank and Jerusalem settlements, then to the election of Hamas and its consequences, and most recently to the Israel/Lebanon war. To be sure, these intervening events are not trivial matters. But neither is a wall that subjugates an entire people.

---

*For a scholarly, if biting, analysis of the Israeli legal response to the ICJ advisory opinion, see Michael Lynk, "Down by Law: The Israeli High Court, International Law, and the Wall," in the *Journal of Palestinian Studies*, Vol. 35, No. 1pp. 5-24 . For a detailed assay of the High Courts role in the occupation see Finklestein [2006, Chapter 9] and pp. 5-24. Kretzmer [2002].

REFERENCES

Aduit, R and Hever, S. (2006). *The Economy under Occupation*. Jerusalem: Alternative Information Center.

Benn, A. "Report: Karni Crossing Operating Far Below Potential." *Ha'aretz,* 21 June 2006, English edition: p. 2.

B'Tselem. (1995). *A Policy of Discrimination*. Jerusalem: B'Tselem.

B'Tselem and HaMoked. (2005). *One Big Prison: Freedom of Movement to and from the Gaza Strip on the Eve of the Disengagement Plan.* Jerusalem: B'Tselem and HaMoked.

Dahleh, M. (5 November 2003). "If This Wall is Built...." Palestine Report. On line: www.palestinereport.org.

Dolphin, R. (2006). *The West Bank Wall: Unmaking Palestine*. London and Ann Arbor: Pluto Press.

Eldar, A. "Peretz Orders Fence Route Reviewed with Palestinians in Mind." Ha'aretz, 19 June 2006. English edition: p. 1.

Finklestein, N. (2005). *Beyond Chutzpah: On the Misuses of Anti-Semitism and the Abuses of History.* Berkley: University of California Press.

Hazboun, S. (2003). "Al-Quds Jerusalem: Socio-Economic Vision". In R. Friedman and R. Nasrallah (Eds.). *Divided Cities in Transition*. Jerusalem: International Peace and Cooperation Center.

Hazboun S. and Baboeram, D. (2003). "An Economic Perspective for Jerusalem."In A. Amin et al, *Envisioning the Future of Jerusalem*. International Peace and Cooperation Center: Jerusalem.

Harel. A. "IDF: At Least One More Year Until Fence Completed." *Ha'aretz*, 17 May 2006, English edition: p. 1.

Horowitz, D. "The Battle for E-1." Jerusalem Post, 18 March 2005: p. 1.
IPCC. (2005). Survey of 1200 Jerusalem Governorate Households, Residents, and Shop Owners.

Khamaisi, R. (2003). "Population and Housing in Jerusalem: Facts and Projections until Year 2020". In R. Khamaisi and R. Nasrallah (Eds.). *The Jerusalem Urban Fabric: Demography, Infrastructure, and Institutions*. Jerusalem: International Peace and Cooperation Center.

Khamaisi, R. and Nasrallah, R. (Eds.). (2003a). *The Jerusalem Urban Fabric: Demography,* Infra structure, and Institutions. Jerusalem: International Peace and Cooperation Center.

Khamaisi, R. and Nasrallah, R. (2003b). "The Jerusalem State of Affairs: Facts, Trends, and Implications". In R. Khamaisi et al. *Jerusalem on the Map*. Jerusalem: International Peace and Cooperation Center.

Klein, M. (September 2003). Apartheid in Jerusalem." *FMEP: Current Analysis*. On line: www. fmep.org.

Kretzmer, D. (2002). *The Occupation of Justice: The Supreme Court of Israel and the Occupied Territories*. Albany: State University of New York.

Lefkovits, E. "Jewish Population in Jerusalem Slips to 66 Percent." *Jerusalem Post*, 24 May 2006: p. 4.

Lynk, M. (2005). "Down by Law: The Israeli High Court: International Law, and the Wall." *Journal of Palestinian Studies*. 35:1.

Mair, L. and Long, R. "Israel's Stranglehold on the Palestinian Economy is Consolidated by a Massive Wall." *Dollars and Sense*. November 2003.

Margalit, M. (2005). *Discrimination in the Heart of the Holy City*. Jerusalem: International Peace and Cooperation Center.

MIFTA. (7 September 2004). «How Dangerous is the Palestinian Economy?» September 7, 2004. On line : www.miftah.org.

Myre, G. "Hamas Rebuffs Palestinian President over Israel." *New York Times*, 22 September 2006: p. A-3.

Palestinian Central Bureau of Statistics. (2003-a). «Household Social Survey of Jerusalem, June 2003.» Press release. On line: www. pcbs.org.

_____(2003-b). «Labor Force Survey Results (October-December 2003).» Press release. On line: www. pcbs.org.

_____(2004). «Household Social Survey of Jerusalem». Press release. On line: www. pcbs.org.

_____(February 2006)» Impact of the Expansion and Annexation Wall on the Socioecomic Conditions of Palestinian Households.» Press conference: pp.7-8. On line: www.pcbs.org.

_____(2001). Jerusalem Statistical Yearbook.No. 3. Jerusalem.

_____(2002). Jerusalem Statistical Yearbook,No. 4. Jerusalem.

_____(2003). Jerusalem Statistical Yearbook. No. 5. Jerusalem.

_____(2004). Jerusalem Statistical Yearbook. No. 6. Jerusalem. On line: www.pcbs.org.

_____(2005). Jerusalem Statistical Yearbook. No. 7. Jerusalem. On line: www.pcbs.org.

_____(2006). Jerusalem Statistical Yearbook. No. 8. Jerusalem. On line: www.pcbs.org.

PASSIA- (2006)- Diary 2006. Jerusalem: The Palestinian Academic Society for the Study of International Affairs.

PENGON. (2003). *The Wall in Palestine: Facts, Testimonies, Analysis and Call to Action*. Jerusalem: Palestinian Environmental NGOs Network.

Rubenstein, D. «The Battle for the Capital.» Ha'aretz,31 March 2005. English edition: p. 1.

Shaoul, I (24 March 2006). «Israeli Announces Plans to Annex More Palestinian Land.»

Counter Currents. On line : www.countercurrents.org.

Shragai, N. «Palestinians Left Outside Jerusalem Wall are Moving into Capital.' Ha'aretz, 16 March 2004. English edition: p. l.

UNCTAD. Report: « Palestinian Economy Has Deteriorated.» United Nations Conference on Trade and Development. August 27,2005. On line: www.jerusalemites.org.

Yoaz, Y. «Court Orders Section of Separation Fence Tom Down.» Ha'aretz, 16 June 2006. English edition: p. A-3.

Yotrng, E. (23 March 2006). «Palestinian Economic Dependence on Israel.» Policy Watch 1088.

The Washington Institute for the Near East. On line: www.washingtoninstitute.org.

World Bank (December 2005). The Palestinian Economy and the Prospects for Recovery. On line: www.worldbank.org.

World Bank. (March 2006). West Bank and Gaza: Economic Update and Outlook. On line: www.worldbank.org.

CHAPTER THREE

Truncating the Right to the City in Jerusalem: A Lefebyrean Analysis

Rassem Khamaisi, ph. D.

I. INTRODUCTION

Continuation of the separation wall construction around Jerusalem has had wide-scale consequences and ramifications in Jerusalem and its surroundings, which have been addressed by various studies and researches [Brooks et. al., 2005; Khamaisi, 2005; Khamaisi and Nasrallah, 2006; Kimhi, 2006]. Those studies revealed the wall's negative consequences and ramifications, including fragmenting the warp and woof of the urban fabric in Jerusalem and hindering the possibility of Jerusalem becoming the heart and capital of any future Palestinian state. The studies also addressed the wall's consequences from the standpoint of Jerusalem being a city divided in reality and suffering from political and ethnic conflict. Nevertheless, various consequences of the wall's construction on Jerusalem are still unclear and must be examined and understood. This study is an additional segment in the chain of research that examines the separation wall's consequences on the city structure and its surroundings. Our goal is to examine the wall's potential to truncate the right to the city for the Palestinian society in Jerusalem.

Our approach is strongly shaped by the Lefebvrean conceptualization of the idea of city citizenship, which was developed by the French sociologist and thinker Lefebvre [Lefebvre 1991; 1996]. This concept was given greater currency by Harvey and developed to the point of becoming the slogan of Radical City Democracy [Harvey 203 and Purcell, 2002]. The construction of the wall around has Jerusalem has fragmented Palestinian Jerusalemite neighborhoods and has isolated them from their surroundings, thereby inhibiting and undermining freedom of movement within the urban network of East Jerusalem, which had evolved organically until it was truncated by the wall [Brooks et. all, 2005]. This fragmentation prohibits realization of the right to the city and enforces an estrangement between the Palestinians and their urban space. They are unable to live freely and they do not have an opportunity to formulate the urban space. Moreover, based on the Israeli's assumption, the wall's path may determine the urban borders of the "unified" Jerusalem as well as the geo-political borders of the State of Israel. The questions raised in light of this assumption are: Would post-wall Jerusalem be a natural city in which it is possible to practice the right to city citizenship after it is transformed from a city in a state of conflict, urban fragmentation and geo-ethnic division into a city whose borders are an extension of the wall?; What will be the nature of the urban networks that will evolve in the wake of the wall's construction?; and Will that transformed situation deprive the Palestinians of ensuring international legitimization for Jerusalem as the capital of their independent state?

The assumption this article seeks to address evolves around the potential of the wall to discredit the idea of the open and stable city, an idea that is advanced by numerous visions for the future of Jerusalem. Moreover, the wall as presently constructed already makes it impossible to realize the right to the city, and it truncates the development of a metropolitan Jerusalem. In fact, it enforces ethnic, national and cultural localization at the neighborhood level and fails to provide a developed public city space, which is one of the major ingredients in the development of a city network in which an equal and free city citizenship right is practiced. Therefore, the completed wall will not only weaken Jerusalem and transform it into a frontier city for the Palestinians as well as the Israelis, it will also exacerbate the national and geo-political conflict surrounding the city.

Our study below begins with a theoretical overview of the concept of the right to the city, which we will attempt to expand to accommodate the reality of a city in a state of conflict, ethnically divided, having huge gaps in living standards between its neighborhoods, and witnessing significant shortages in the provision of infrastructure and services in the Arab Palestinian neighborhoods [Khamaisi and Nasrallah, 2003]. We will seek to answer the question, Is it possible to utilize and apply the idea of the right to the city in the instance of Jerusalem, a paradigm case of a nationally and ethnically divided city? [Bollens, 2000; Auga et. al., 2005] The second part of this study presents a brief overview of the evolution of the geo-political reality of Jerusalem, explaining how the right to the city has been minimized and truncated. The third part addresses the effects and ramifications of the wall through a discussion of the components of the concept of the right to the city, especially in the wake of minimized public spaces, truncated neighborhoods, and transformation of the city from an urban space with a semi-integrated functional network based on national and geo-ethnic affiliation into a city formed of secondary ethnic concentrations based on the levels of neighborhoods, village and conglomerates that are isolated and have no ties among them. Last, we conclude this study with an attempt to outline some of the integrating, albeit contradictory, components between the right to the city and the idea of the open city which is aborted by the wall's construction. Furthermore, we shall indicate some of the steps that must be taken for the sake of reviving the city functionally and developing an urban network capable of forming the heart of the future Palestinian state and the center of the city of Israel, this instead of the deep-rooted state of conflict which threatens Jerusalem's development and prosperity. We shall argue for the proposition that ensuring the right to the city for the Israelis hinges on ensuring the right to the city for the Palestinians, otherwise the state of conflict in the city will worsen and lead to a scenario of self-destruction.

II. THE RIGHT TO THE CITY

The Concept of the Right to the City and Fencing

Before the concept of "The Right to the City" was proposed, urbanologists viewed national citizenship and political centrality as the key factors which determined the city's resources and shaped its decisions in isolation from the role and right of a city's citizenry and its inhabitants to participate in making decisions concerning the nature of the city and the means of producing and managing its space. Under a regime of national citizenship and political centrality, the city's citizens and inhabitants had to accept the central governmental decisions imposed on them, and any right to participate in the formulation and production of the space in which they lived was not recognized. The notion that all of the city's citizens are equal was unacceptable [Jabarin, 2006; Purcell, 2003]. The concept of the right to the city stems from guaranteeing people's rights in the city as equal citizens who should have the ability to move spatially and functionally within the city's surroundings without impediments or administrative, physical or cultural/national barriers [Fenster, 2006]. This concept evolved in response to the deliberate and direct restrictions of global geo-political and economic transformations, which imposed political, economic and functional structures that handicap an individual's rights in the city space as it is controlled by the central government, multinational companies, or globalization [Swyngeodouw, 2000; Falk, 2000]. This national central control may lead to stripping citizens of their right to participate in formulating decisions concerning designing, planning, managing and producing the city space [Holston and Appadurai, 1999]. The urbanization process that the whole world is undergoing and the sharp population increases in the cities, in addition to concentration of the economic resources and governance and decision-making centers in the cities, has attracted researchers who are interested in attempting to understand the formation of urban spaces and people's movements within them, and who are monitoring the nature of the relations evolving among city residents in states of stability and conflict [Harvey, 2003]. Lefebvre's concept of the right to the city evolved from a reality in which the city represents society's trackings on the ground both in terms of its tangible physical presence as well as its intangible impact that evolved from taking decisions and formulating ideas that determine the city's model and the formation of its structure. The right to the city concept presents itself as a noble form of rights: the right to freedom, and individual and personal rights within the scope of participation and involvement in the various societal structures, which include the rights to living, housing and work. The right to the city idea also includes the right to creativity, participation and allocation [Lefebvre, 1996].

Moreover, the concept of the right to the city originated from the *production* of the city space; therefore, whoever lives in the city and interacts with it [which is to say, produces it] is entitled to demand the right to the city [Lefebvre, 1991]. The right to the city is not limited to those who live in the city however, but includes as well those who work in it, interact with it, visit it and feel attachment and belonging to it, and those who use its urban and service space and network.

Lefebvre and other researchers who discussed the concept of the right to the city summarized it in two major principles: The right to participation and The right to appropriation [Salmon, 2001; Lefebvre, 1991; 1996] These two rights include equality of participation in using the city space and in formulating and producing it culturally, spatially and ideologically. These concepts are based on the expansion of the personal right in a participatory national liberal democracy to the community or urban level. The freedom of movement within the urban space facilitated the right of location in the city in accordance with both the individual and the economic community's goals . Based on the above, the metropolitan space was defined as an urban space enjoying structural contiguity, divided politically and administratively but integrated functionally and economically, and enabling an individual, a family or an investor to settle freely wherever they deem appropriate, taking into consideration their abilities, available economic resources, and cultural, national and ethnic desires and preferences [Heinelt, 2005]. If we add to this definition the right to the city by participating in managing and formulating the space and appropriation in it, then this concept forms a theoretical foundation for understanding the contradiction between the reality of Jerusalem, the ramifications of the wall's construction, and truncating and fragmenting the urban space on one hand, and denying the right to the city for the Palestinian people and society, who presently do not enjoy the right on the national level and are being deprived of the right to the city on the local level, on the other hand.

Several scientific conferences were held for the purpose of reviewing and assessing the right to the city; eventually it was recognized as a basic human right which must be preserved and guaranteed even in cases of extraordinary developments such as wars. The proposed international declaration for endorsing the right to the city presented the components of the humanitarian right to the city. It stipulated: "The right to the city includes internationally-recognized human rights to housing, social security, work, appropriate living standards, recreation, information, organization and freedom of assembly, water and food, liberation from de-possession, participation and self expression, health, education, culture, privacy and security, a safe and healthy environment, compensation and legal treatment in case of being subject to a violation, and the collective agreed upon and endorsed human rights, which are guaranteed for all human beings under all circumstances." Moreover, "...the right to the city incorporates such other urban human rights as the right to occupy and own land, the provision of public transportation, energy, and basic infrastructure, availability of skills and skill development, and obtaining public goods -- including natural resources and financing –all as basic and necessary practical elements. The right to the city outlines in its context the countries and local authorities' obligations to respect diversity and the equal rights of the various ethnic, lingual, gender, religious and cultural groups. The right to the city stipulates that all residents of a city possess mutual humanity from which stems the individual and collective rights to obtaining and maintaining a living place in security, peace and dignity regardless of the civic situation" [The Third International Social Forum, Porto Allegro, January 2004, www.hic-mena/documents].

Our attempt to discuss the wall's ramifications in accordance with the concepts of the Lefebvrean idea of the right to the city may be criticized, especially in light of the fact that the idea of the right to the city was devised for cities where there are no geo-political or national conflicts and whose national realities are decided. The only types of conflicts that characterize those cities are class, socio-economic and ethnic conflicts between the authentic groups and the immigrants, and between the various economic classes in them. The residents of those cities are subject to the central government, but the right to the city accords them the right of city citizenship. Jerusalem obviously suffers from a conflict over its geo-political reality and future [Khamaisi and Nasrallah, 2006]; however, we believe that the application of the concept of the right to the city's situation will shed light on the state of Jerusalem, including the contradictions the city suffers from on the individual, collective and national levels which will be further exacerbated by the construction of the wall.

Therefore, the question to be answered in this article is: "Does the construction of the wall contribute to preserving the right to the city for those who live in it or interact with it?" In order to answer this question, we will review the development of the Israelis' denial of the Palestinian right in Jerusalem through rejection of the Palestinians' participation, prohibiting any possibility for their involvement in formulating and producing the space and sharing the resources, and fragmenting the city and transforming it from a central city into a frontier city, thereby leading to the creation of a diseased city that is dying because of the wall.

Regardless of the Palestinians' non-participation in formulating and producing the urban space, what is the nature of the space they have produced as an alternative, and how did Israel influence the creation/production of such space? Is participation in the space the only means for realizing the Palestinians' right to the city or do the Palestinians have their own space, which existed before Israel? If so, how did they deal with this space since the occupation and how did they create alternative spaces in Jerusalem's surroundings? And how did the wall contribute to weakening those spaces and exacerbating the problems in Jerusalem by generating a population movement into the city which settled in poor and densely populated neighborhoods that are characterized by the phenomenon of random construction?

The Process of Contraction of the Right to the City

The construction of the wall and the fence around Jerusalem has fragmented the neighborhood networking and capped a process of contraction of the Palestinians' right to the city as citizens living in it and witnessing its fate. The contraction process began in the middle of the nineteenth century, when foreign colonial missions came to Jerusalem in an effort to control its space. From that time, the urban space in Jerusalem began extending and expanding outside the ancient walls surrounding the Old City [Mustafa, 1997]. At the same time, Jerusalem continued to develop within the Old City walls, and its citizens and residents lived in accordance with the traditional models of inhabitance and space management [Akbar, 1995]. Moreover, over the years the villages surrounding Jerusalem expanded from their nuclei and developed, producing rural spaces that grew and developed in an integrated organic manner that balanced the needs, the capabilities and the means of consumption and production. Contiguity and integration between the neighborhoods that developed around the Old City and those that expanded from the villages were achieved eventually to form the city space of Jerusalem. This urban space had developed in an integrated organic manner, balancing the traditions, the needs, and the available means of consumption and production. However, the foreign missions and the immigration waves of the Zionist Movement settled in Jerusalem and introduced new urban patterns in the physical, functional and administrative structure of the city [Ben Arieh, 1979]. In 1863, the Jerusalem Municipality was established as an appointed local governance representing the central governance in Istanbul. The year 1917 was a major turning point in Jerusalem: the city was occupied by British forces during World War I; the British Mandate was declared in Palestine;

and the mandate's central institutions such as the High Commissioner settled in Jerusalem. Hence, Jerusalem became a central administrative and political city for the British Mandate in Palestine in addition to its historic, spiritual, religious and symbolic centrality. The urbanization process and urban development continued to expand and included the establishment of modern Palestinian Arab and Jewish neighborhoods outside the wall, neighborhoods which were based on national, class and cultural affiliations. Each ethnic/national group lived in isolation from the other [Tamari, 2002]. In the second decade of the twentieth century, conflict broke out between the Jews and Palestinian Arabs. That conflict reached its peak in 1948, when the city was divided geo-politically and physically, and the right to Jerusalem was limited: freedom of movement and settlement was controlled and inhibited within the city's space. During the British Mandate period, the official Palestinian Arab participation in formulating the space, through managing, planning and developing it, was restricted, and the Palestinian Arabs' participation in city citizenship was limited. In fact, the British High Commissioner and his arms were the central body that managed the city's space and formulated its urban network, while the citizens who lived in the city and those who interacted with it and those who immigrated to it for residence or work were practically neutralized in the process of formulating the space and did not represent a central factor in producing it. This does not mean that they did not produce their own organic space through which public space was produced on the level of the neighborhoods. Rather, a Palestinian Arab space evolved through the Palestinian Arabs' production of the space as consumers of it and through meeting their needs and providing their spatial consumption. This space evolved in accordance with accumulation of the production of the private space; therefore, a significant shortage in producing and providing the public space was witnessed.

The turning point in inhibiting and truncating the right to the city came in the wake of the 1948 War and the endorsement of the physical and geo-political division of Jerusalem into two parts. The western part of Jerusalem was subject to Israeli control, while the eastern part, including the Old City, fell under Jordanian control. This physical division included the establishment of a separating border fence inside the city's structure. The war transformed Jerusalem from a geographically, administratively and politically central city into a divided border city suffering from security instability [Benvenisti, 1996]. The eastern part of Jerusalem became the center of the West Bank area, which was annexed to the Hashemite Kingdom of Jordan and followed Amman as the main central city in the Kingdom. Between 1948 and 1967, the right to the divided city was subject to checkpoints and barriers that prevented appropriation and participation in space formulation. In fact, the city structure produced as a consequence of the war was fragmented since the city itself was divided by physical borders that made it impossible to travel between its two parts. The factors determining movement inside the city and into it was the policies of the central Israeli government in the western part of Jerusalem and the Hashemite Kingdom of Jordan in the eastern part of the city. During the period of geo-political division, Jerusalem suffered from backwardness and its role was minimized in spite of the fact that West Jerusalem was declared the capital of the State of Israel and East Jerusalem remained the spiritual and religious center of the Arabs and Muslims as well as a regional center and the second most important city in the Hashemite Kingdom of Jordan. During this period, it was impossible to address the right to a divided and partitioned city [Wasserstein, 2002]. It is true that elections were held in West Jerusalem for electing representatives in the Israeli Jerusalem Municipality, while representatives in the Arab Jerusalem Municipality in East Jerusalem were appointed; but in both cases the central governments dominated the passing and making of decisions which led to producing the city's spaces and formulating the movement of citizens within them. It is worth noting here that the Israeli neighborhoods developed in West Jerusalem in accordance with predetermined planning, direct public sector intervention in providing housing, and allocation of lands to public institutions in order to transform West Jerusalem into a capital, while housing development in East Jerusalem depended on self-initiated private construction; therefore some neighborhoods evolved without official initiated planning. Furthermore, the city's subordination to Amman made it lose the national institutions which should have developed in it.

This physical and geo-political division ended in the wake of Israel's occupation of the entire West Bank including East Jerusalem in 1967. Following the occupation, the Israeli authorities officially controlled Jerusalem and sought to Judaize the space by the establishment of Israeli settlements in East Jerusalem. The Israeli settlements isolated the center of East Jerusalem and the Old City from the surrounding Jerusalemite neighborhoods and the villages that were annexed to East Jerusalem space in accordance with a decision by the Israeli authorities, e.g., Beit Hanina, Kafr Aqab, Al Issawiya, Sur Bahir, etc. Israel annexed those villages and their lands to Jerusalem in an effort to expand the lands under its control [Khamaisi and Nasrallah, 2003]. The Israeli authorities also confiscated more than 25,000 dunums of Arab lands for the purpose of establishing Jewish settlements which was part of their policy to fragment and truncate Palestinian spatial continuity. Moreover, the Israeli authorities used spatial planning as a legalized means of control by controlling and inhibiting the Palestinian expansion [Khamaisi, 2003]. Hence, the Palestinian right to the city was minimized to the level of the neighborhood and the village, while the public space fell under Israeli administrative control and became subject to the Israeli authorities' decisions [Khamaisi and Nasrallah, 2006].

Since the Israeli occupation in 1967, Palestinian Jerusalemites have refused to take part in the local government and in managing, formulating or producing the space by participating in the Jerusalem Municipality. Although Israel granted the Palestinian Jerusalemites the right of permanent residency in the frame of its unilateral annexation of the occupied Jerusalem under its official sovereignty in contradiction to international legitimacy resolutions, it has refused to grant Palestinians in Jerusalem the right of citizenship. The goal sought by the Palestinian Jerusalemites is to end the occupation, not to attain equality under Israeli control as citizens in the state of Israel. Thus, official and public Palestinian participation in producing the public city space as a major component of ensuring their right to the city, is unthinkable through Israeli occupation institutions because the occupation makes it impossible to realize this right since the occupation itself, by definition, is imposed. Nevertheless, the Palestinian Jerusalemite society witnessed significant economic prosperity and relative housing growth between 1967 and 1993. This included a population increase from 68,000 to over 200,000, and an housing increase in the Palestinian villages annexed by Israel in 1967, an area which is known today as East Jerusalem. This relative prosperity and housing expansion occurred without the formation of an urban housing network in which public space is provided to ensure the right to the city for the city's inhabitants as well as those who interact with it. The goal formulated by the Israeli authorities was to ensure judaization of all of Jerusalem to become the capital of the state of Israel and its political center, and even the world capital of the Jewish people. In order to realize this goal, administrative, planning and geo-political restrictions were imposed on the Palestinian existence in Jerusalem to achieve a geo-demographic goal to limit the Palestinian population in Jerusalem to 30% or less of the total population of Jerusalem Municipality as that areas is defined by Israel [Misselwitz et. al., 2006]. The planning of the wall's path took this geo-demographic objective as a central component, as we shall illustrate later. It is worth noting here that between 1967 and 1993, the Palestinian freedom of movement and settlement in the city space of East Jerusalem was restricted, especially from the villages surrounding the Old City. In the meantime, Palestinian settlement in West Jerusalem was prohibited for geo-political reasons by Israeli prohibitions and Palestinian reluctance. This means that the concept of a functional metropolis was not realized in the Jerusalemite reality, although the regional spatial concept and the political and administrative divisions were realized as the Jerusalemite urban space extended from Bethlehem in the south to Ramallah in the north. [Khamaisi, 2003].

The year 1993 witnessed a truncation of the Palestinian right to Jerusalem following the city's closure and the denial of free Palestinian movement into it from its surroundings which nourish the city. This closure occurred through the imposition of permanent and mobile (flying) military checkpoints on the roads leading to and out of Jerusalem. Those checkpoints weakened Palestinian movement into Jerusalem and inhibited its development. They allowed Israeli settlers to travel from the settlements surrounding Jerusalem into the city, while Palestinians who did not possess the right of permanent residency in the city were not allowed to enter it except after obtaining special permits which are impossible to obtain in most cases for either security or bureaucratic reasons. In the year 2003, those checkpoints began a transformation into a separation wall undermining functional and administrative extension and continuity between Jerusalem and its surroundings. The wall fragmented Palestinian neighborhoods located within the administrative borders of Jerusalem which were determined by Israel in 1967. It must be pointed out here that the closure and truncation of the Palestinian right began to worsen at the beginning of the First Intifada in 1987, which resulted in the closing the city for free Palestinian movement by means of military barriers and checkpoints on the roads. Later, the Second Intifada broke out in 2000 and eventuated in the decision to establish the separation wall in 2003, a wall that surrounds Jerusalem and effectively annexes the surrounding Israeli settlements to the city while fragmenting the Palestinian neighborhoods on its outskirts.

The wall also has caused a division between the heart of the city -- the Old City and its surroundings -- and the nearby Palestinian neighborhoods which had become parts of the city's urban and functional network [Brooks et. al, 2005]. In 2006, a wall was constructed in the northern perimeter, isolating Kafr Aqab and Qalandiya from the Atarot Industrial Zone, and the wall also divides the main Jerusalem-Ramallah Road from Qalandiya to Dahiyat Al Bareed into two separate parts along its midline. Furthermore, construction works are now underway that will divide Dahiyat Al Bareed into two areas -- one in East Jerusalem and another on the West Bank side of the wall. Similar divisions include isolating the Abu Dis area from Ras Al Amud. In fact, inspection of the wall's path reveals that ethno-demographic considerations and the residents' housing locations in accordance with national affiliations represented a basic tenet in charting the wall's path. For example, Israel kept outside the separation wall approximately 55,000 Palestinian Jerusalemites who hold Israeli identification cards that accord their holders the right of permanent residency in Jerusalem and entitle them to receive the services provided by Israel to its residents (see **Map 2**).

Based on the above discussion, it is clear that the Palestinian right to the Holy City underwent a process of control and restriction until it was substantially reduced. That process began with the development of ethno-national neighborhoods at the beginning of the twentieth century and continued through the middle of the twentieth century and in the wake of the establishment of the State of Israel in 1948. In spite of the Israeli unification attempt following occupation of the Palestinian territories in 1967 and the annexation of the occupied East Jerusalem into Israel, this rhetorical, official, selective unification on the basis of ethnic affiliation did not realize the right to the city. In fact, the attempt to annex the area kept it divided and fragmented even though the physical barriers between the Palestinian and Israeli sections were abolished following the city's occupation in 1967. The enforced ethno-national fragmentation continued and inhibited any free participation pertaining to movement, and settlement within the city's borders, or in the formulation of the urban space [Cohen, 1980].

The First Intifada marked the beginning of developing a spatial separation, which eventually became military/security closure by means of the wall's construction. During this period, the security and trust space within the city and its surroundings shrank, while fear space and areas of distrust expanded. The security and trust space shrank to the level of the neighborhoods, while the fear space included seam areas between the Palestinian and Israeli neighborhoods. Following the closure, the wall was constructed to isolate the city from its surroundings and exacerbate the city's fragmentation and division on ethno/national, demographic and spatial bases. The Israeli claim concerning providing personal and public security in addition to national geo-demographic security was a major motivator for constructing and determining the path of the separation wall, but also undermined the possibility of providing and developing the right to the city for its citizens and residents, as well as whoever else claimed that Jerusalem is their city and center. Hence, Palestinian Jerusalemites have not enjoyed the right to citizenship since Israel's occupation of Jerusalem in 1967; it led to their absence and exclusion from taking the official collective decision in formulating and forming the city space and producing Jerusalem's structure and network in response to their requirements and desires.

The geo-political and ethno-demographic transformations in Jerusalem's reality inhibited local participation in devising, formulating and shaping the space and its urban network. Thus the formation of the Jerusalemite space has been imposed on the city from above (the central authority) in response to geo-political considerations and by means of Israeli governmental intervention; the role of the citizens/residents in participating in forming the space has been limited and differs between the Israelis and the Palestinians; Israelis participate in electing their representatives in the local government and in reviving their civic society, while the Palestinians refuse to participate in shaping and forming the space, and even resist the decisions imposed on them. This imposition of decisions affirms the Israeli rejection of a Palestinian right to the city. The rejection is enforced and underscored by the wall's construction.

Rejection of the Right to the City following the Wall's Construction

Some may think that the wall's effect on the Palestinian's the right to the city is based on a technical or functional viewpoint, implying that dismantling the barrier will restore the right to city and render it an open city offering freedom of movement and settlement. Israelis argue that the constructed wall is a "temporary fence" that can be dismantled and removed in the case of stability and agreement on a geo-political arrangement, although the history argues that whatever Israeli measure that is introduced as "temporary" becomes a permanent component of the occupation. In other words, the position that the wall's construction is a technical matter is false, and the wall is indeed constructed to realize geo-political goals which can and be presented as a basis for future borders. We argue that the wall's construction in the case of Jerusalem is a central component in the Israeli rejection of the Palestinian right to Jerusalem both spatially and functionally. In this section of this article, I will overview and discuss the means of the wall's transformation into a major factor in fragmenting and dividing the Holy City and in maintaining Israel's rejection of the Palestinian right to the city, whether by participation, appropriation, or ensuring the right to citizenship.

The decision to construct the wall and fence surrounding Jerusalem stemmed from primarily security considerations. The concept of security in the Israeli interpretation is broad and includes personal individual security as well as public and national security. Before the wall's construction, geopolitical, ethno-demographic, administrative and spatial policies were devised for the sake of ensuring Israeli control over Jerusalem in order for it to form the capital of the State of Israel and the Jewish people [Hoshen et. al, 2004]. Therefore, the Israelis worked tirelessly on changing the nature of the city, and ensuring that a Jewish majority lives in it. The borders demarcated in 1967 as Jerusalem's municipal borders were based on geopolitical and demographic considerations [Hazan, 1995], and the wall's construction came to consolidate those considerations. The question raised in the wake of the wall's construction is: "Will the right to the city be provided to those who inhabit it, or does the wall simply represent an additional step in the rejection of the Arab Palestinian right to the city?" We will provide below a brief answer to this question by outlining the wall's ramifications and effects on the city's structure and network, on movement within it, and on its relations with its urban and geo-political surroundings. We shall discuss the wall's ramifications from the standpoint of the Lefebvrean idea and through its four components which underlie the realization of the right to the city: participation, appropriation, space production, and urban citizenship.

The Right to City Participation following the Wall's Construction

The right of Palestinian Jerusalemites to participate in decisions and to play a major role in the distribution of resources has become very uncertain in the wake of the wall's construction for two main reasons. The first is the Israeli desire, through governance and domination on the central as well as the local levels, to enforce the judaization of Jerusalem and transform it into a city with a Jewish Israeli majority. Immense resources are being allocated for this purpose. Thus, development gaps between the Israeli and Palestinian neighborhoods are maintained, and Palestinian public and private sector investment in developing Palestinian neighborhoods is prohibited or at least impeded; this pushes the Palestinian upper and middle classes to abandon those neighborhoods, and it contributes to a reduction of the Palestinian presence in the city. The Israeli government and Jerusalem Municipality repeatedly makes pledges to provide and allocate resources for developing the Palestinian neighborhoods in Jerusalem, including re-planning them, but these rhetorical pledges are not accompanied by the allocation of appropriate resources to ensure effective Palestinian participation. The Israeli government and Jerusalem Municipality reject the principle of equal Palestinian participation in managing the city and sharing its resources in accordance with agreed-upon principles and criteria. Moreover, the Israeli government and Jerusalem Municipality devise and implement policies that ensures their ownership of Jerusalem and marginalizes the Palestinians living in the city as a minority to be provided with a minimum level of resources for which to fight a battle of survival. The wall's construction presents the Israeli government with a dilemma: if it wishes to annex the Palestinian Jerusalemites left within the wall, whose number stands at approximately 200,000, as permanent residents then it has to provide them with resources and accept their participation in making decisions pertaining to managing the city. This is rejected by the Israeli government and the Jerusalem Municipality [Garb, 2004]. The Israeli rejection will be enforced in the wake of the wall's construction and will lead to a deterioration of the conditions in Palestinian neighborhoods and contribute to the transformation of those neighborhoods into peripheral isolated enclaves separated by the wall from adjacent Palestinian neighborhoods. This is all done in the name of the Judaization of Jerusalem.

The second reason pertains to the Palestinian position on participation. Palestinian Jerusalemites living in the city, as well as those interacting with it and aspiring for it to be the capital of the Palestinian state and its economic, cultural and administrative heart, reject participation with the Israeli occupier. Transformation of the issue of Jerusalem from a geo-political and occupation issue into an issue of ensuring citizenship and services is inconceivable from a Palestinian standpoint. Palestinians also reject transformation of the issue of Jerusalem into a functional issue or an issue of services in the wake of the wall's construction, and this is exactly what the Israelis seek to make out of the issue of Jerusalem. Therefore, Palestinians refuse to participate in the municipal elections. They are also suspicious and disapproving of the local administrations set up by the Israeli Jerusalem Municipality although many of those administrations are manned by Palestinians. Undoubtedly, the wall's construction and the physical isolation of the Palestinian Jerusalemites from their brethren in Jerusalem's surroundings, including the cities of Ramallah and Bethlehem, presents the Palestinian Jerusalemites with their own dilemma: they possess conditional residency rights in Jerusalem and can theoretically demand participating in making decisions and sharing resources and power, but the Israeli government's efforts to transform the issue of Jerusalem from a sovereign political negotiation issue into a municipal services issue implicitly discredits the viewpoints presented by some Palestinian Jerusalemites to participate in the municipality in order to create a Palestinian lobby in the Jerusalem Municipality that will protect certain Palestinian interests. On another hand, the Israeli government and the Jerusalem Municipality impose their policies and decisions, and even their taxes on the Palestinian Jerusalemites who are obliged to adhere to the Israeli law without enjoying services in return for those taxes. In other words, the Palestinian Jerusalemites fulfill their duties, including their imposed financial obligations, in return for their conditional residency without receiving proportional municipal services and civil rights. This reality has existed since 1967, but it will be exacerbated in the wake of the wall's construction because it will transform the issue of the Palestinian Jerusalemites into a functional and service issue, and they will become connected to their Palestinian state through border crossings erected along the wall. The rejection of equal mutual participation of the Palestinians and Israelis in the issue of Jerusalem is a central component in undermining and truncating the Palestinian right to Jerusalem. The impossibility of participation maintains the class and national segregation in Jerusalem and exacerbates the differences between the East and West Jerusalem, inequalities which hinder security and stability and deny collective responsibility for managing the city and distributing or sharing the resources and power in it.

Denial of the Right to Appropriation following the Wall's Construction

Providing the right to appropriation represents one of the major components of the right to the city. Lefebvre [1996] pointed out that appropriation is a spatial practice whose growth was proper, appropriate and natural for the sake of meeting and expanding human needs and potentials. The right to appropriation includes the residents' right to free utilization and occupation of the urban space and free personal access to it without any hindrance [Capron, 2002]. Lefebvre [1996] explained that the right to appropriation also has a broader meaning, which includes the right to produce and occupy the general space in accordance with the residents' needs and requirements. This broader definition assumes that one of the components of appropriation is the production of urban space and surroundings in a manner that enables residents to exercise its use fully and completely. Undoubtedly, the wall's construction is a process of producing a space that the Palestinians have no role in creating, do not possess the right to appropriation in, and even oppose, although the Israelis claim that Palestinian violence threatened Israeli security and formed the motive for the wall's construction. Given the fact that the wall isolates Palestinian Jerusalemite neighborhoods from each other [as in the case of the Dahiyat Al Bareed area, and in the isolation of Beit Hanina Village from New Beit Hanina] it restricts appropriation to the level of private personal space and cancels the public city space which must serve the Palestinian Jerusalemite citizens.

Inspection and analysis of land uses and appropriations in the Palestinian Jerusalemite neighborhoods reveals that the idea underlying the planning of those neighborhoods was to avoid the creation of public city spaces in them [Khamaisi, 2003; 2006]. Detailed master plans were devised for each neighborhood or village in accordance with a restrictive methodology whereby land uses were not appropriated adequately for general purposes aimed at serving the populations or being utilized by the population of the entire city. The planning and administrative concept imposed by the Israeli government was counteracted by a traditional local/village concept in the neighborhoods and villages that were included in the administrative borders of Jerusalem Municipality following the occupation of 1967, such as Shu'fat, Sur Bahir, Um Tuba, and Al Issawiya. This traditional concept was unsupportive of appropriating private lands for public purposes and avoided attracting immigrants. The divergence of these contradictory interests resulted in an absence of public city space and further fragmentation of the functionally disintegrated urban structure in East Jerusalem. The wall's construction enforces this fragmentation on two levels: the first is isolation of the neighborhoods' structures into parts on the inner side of the wall and others on its outer side, and the second is enforcing a continuation of the local/village nature in spite of the urbanization process in the Palestinian neighborhoods without forming any public city space. Given the fact that the national geo-political role of East Jerusalem was marginalized and truncated following the wall's construction as Palestinian governmental and administrative centers settled outside the wall, the need for providing the public city space became a luxury and essentially not required because functional subjugation was enforced between the neighborhoods as urban units by the local and governmental authority which possesses the resources and the power. Of course, this reality did not fulfill the Palestinian needs and potentials in Jerusalem.

The wall's effects on enforcing denial of the Palestinian right to appropriation in the city were felt on the tangible level in the severing of transportation and the failure to provide a road network connecting the Palestinian neighborhoods and contributing to free movement into them, between them and within them. Meanwhile, no lands were appropriated for public city purposes that exceeded neighborhoods' uses like a municipal soccer stadium, a service center, a public library, a court, etc. The formulators and managers of the space in the Jerusalem Municipality and the Israeli government claim that Palestinian Jerusalemites can theoretically use the public space that was created to serve the Israeli Jews in West Jerusalem. They argue that Jerusalem is a united city and no duplications in land uses should be created on the collective city level. But practically, Palestinians are barred from using this public space, which came at their expense and does not meet their needs and desires. Hence, the Palestinian occupation and utilization of the city space is shrinking to that occupied by their bodily physical existence. Moreover, their continuity with their Palestinian surroundings which feed them functionally -- including the West Bank, Gaza Strip and the entire Arab and Muslim world -- has been severed, creating a structural crisis and minimizing population mobility from the city level to the local level in the neighborhoods or the village, thereby causing further fragmentation not only in the spatial distribution within the city's various parts, but even inhibiting development of a civic leadership representing the population and presenting the interests of the Palestinian Jerusalemites. In fact, what happens and what is being developed is the phenomenon of traditional local groups trying to represent people's interests on the local level. This phenomenon was witnessed in dealing with the Israeli government to determine the wall's path, when local groups sought to conduct minimal localized modifications on the path of the wall to minimize local damages and possibly ensure local contiguity [such as Dahiyat Al Bareed, Sur Bahir, and Abu Dis] after losing hope in the possibility of stopping the wall's construction on the collective level. Moreover, Palestinian collective representation concentrates on the geo-political dimension as a central factor in changing and improving the reality of Jerusalem and does not give enough weight to the functional living role for the Palestinian residents. Similarly, the national Palestinian collective representation prohibits the local representation from granting legitimacy to space appropriations imposed by the Israelis. This reality will worsen following the wall's construction. The shortage of land that is allocated for public uses will not allow new economic opportunities within the Palestinian Jerusalemite society, and the separation of the Palestinian Jerusalemite society from its Palestinian extension on the outer side of the wall, will lead to two contradictory, albeit integrated, operations. On one hand, Palestinian entry into Jerusalem will decrease, transforming the city from a national center and central city that provides services to the entire Palestinian population [e.g., educational, health and tourist services] into a city lacking such services after they deserted Jerusalem or were forced to relocate to the outer side of the wall in order to serve the Palestinians living outside the city and on the outer side of the wall. On the other hand, the number of consumers of such services inside Jerusalem will decrease constantly due to the decreasing Palestinian Jerusalemite population inside Jerusalem and on the inner side of the wall. This trend will make it economically and functionally unfeasible to maintain the existence and development of such institutions, leading to their closure and relocation to the outer side of the wall. In return, this reality exacerbates the Palestinian Jerusalemite subjugation to Israeli city service institutions which do not meet their needs.

Therefore, the wall's construction will prevent providing the right to free Palestinian appropriation in Jerusalem, leading in the end to a void in public and private spatial formation in East Jerusalem and transforming it from a city that had begun to formulate its urban structure into a collection of local residential concentrations that are fragmented, existing without city components, and lacking a city center that unifies, serves and polishes them.

Production of the City's Space on the Outer Side of the Wall

The wall's construction remade the Jerusalemite physical city space and its relations with its inside and surroundings. The production of space goes far beyond the process of planning physical sites in the city to actually formulating and producing whatever has to do with life in the city. Providing the right to the city and producing the space require reshaping power relations and the distribution of resources, and transferring them from the central authorities to the local residents and their representatives, taking into consideration equality in the distribution of resources in accordance with needs in order to prevent the creation of gaps among the residential groups regardless of their national or ethnic belongings and affiliations. We cannot expect demarcation of the borders of the city's space, which is imposed by the Israelis through construction of the wall and the separation fence, to reformulate/reshape power relations and the distribution of resources and production of the space, especially in light of the experience of mixed Arab/Jew cities in Israel, such as Jaffa, Tel Aviv, Lod, Ramle, Haifa and Akko, in which that Jewish groups dominate Arab groups. Although both groups are citizens of the state, Arabs in those cities suffer from dual discrimination on the national and city levels [Falah, 1996]. Reduction of the Palestinian Jerusalemite population on the inner side of the wall may alleviate the perceived ethno-demographic pressure that accompanies the formulation of urban policies and plans in Jerusalem at the hands of Israeli government apparatuses and the Israeli municipality. Alleviation of the ethno-demographic pressure and transformation of the Palestinian Jerusalemites into a divided and fragmented minority having no collective city leadership and no functional city institutions capable of demanding the redistribution of resources and taking decisions concerning production of the space increases the deterioration of the living conditions for the Palestinians, including the level of services and infrastructure. Rejection of the principle of a Palestinian Jerusalemite collective demanding to share the resources and power under Israeli sovereignty represents an additional pretext for Israeli decision makers and distributors of resources to overlook Palestinian needs. The reduction of resources allocated for the Palestinians, coupled with the increase of urban life requirements, contribute to widening the gaps between what it provided by the municipality and what is required by the citizens.

The Palestinian nonparticipation in producing the space and sharing the resources and urban decisions will exacerbate the Palestinians' estrangement in the city's space and force them to produce the space without taking their interests and needs into consideration. Gaps between the Israeli and Palestinian neighborhoods will be widened. Those gaps include the lack and unavailability of services and infrastructure, the disappearance of economic and administrative opportunities, and the deterioration of the quality of life. The widening gaps will increase the spaces of estrangement and fear between the Israeli and Palestinian societies and increase instability, especially as the younger generations enter the chain of demanding appropriate city services in the era of globalization and openness. Those young generations will not be indifferent to the production and imposition of the imposed space without having an effective role. In other words, Israel's refusal to share production of the city's space will threaten stability in the city and lead to conflicts that may reach the level of violent confrontations between the Palestinians and Israelis within the city's space, conflicts based on the gaps and the control of resources and packaged by the national geo-political conflict.

It is worth pointing out here that the wall will, firstly, isolate the spaces inside the city from their suburbs as well as from the surrounding cities. Meanwhile, weak neighborhoods will evolve between such cities as Ramallah and Jerusalem. Those neighborhoods will evolve randomly. Also, the space inside East Jerusalem will become comprised of separate disintegrated or heterogeneous spaces. The first such space is the Old City and its surroundings, which suffer from economic weakness coupled with residential concentration. The surrounding commercial centers will be weakened and civil cultural life will become isolated and start moving to the cities outside the wall or the western part of

Jerusalem. Secondly, consider the space comprised of the Arab villages and neighborhoods, which do not enjoy any contiguity or integration among each other. These neighborhoods will keep random urban openness in order to meet the population increase, but they will not be able to attract positive migration to them or provide national-city services in them. They may be transformed into something similar to ghettos besieged by the wall as well as by the urban restrictions imposed by Jerusalem Municipality and the Israeli government. The third space is the Israeli neighborhoods and settlements that are isolated from the urban expansion west of Jerusalem by Palestinian neighborhoods west of the wall; these Israelis live in a state of conflict and heterogeneous competition. The wall will cancel, or at least freeze, the functional and spatial relationship between the Palestinian neighborhoods within the wall and others outside it, and will dwarf the role of Jerusalem and transform it from a central city in the heart of a nation to a partitioned peripheral city suffering from the absence of a connected hinterland that feeds and pushes it.

The Wall's Construction and the Dilemma of the Right to Citizenship

The idea of ensuring the right to the city originated from the individuals' possession of the right to participate in decision-making on the national level, although their participation on the city level is limited. Part of the right to the city is the individual and the society's right to formulate their opinions, ideas and demands in regards to the extent of their activeness in the city space, and to make their opinions heard. This means that the right to the city enforces democratic participation locally as well as on the national level. The questions we put forward here are: Does the wall's construction rearrange the relationship between the Israeli and Palestinian Jerusalemites to provide city democracy, or do Palestinian Jerusalemites continue to be deprived of participation in the Jerusalemite citizenship? and What is the answer's meaning for the reality of Jerusalem beyond the wall?

To answer these questions it is necessary first to present the reality before the wall's construction. Analysis of the reality demonstrates that it contradicts the concept of the right to the city. Palestinian Jerusalemites have not been granted the right to participate in the Israeli national elections (for the Knesset) although they were granted the right to participated in the municipal elections. Participation in the national Palestinian elections was granted to the Palestinian Jerusalemites for the elections of the Palestinian Legislative Council in 1996 and 2006, but they were not allowed to form a Palestinian municipality. In return, and as pointed out earlier, Palestinian Jerusalemites do not exercise the right of local election to participate in the municipal decision-making process. This refusal represents part of the rejection of the occupation on one hand, but on the other hand full citizenship was not granted, or was not imposed, by Israel on the Palestinians for internal Israeli considerations (demographic and political). Instead, they were only granted permanent residency rights and most of them retained Jordanian nationality and citizenship even after Jordan's disengagement with the West Bank in 1988.

We do not expect this reality to change following construction of the wall. The Palestinians will remain deprived of the provision of citizenship rights and participation in the decision-making process. After construction of the wall, a new Jerusalemite ethnic group may evolve in Israel. It will be a minority deprived of the citizenship rights but subject to the Israeli law. It will not be allowed to participate in national elections but   it will reject local elections. This contradictory reality will deepen the contradictions within the Jerusalemite Palestinian society and place it in a dilemma on the individual as well as the societal levels, and this includes the individual behavior within the space. Furthermore, this reality will stand regardless of serious demands by the Palestinians in Jerusalem to change the urban reality and its acceptance by Israel and the Jerusalem Municipality, which controls the space and movement within it, and possesses the power and the resources to produce it.

Construction of the wall, the derailment of the urban expansion among the Palestinian neighborhoods, and the uprooting the Palestinian personal affiliation from the Palestinian political center are all factors which will intensify the contradictory nature of the status quo. The situation may evolve to a re-drawing of a distinct Jerusalemite identity as a way out of these crises and the contradictory conditions as part of re-devising the official citizenship in return for globalization as proposed by Purcell [Purcell, 2003]. Purcell uncovered three major changes in crystallizing the citizenship and affiliation in the era of globalization, which were:

* Re-measurement of citizenship;

* Redoing the geographic distribution of citizenship;

* Re-guiding citizenship away from the nation, which is considered the dominating political society, as well as away from the citizens, who are considered homogeneous entities.

Here, the idea of the multi-layered citizenship replaces a mode of citizenship based on the democratic liberal model [Yuval-Davis, 2000]. This local model of citizenship is enforced by the fact that it stems from the concept of the right to the city, which was proposed by Lefebvre when he focused on inhabitancy as a basis for ensuring the right to the city [Lefebvre, 1991]. Here we raise the issue of pushing the Palestinian Jerusalemites to develop a new kind of citizenship in the wake of the wall's construction, especially in the reality of the contradiction to which they drifted without having any role in its production.

It must be pointed out here that the suffering arising from the denial and truncation of the right to the city includes Jerusalemite males as well as females, and women are expected to suffer even more from the lack of required services in the city. This conclusion was reached by various studies that focused on the gender reality in the city's surroundings [Fenster, 2004; 2006].

In sum, construction of the wall raises issues pertaining to the problem of citizenship versus residency, and political participation on the national level versus the local level. These problems will worsen in the wake of the wall's construction and will generate efforts to resolve them. These issues have ramifications and consequences on the daily lives of the Palestinians and the Palestinian existence in Jerusalem, especially in light of the fact that the distribution of financial resources and lands in the Jerusalemite reality, as is the case in the Israeli reality in general, is organically tied to national and ethnic affiliation. The wall was constructed to enforce the Jewish and Israeli identities of Jerusalem, and this enforcement cannot occur in a vacuum, especially the absence of equal citizenship and equal geo-political participation, which are inhibited by the wall. In fact, the wall prohibits even thinking about these issues since it is an outgrowth of the Israel ideology embodied in the slogan, "We are here and they are there," a stance that adds to residential separation and the prevention of spatial participation.

III. SUMMARY AND CONCLUSIONS

The wall's construction created and continues to create the space of the city of Jerusalem and the relations between the residents and inhabitants of the city. The wall determines and controls the Palestinian right in the city. We have tried in this chapter to analyze the ramifications of the wall and its effects on the right to the city stemming from the Lefebvrean idea and concept of citizenship. Although we realize that this concept may be inappropriate for analyzing the conflict ridden situation of Jerusalem, it adds a relevant additional dimension to our understanding of the relations in the conflict. In a previous study we discussed the wall's effects on Palestinian citizens [Khamaisi, 2005]

We demonstrated that the wall will truncate the Jerusalemite urban space and lead to its fragmentation and increase the spaces of fear within the city. Moreover, construction of the wall has undermined the development of Jerusalem as an urban, political and administrative heart of the Palestinian state, and deformed the natural organic development of the Jerusalemite urban state and its linkage with the cities and villages surrounding it, which feed it and enforce its development.

But in this study we tried to focus on the means of denying the right to the city following construction of the wall. The traditional localization in the neighborhoods and villages will be consolidated; therefore no urban rural state will be developed while the freedom of movement within this space shrinks. The result of the construction of the wall is the formulation and production of a space that is incapable of ensuring equal Palestinian participation in developing this space, and undermines fair and equitable distribution and sharing of resources, and participation in the urban divisions. The incomplete residency/citizenship that is conditionally imposed on the Palestinian Jerusalemites confuses and leaves them with a dilemma that they have no ability to manage in a situation characterized by a contradictory fluctuation between the ethnic and national affiliation and belonging on the local and societal level on one hand, and between meeting the political national aspirations and the providing of the living conditions within the urban space on the other hand.

Undoubtedly, the wall transforms Jerusalem from the state of centrality to a state of marginalization as a peripheral border city. This transformation leads to minimizing the general space until its absence, which means that the city becomes comprised of discontinuous and heterogeneous residential groups with varied levels of infrastructure and qualities of life. All of this makes it difficult to utilize Jerusalem as a central city and an urban heart for the state of Palestine. And there may be no short term solutions to these dilemmas.

We must point out here that construction of the wall practically undermines the concept of the open city, which is integral to the concept of the right to the city. The concept of the open city is still being undeveloped in the case of a city divided ethnically, culturally and politically. The concept of the open city does not mean nonexistence of administrative or political borders within the city. Rather, it means that those borders are permeable so that an individual, a family or an economic activity can move and settle freely within the city's space and can cross those borders easily and fluidly. The concept of the open city rejects the erection of physical borders within the city and within its surroundings. The construction of the wall has practically cancelled the idea and the vision of the open city, which is being demanded by a multitude of citizens and activists for the sake of devising a geo-political arrangement for the future of Jerusalem. In return, as the idea and the concept of the open city are eroded, the wall undermines the concept and the idea of the right to the city. This right is theoretically true for the Israelis, but the Palestinians are deprived of it. However, the wall increases the formation of spaces of fear within the city, thereby leading both ethnic groups to a feeling of insecurity in the city, and thereby pushing towards more polarization within the city among the ethnic/national groups.

In the end, it must be pointed out that the wall cannot ensure stability and prosperity for the city; on the contrary, it will maintain the state of conflict in it. Experiences of divided cities like Berlin, Nicosia, Beirut, Johannesburg, and Belfast confirm that the wall in the city's space cannot transform it into a central city. On the other hand, the removal of walls has contributed to the development of the cities and restoration of their centralities as in the case of Berlin. Meanwhile, the Israeli desire to legitimize its control over Jerusalem following construction of the wall is not materializing. This means that there is no alternative to proposing agreements that ensure the Palestinian right in the city for all its citizens in order to push the city toward stability, development and prosperity since the wall blocks such a vision for the city. This also means that both the Israelis and the Palestinians must guarantee their mutual interests in ensuring the right to the city. Further increases in Israeli domination over Jerusalem following construction of the wall cannot transform the city into an Israeli center, and the Israelis must realize that their interests in Jerusalem cannot be ensured through the erection of walls, but rather through recognition of the Palestinians' right to the city and facilitating the realization of this right through reproducing the space in a way that creates a Jerusalem that forms the heart and capital of the Palestinian state.

It can be concluded from the study that it is impossible to realize the concept of Israel's right to the city even after establishing the wall and imposing Israeli control over the east as well as west of Jerusalem because the city is being transformed into a border or frontier city. On the other hand, the wall has effectively ruled out the idea of Jerusalem becoming the capital of the Palestinian state and its political, administrative, and functional heart, transforming it instead into a truncated marginalized city. In fact, there is presently no physical, spatial, functional or even social integration between the Arab neighborhoods inside the city. The fragmentation created by the wall and Jerusalem's isolation from its surroundings contribute to the virtual lack of contiguity and integration between the Old City and its surroundings. This includes its connections with the commercial centers in Sheikh Jarrah and on Salah Eddin Street, on one hand and with its surrounding neighborhoods and villages which have developed small secondary centers and formed additional neighborhoods which serve them on the other. The above developments have caused a decline in the number of Palestinian national institutions in Jerusalem; several institutions have deserted Jerusalem for the surrounding cities such as Ramallah. By contrast, the wall created areas outside the wall that used to be affiliated with Jerusalem but were excluded outside the wall and now suffer from a dual marginalization. Kafr Aqab is but one example.

Consider, the wall's construction pushes Jerusalem into further deterioration and decline, accelerating negative migration from it, especially among members of the upper and middle classes. The fact that only the poorer classes do not leave Jerusalem will exacerbate the conflict in it, especially in the wake of its transformation into a frontier city. These negative ramifications will increase in the wake of Israel's implementation of the proposed unilateral "convergence/consolidation/realignment" plan, thereby exacerbating the city's deterioration, even if the plan entails the removal of Palestinian neighborhoods outside the wall.

In conclusion, the argument of this study underscores the need to stop the process of building the wall, for the sake of the city and its citizens, as well as for the sake of ensuring civil rights in Jerusalem. Continuing to ignore the immense dangers imposed by the wall on Jerusalem, in the short or long term, constitutes a crime against the city, its citizens and its lovers.

REFERENCES

ENGLISH SOURCES

Auga, M., Nasrallah, R., Hasson, S. and Stetter, S. (2005). *Divided Cities in Transition Challenges Facing Jerusalem and Berlin*, IPCC, Jerusalem.

Alterman, R. (2001). "National-Level Planning in Israel: Walking the Tightrope between Centralization and Privatization," in *National-Level Planning in Democratic Countries: An International Comparison of City and Regional Policy -Making*, edited by R. Alterman, University Press, Liverpool: pp. 257-288.

Benvenisti, M. (1996). *City of Stone: The Hidden History of Jerusalem*, Berkley: University of California Press.

Boal, F. (1997). "From Undivided to Undivided: Assimilation to Ethnic Cleansing," Paper presented at the NETHUR Workshop on The Undivided City, Den Haag, 1997, 10-11.

Bollens, S. (2000). *On Narrow Ground: Urban Planning amidst Ethnic Conflict in Jerusalem and Belfast*, New York: State University of New York.

Brooks, R., Nasrallah, R., Khamaisi, R. and Abu Ghazaleh, R. (2005) *The Wall of Annexation and Expansion: Its Impact on the Jerusalem Area*, IPCC, Jerusalem.

Cohen, S. B. (1980). *Jerusalem Undivided*, Herzl Press, New York.

Cuthbert, A. (1995). "The Right to the City: Surveillance, Private Interest and the Public Domain in Hong Kong," in *Cities*, vol.12, no. 5, pp. 293-310.

Falk, R. (2000). "The Decline of Citizenship in an Era of Globalization," *Citizenship Studies*, 4:15-18.

Falah, G. (1996). "Living Together Apart: Residential Segregation in Mixed Arab-Jewish Cities," *Urban Studies*, 33: pp. 823-857.

Fenster, T. (2004). *The Global City and the Holy City: Narratives on Planning, Knowledge and Diversity*, London: Pearrson.

Goodwin, M. and Painter, J. (1996). "Local Governance, the Crises of Fordism and the Changing Geographies of Regulation," *Transactions of the Institute of British Geographers*, no. 21, pp. 635-648.

Harvey, D. (2003). "The Right to the City," *International Journal of Urban and Regional Research*, vol. 27, no. 4, pp. 939-941.

Heinelt, H. (2005). *Metropolitan Governance in the 21st Century, Routledge*, London.

Khamaisi, R. (1997). "The Metropolitan Area of Jerusalem: Normal or Truncated? El *Syassa El Falestenia (Palestine Policy)*, vol. 4, no. 14, pp. 32-49.

Khamaisi, R. and Nasrallah R. (eds.) (2003). *The Jerusalem Urban Fabric: Demography, Infrastructure and Institutions*, IPCC, Jerusalem, p. 432.

Khamaisi, R. (2003). "Land Use and Ownership in Jerusalem," in Khamaisi, R. and Nasrallah, R. (eds.), *The Jerusalem Urban Fabric: Demography, Infrastructure, and Institutions, IPCC, Jerusalem*, pp: 198-230.

Khamaisi, R. et al. (2006). *"Jerusalem on the Map,"* 2nd ed., IPCC, Jerusalem.

Lefebvre, H. (1991). *"Critique of Everyday Life,"* Verso, London.

Lefebvre, H. (1991a). *"The Production of Space,"* Blackwell, Oxford.

Lefebvre, H. (1996) . *"Writings on Cities,"* Blackwell, Cambridge.

Mitchell, D. (2003). *"The Right to the City: Social Justice and the Right for Public Space,"* The Guilford Press, New York.

Misselwitz, P. et al. (2006), *City of Collision: Jerusalem and the Principles of Conflict Urbanism, Birkhauser* Publishers, Berlin.

Purcell, Mark, "Excavating Lefebvre: The Right to the City and its Urban Politics of the Inhabitant," *Geojurnal* 58 (2002): 99-108.

Roman, A. (ed.) (2003). *The Jerusalem Lexicon*, The Jerusalem for Israel Studies, Jerusalem. (in Hebrew.)

Salmon, S. (2001). "The Right to the City Globalism, Citizenship, and the Struggle over Urban Space," Paper presented at the 97th Annual Meeting of the Association of American Geographers, New York.

Tamari, S. (ed.) (2002). *Jerusalem 1948: The Arab Neighborhoods: Their Fate in the War*, Jerusalem: The Institute of Jerusalem Studies and Babil Resource Center.

ARABIC AND HEBREW SOURCES

Akbar, M. J., (1992), *Earth and Building in Islam*, Dar – al Qebla, Jadda, (in Arabic).

Mustafa, W., (1997), *Jerusalem: People and Building*, JMCC, Jerusalem (in Arabic).

Ben- Arieh, Y., (1979), *City in Mirror of the period- the New Jerusalem in its Beginning*, Yad Ben –Zvi Press, Jerusalem (in Hebrew).

Choshen, M. and others, (2004), *Sustainable Jerusalem, Issues in Development and Conservation*, Jerusalem Institute for Israeli Studies, Jerusalem, (in Hebrew).

Hazan, A., (1995), *Jurisdiction of Jerusalem 1948-1993*, Jerusalem Institute for Israeli Studies, Jerusalem, (in Hebrew).

J'abarin, J.,(2006), Right of City; The Crisis of Sehab –al-Den in Nazareth, *Makan*, Adala, vol. 1, pp: 7-20 (in Arabic).

Fenster , T.,(2006), Right of City and the Gender Dally Life , *Makan*, Adala, vol. 1, pp: 33-42 (in Arabic).

Khamaisi, R., (2006), *Conflict Over Housing: The Housing Sector in Jerusalem: Existing Situation, Barriers, Needs and Future Policies*, IPCC, East Jerusalem (in Arabic).

Khamaisi, R. and Nasrallah, R., (2006), *Jerusalem: The City of Lost Pease*, IPCC, East Jerusalem (in Arabic).

Kimhi, I. (ed.) (2006). *The Security Fence in Jerusalem: Its Impact on the City Residents*, The Jerusalem Institute for Israel Studies, Jerusalem (in Hebrew).

CHAPTER FOUR

The Wall and the Enclaves:
Case Studies in Disrupted Communities

Abdalla Owais, ph. D.

The separation wall has not only isolated East Jerusalem from the West Bank, but it has also stripped it of the most important factors a city needs to expand its geographic and demographic space. Normally, expansion reflects a city's activity and activism in a bordering area, and comes as a validation of its strength and its critical role on the local and regional levels. Just so, in the past, it was natural for attractive communities to grow at Jerusalem's peripheries; they facilitated its development and expansion and transformed the localities surrounding East Jerusalem into regionally important demographic and economic magnets. The development was not the result of a discrete phase of the city's life, but was rather a continuation of the evolution of the social, economic, cultural and geographic linkages between Jerusalem and its suburbs.

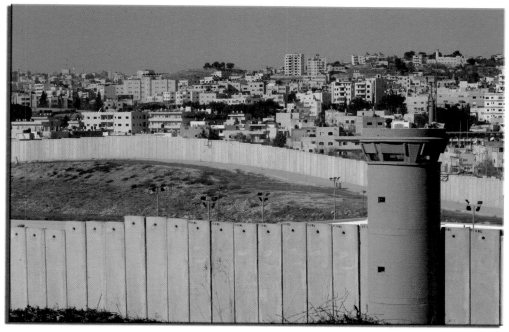

The wall in Qaladiya. Jan 2007.

These hubs of attraction evolved in various suburbs of East Jerusalem such as Al Eizariya, Abu Dis, Ar Ram, Bir Nabala, Anata and several others. These suburbs share a common characteristic, which is their location on the regional transportation axis connecting the south and north of the West Bank (Bethlehem-Jerusalem-Ramallah), or the western-eastern transportation axis (Jerusalem-Jericho-Amman).

The suburban areas began playing a significant role in developing the city's economy when investors from Jerusalem and outside it became interested in them, particularly in the real estate and construction sectors. In fact, those communities became the Palestinian Jerusalemites' strategy to avoid the oppressive housing crisis and excessively high rents in East Jerusalem and allowed them to live within a few kilometers of the city.

The decision to build the separation wall in and around Jerusalem, which was taken by the Israeli occupation authorities in 2002, has prevented any future interaction between the city and its suburbs. The wall has isolated and truncated the neighborhoods from the city and transformed them into marginal peripheral communities after they had become central points of attraction. Moreover, the wall cut the main roads linking East Jerusalem with the West Bank, leading to the economic collapse of many suburban communities and inflicting huge damages on their social and urban structures.

The decision to build the wall coincided with Israel's plans to restructure the city and to use the wall to set the actual borders of the so-called Greater Jerusalem. One of the most important elements of the plans placed Palestinian housing centers (e.g., Kafr Aqab, Shu'fat Refugee Camp and other areas located within the East Jerusalem borders) on the outer side of the wall. Another element was to isolate and truncate Palestinian suburban residential concentrations to prevent them from becoming an extension of East Jerusalem. The separation wall places them in demographic ghettos or enclaves, effectively surrounded by the wall and cut off from East Jerusalem and many other Palestinian communities. That strategy has resulted in the creation of a number of enclaves in and around East Jerusalem. Four such enclaves are the focus of the case studies which follow.* Our research in the enclaved communities has centered on the impact which ghettoization, created by the wall, has had upon the social life, economic well-being, and health and education in these communities. The housing enclaves include:

- **Ar Ram and Dahiyat Al Bareed**
- **Shu'fat Refugee Camp and Anata**
- **Al Eizariya, Abu Dis and As Sawahira Ash Sharqiya**
- **Bir Nabala, Al Judeira, Al Jib and Beit Hanina Al Balad**

These communities now have less area for urban expansion and fewer dunums for agricultural use because most of their open space has been placed on the other side of the wall from the communities. They have also suffered from a decline in population as the result of an emigration of Palestinians who held the blue ID card that allows them to enter and live in East Jerusalem. These communities were classified in the Oslo II Agreement as "Area C" territory, which means they were under Israeli control: they cannot be developed without Israeli authorization. **

The projected length of the wall in Jerusalem will exceed 100 kilometers. To date it has isolated Arab residential concentrations whose combined population in 2006 was estimated at approximately at 187,000; they occupy an area that has been reduced from 286,500 dunums (71,400 acres) to a mere 75,000 dunums (19,000 acres).

The "facts on the ground" imposed by Israel on these areas have left the residents with enormous challenges and extremely difficult conditions that affect every aspect of their lives. In this chapter, we shall illustrate the living conditions facing residents of these ghettos and demonstrate the extent of the deterioration and suffering inflicted on their lives as a result of the wall. We will see that the separation barrier has rendered East Jerusalem suburbs isolated fragmented entities that are unable to perform their roles in an ordinary manner and unable to maintain their continuity with their natural environs except through gates whose closure and opening is arbitrarily controlled by the Israelis.

---

*A note on the sources of this chapter. The author and IPCC staff members conducted extensive field research in the enclaves throughout 2005 and the first half of 2006. Each community was visited for the purposes of interviewing and field observations; most communities were visited several times. Interviews were held with the community local councils and refugee camp administrators, and many were able to provide not only their opinions and observations but also statistical reports on their towns. Interviews were also conducted with a wide array of professionals and local residents, including lawyers, labor leaders, school administrators, bus drivers, students and an untold number of ordinary residents. Data were also gathered from a number of government and NGO agencies including: the Ministry of Education, the Ministry for Jerusalem Affairs, the Palestinian National Authority Survey Department, UNRWA, the Women's Center of Shu'fat Refugee Center, the Palestinian Planning Center, B'Tselem, and the General Union of Palestinian Workers.

** All of the occupied territories were classified under the Oslo Accord of 1993 either as Area A (the Palestinian Authority exercises both civil and security jurisdiction), Area B (the Palestinian Authority exercises civil jurisdiction while security jurisdiction is shared with the occupation authorities), or Area C (both civil and security jurisdiction are exercised by the occupation authorities).

Figure IV: 1 Jerusalem Transport Routes Before and After the Wall

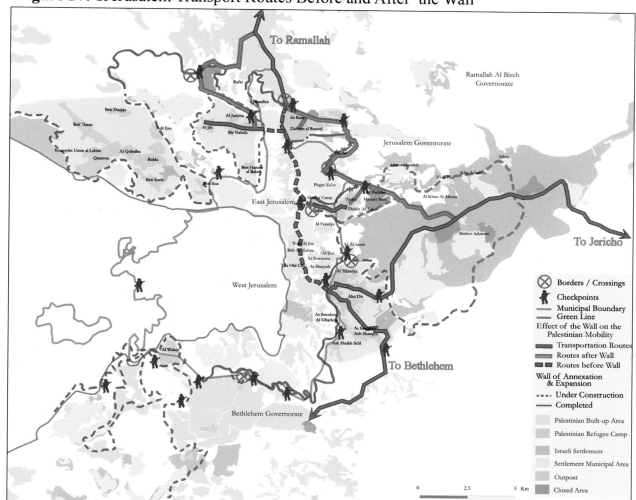

I. THE AR RAM/ DAHIYAT Al BAREED ENCLAVE

Ar Ram is located eight kilometers north of the Old City of Jerusalem, on a rise 870 meters above sea level. Ar Ram evolved on top of an archeological site known in the past as Ar Ramah, the hill. It was known during the Roman era as Aram. The Arabs later altered the name to Ar Ram. The combined area of Ar Ram and its twin adjoining town Dahiyat Al Bareed is 5,598 dunums (1,375 acres), most of which has been confiscated by Israeli occupation authorities, leaving the community with 2,700 dunums (675 acres), of which 2,100 dunums (625 acres) are classified as Area B and the remaining 600 dunums (150 acres) classified as Area C. Presently, the community is bordered on the north by Kafr Aqab and Qalandiya, on the east by Jaba' and the Giv'at Binyamin Israeli settlement, on the south by Beit Hanina Al Balad and the Neve Ya'akov Israeli settlement, and on the west by the Atarot Industrial Zone and Bir Nabala.

The location of Ar Ram/Dahiyat Al Bareed played a significant role in attracting many Jerusalemites and West Bankers. It is situated midway between Jerusalem and Ramallah on a critical transportation route that links East Jerusalem with the northern and southern cities of the West Bank. Moreover, the Ar Ram Junction is the main connecting point between Jerusalem's northern and northwestern suburbs. Ar Ram's location helped it attract investors and a labor force; investments surged in tandem with increases in population. Naturally, the most significant investments were in the real estate and construction sectors in response to the demand for housing. Easy access to Jerusalem and Ramallah also attracted various international, NGO, and PA organizations.

The commercial area in Ar Ram. Nov. 2006.

Figure IV: 2 Ar Ram, Dahiyat Al Bareed Enclave

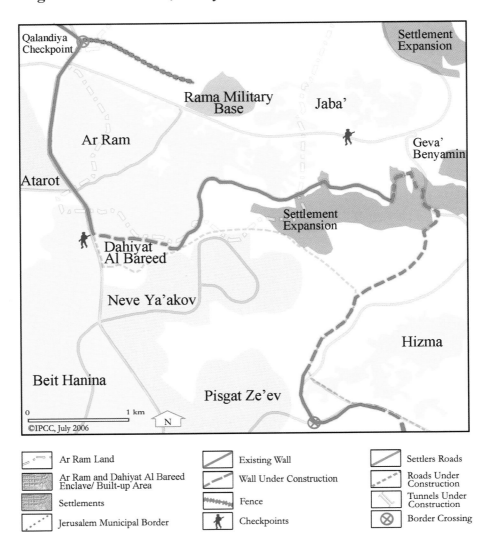

This prosperity lasted until 2002, when Israel approved plans for the wall. Moreover, the main roads in the community, such as the Jerusalem-Ramallah Road and the Ar Ram Junction, were closed or disrupted, and this led to a rapid deterioration in an economy whose prosperity was quite dependent on the community's role in traditional East Jerusalem and north/south West Bank traffic patterns.

According to the Ar Ram Local Council, the pre-wall population in 2002 was approximately 60,000; this is far larger than the PCBS estimate which does not include Jerusalem ID holders residing in the enclave. Jerusalem ID holders (representing 60% of the population) and expatriates from other West Bank areas made up the overwhelming majority of the population. However, the population began decreasing when the occupation authorities announced their plans to build the separation wall and implemented the first segment of it in Ar Ram between Qalandiya and Dahiyat Al Bareed. By 2005 the population had dropped to approximately 50,000; still most were Jerusalem ID holders, with the balance being West Bank ID holders and some were even Israeli ID holders. The demographic diversity in Ar Ram created a multitude of interconnected relations with the population and institutions of East Jerusalem and with the Palestinians who lived within the Green Line. These interconnections included the economic, educational, health and social aspects of life.

The Separation Wall

The wall running in the middle of the Jerusalem-Ramallah road in the area of Ar Ram. Nov 2006.

The completed wall will surround Ar Ram and Dahiyat Al Bareed on three sides—north, east, and west. The western section currently underway incredibly will run along the middle of the Jerusalem-Ramallah Road, dividing this main thoroughfare into two segments: one side of the wall the road will be considered within Jerusalem; the road on the lanes on the other side of the wall will, from the Israeli point of view, be considered West Bank territory. The western section will join the southern section south of the Qalandiya Checkpoint. On the east, Ar Ram will be isolated from the road that leads to Hizma, and in the south, Dahiyat Al Bareed will be isolated from the Neve Yaqov Israeli settlement by barbed wire and patrol roads. The wall will transform the area into an enclave with eventually only two controlled outlets. It will be separated from East Jerusalem, Bir Nabala, Al Judeira, Al Jib, and Beit Hanina Al Balad by the wall.

Wall construction in Ar Ram began on May 15, 2005, with a segment extending from the town's northern border with Qalandiya southward towards Dahiyat Al Bareed south of Ar Ram. The wall along the middle of the main road from East Jerusalem to Ramallah runs 2.4 kilometers and isolates Ar Ram from East Jerusalem on the west. In the south and east, a 3.5 kilometer segment of the wall isolates parts of Dahiyat Al Bareed from Ar Ram and runs to a point south of Jaba Village.

There, the wall will connect with the northern segment, which extends from the Qalandiya Crossing to south Jaba', creating from Ar Ram and Dahiyat Al Bareed a demographic ghetto that no one can enter on leave except via two checkpoints: the first in the north towards Jerusalem and Ramallah, and the second is planned to be south of Jaba' towards Hizma and the Anata area villages and from there towards the villages and towns south of East Jerusalem.

Wall construction has not only isolated the community from East Jerusalem, but also part of the Dahiyat Al Bareed neighborhood was severed from the community, placed on the East Jerusalem side of the wall in preparation for annexing it to Jerusalem. On June 22, 2005, an Israeli court issued an injunction ordering the army to suspend wall construction in Dahiyat Al Bareed until a final verdict on the lawsuits concerning its path is made. The occupation government altered the path of the wall in accordance with the request of some of the international, PA, and NGO institutions seated in Dahiyat Al Bareed. It was displaced northwards, thereby annexing parts of Dahiyat Al Bareed (100 buildings) to the municipal borders of Jerusalem and isolating them from Ar Ram. This measure led to the isolation of at least twenty-one organizations. The "inconvenience" of the wall and the division of Dahiyat Al Bareed forced several of them to close their offices there and move to Ramallah or other cities.

The wall under construction in Dahiyat Al Bareed. Jan 2007.

Following is a list of some of the institutions that are in the part of Dahiyat Al Bareed that has been split off from the community by the wall and effectively annexed to East Jerusalem:

- World Bank
- Egyptian Land Bank
- The Academy for Educational Development
- The Women's Studies Center
- Arab Studies Society—Geographic Information System (GIS)
- The Central National Committee for Rehabilitation of he Handicapped
- Norwegian Consulate
- The Welfare Consortium
- The Rosary Convent and School
- The Orthodox Club

At this writing, wall construction has not been completed, but on April 14, 2006, concrete blocks and barbed wire were placed alongside the planned path of the wall to prevent access towards

Jerusalem except for residents of Dahiyat Al Bareed. On another hand, it is still possible to travel from Jerusalem towards Ar Ram and Ramallah via the Dahiyat Al Bareed Checkpoint south of Ar -Ram. Actual construction of the wall's foundations in Dahiyat Al Bareed began on July 3, 2006. The Dahiyat Al Bareed Checkpoint is due to be closed in the near future, once wall construction is completed.

In the northern part of Ar Ram, no concrete wall is planned to be constructed due to the rocky terrain that forms a natural barrier. The occupation authorities are content with erecting a fence four meters high that extends from the south of Jaba' village to the Qalandiya Crossing. A segment of Road No. 45, which links Israeli settlement blocs in the Binyamin area (near Ramallah) with Jerusalem as well as with Tel Aviv and the coastal area via Qalandiya Crossing, lies just outside this segment.

The Economy

During the nineteen eighties and nineties, economic conditions in Ar Ram reached high levels in comparison with other West Bank cities. As we have noted, this prosperity largely can be attributed to Ar Ram's strategic location near the road connecting Jerusalem with Ramallah, as well as connecting Jerusalem suburbs with each other, particularly via the Ar Ram Junction which connects northern, northwestern and eastern Jerusalem suburbs with each other. Ar Ram's strategic location also made it a storage center for goods and containers coming from the Ashdod Port in Israel before their distribution to the rest of the West Bank. These attributes made Ar Ram an attractive center for investors and the labor force from the entire West Bank, including East Jerusalem, and contributed to increasing per capita income to levels paralleling those in urban East Jerusalem.

Moreover, Ar Ram was attractive to East Jerusalemites not only because of its proximity to East Jerusalem but also because of the availability of comparatively affordable housing. This led to a construction boom to meet the demand for apartments and office spaces. In fact, the extraordinary demand in the real estate market prompted investors to demolish old houses to build huge buildings with larger residential capacities. However the construction and real estate sectors were adversely affected by Israel's announcement of its intention to build the wall and by the promulgation of special laws which revoked the right of Palestinians carrying Jerusalem ID cards to live outside of the J1 East Jerusalem area. Ar Ram and Dahiyat Al Bareed are in the J2 area, which Israel—but not the PA--considers to be the West Bank. Nowadays there are scores of multi-story buildings in Ar Ram that are vacant because they were deserted by residents or businesses, and there are also scores of large buildings whose construction has not been completed since their owners are discouraged by the vanishing market for them.

The community's economic prosperity began regressing concurrently with wall construction. A significant number of commercial outlets have been closed since 2002, when the Israeli authorities declared their intention to build the wall. The Ar Ram Local Council estimates that 550 commercial enterprises on the main streets of Ar Ram and Dahiyat Al Bareed have moved out or gone bankrupt. In the meantime, many of the companies and commercial and service offices that stayed in Ar Ram have shrunk due to the difficulty of moving goods in or out of the area and to the access problems the wall created for their clients. Furthermore, the inability of the local labor force to access jobs in East Jerusalem or cross to the other side of the Green Line caused unemployment rates to surge above 50% to an estimated 10,000 jobless persons. This naturally led to a deterioration of family income levels and a rapid wave of immigration to Ramallah and the rest of the West Bank.

Approximately 20 institutions and companies, and dozens of shops and businesses based in Ar Ram alone closed down. For example, 88 of the 312 commercial outlets on the main Jerusalem - Ramallah Road, which was bisected by the wall from Qalandiya Crossing to Dahiyat Al Bareed south of Ar Ram, are closed.

Construction froze in Ar Ram due to the economic depression that was generated by the construction of the wall. Thousands of residences have become vacant as Jerusalemites migrate back to Jerusalem. Jan 2007.

In short, the area economy has been dealt a huge blow. Its economy was largely based on its location and its easy access to East Jerusalem and other surrounding communities. With the continuing threats to East Jerusalem ID holders who live outside city boundaries in such towns as Ar Ram and Dahiyat Al Bareed, out-migration of Blue Carders is expected to continue in the coming years. This bodes no good for the Ar Ram/Dahiyat Al Bareed enclave.

Social Sector

Many of the community's residents who held the East Jerusalem ID card have returned to the city, some leaving behind members of their extended and even immediate families who hold West Bank IDs. This has fractured family relations and social ties. But in spite of the emigration of many Jerusalem ID holders from Ar Ram, a large number of Jerusalemites continue to live in the town. The Ar Ram Local Council estimates in its report on April 9, 2006 that while the percentage of Jerusalemites who have moved out of the town has reached 15%, Jerusalemites remaining in Ar Ram/Dahiyat Al Bareed still constitute 50% of the total population. Some of those who stayed in Ar Ram have investment ties; others do not want to sever family or marital ties with persons who hold West Bank IDs and who therefore cannot live in East Jerusalem. Still other Blue Carders who have remained in Ar Ram simply do not have the financial means to live in East Jerusalem.

Other social effects arise from the division of the Dahiyat Al Bareed area. The path of the wall in Dahiyat Al Bareed split off a section of the community from the rest of the town and prohibited residents who carry West Bank ID cards from entering that section. The inability of Palestinian relatives carrying West Bank ID cards to reach those residents has created considerable social suffering. Furthermore, the wall's construction has made it impossible to access places of worship in Jerusalem and the closed areas.

In conclusion, the social continuity in Ar Ram and Dahiyat Al Bareed, which was based on decades of interactions, is subject to collapse now just as it is in other areas of the governorate that have been isolated and truncated from East Jerusalem.

Transportation

Ar Ram represented a connecting point for East Jerusalem with Ramallah and with other cities in the north of the West Bank. Ar Ram's roads also connected the suburbs north, northwest, and northeast of Jerusalem throughout the years preceding the wall's construction. This strategic location made Ar Ram the main access point for all transportation means to the areas surrounding East Jerusalem.

A traffic crisis in Ar Ram began after the occupation authorities decided to restrict Palestinian travel along the roads adjacent to the Neve Ya'akov and Pisgat Ze'ev Israeli settlements. Those roads formerly connected East Jerusalem with Ar Ram and Ramallah and allowed drivers to avoid congested areas. The Israeli restrictions have forced traffic flow between Jerusalem and Ar Ram and Ramallah to pass through Shu'fat and Beit Hanina and then along the main road through Dahiyat Al Bareed and Ar Ram.

Qalandiya Checkpoint 2004.

Qalandiya Checkpoint 2007.

The traffic problem between Qalandiya and Dahiyat Al Bareed was exacerbated by wall construction in the middle of the Jerusalem-Ramallah main road. The Ar Ram Junction, which connects northern, northwestern, and northeastern suburbs of Jerusalem with each other, lies on this road; therefore, wall construction lead to enormous traffic jams, particularly during the morning and afternoon rush hours. This forced citizens to leave much earlier in order to get to their work places or schools on time. On April 16, 2006, the wall was completely closed, making access to the northwestern suburbs and villages of East Jerusalem through Ar Ram Junction impossible and forcing commuters to detour through the Qalandiya Refugee Camp three kilometers north of Ar Ram Junction, before heading down a new road. The distance from the Ar Ram Junction to Bir Nabala used to be approximately 500 meters; in the wake of the wall it has become a drive of approximately 15 kilometers. This complication is reflected in dramatic increases in transportation costs to the thousands who move about in this area daily.

Figure IV: 3 Transport Routes in Ar Ram/Dahiyat Al Bareed Enclave Before and After The Wall

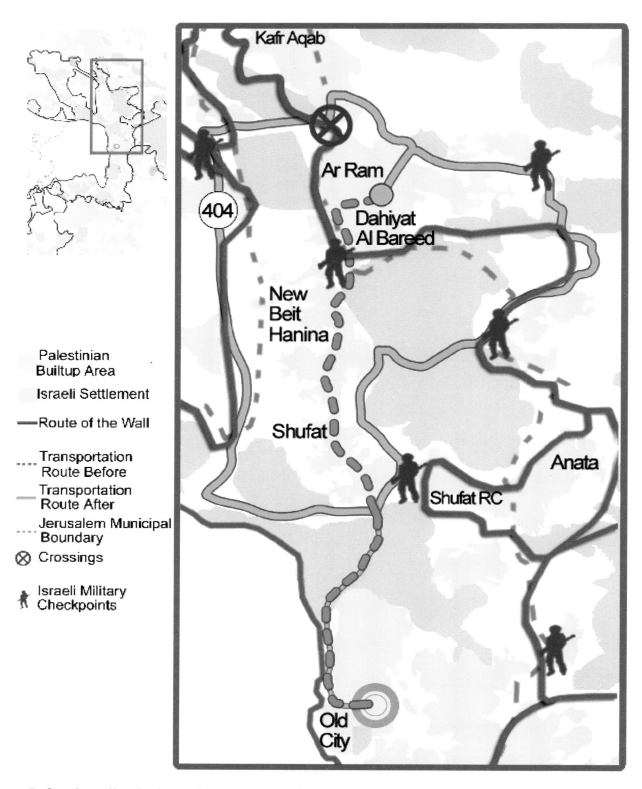

Before the wall, Palestinians from Ar Ram and Dahiyat Al Bareed simply moved south along the main axis of Jerusalem - Ramallah road a distance of merely 5 km to the center of Jerusalem, which required only 10 minutes in travel time. After the constructions of the wall, Palestinians are not allowed to enter the city unless they have permits, which are rarely obtained. In that case, they have to travel into Ramallah and then transit the Qalandiya Checkpoint (which the Israelis call the Atarot Terminal), then travel along Roads No. 45 and 404/4 to reach the same destination- - a distance of at least 14 km and requiring at least 30 minutes, not considering the waiting times at the checkpoints. Only Jerusalem ID holders can take an alternative 13 km route to enter the city through the Hizma Checkpoint.

Table IV: 1 Transportation Costs between Ar Ram and Neighboring Areas

Destination	Fares prior to wall construction (in NIS)	Fares after wall construction (in NIS)
Ramallah	3	4 (an increase of 33%)
Jerusalem	3.5	6.5 (an increase of 86%)
Al Eizariya and Abu Dis	5	8 (an increase of 60%)
Bir Nabala	1.5	5 (an increase of 233%)

These hikes in transportation costs impact negatively on the freedom of movement as well as on commercial activity in Ar Ram. They also impact negatively on social ties, especially among elderly people who cannot cope with the physically stultifying and psychologically humiliating circumstances that exist at checkpoints, even though they have close ties with family members in the areas on the other side of the wall.

Education

There are fourteen schools in Ar Ram and Dahiyat Al Bareed. They serve the town and nearby villages, as well as areas within East Jerusalem's borders. An additional 5,000 pupils living in Ar Ram and carrying Jerusalem ID cards go to schools in New Beit Hanina and Shu'fat Village, as well as other schools within East Jerusalem. The erection of checkpoints and construction of the wall made it impossible for West Bank ID holders to go to schools within East Jerusalem. On the other hand, delays and complicated measures at checkpoints have prompted East Jerusalem residents to abstain from sending their children to schools outside the city, including Ar Ram schools, and many East Jerusalem ID holders who are residents of Ar Ram now abstain from sending their children to schools within East Jerusalem. **Table IV: 2** below presents the governmental and private schools in Ar Ram, and the number of their pupils from inside and outside Ar Ram.

Table IV: 2 Schools and Enrollments in Ar Ram/Dahiyat Al Bareed

School	Type	Pupils		Teachers	
		No. of Pupils	(From outside Ar Ram)	No. of Teachers	(From outside Ar Ram)
Ar Ram Boys Secondary School	Government	382	74	20	16
Ar Ram Girls Secondary School	Government	382	28	18	9

Table IV: 2 (continued)

Ar Ram Girls Basic School	Government	353	0	13	7
Mu'ath Bin Jabal Basic School	Private	15	0	2	2
Bridge Academy	Private	208	0	16	16
Holy Land School	Private	133	73	14	9
Al-Majd Basic School	Private	101	0	8.5	2.5
Al-Fares Basic School	Private	35	0	2	1
Al-Ma'aref Al-Islamieh Basic School	Private	30	0	3	1
An-Nahdah Al-Islamieh School	Private	461	0	18.5	13.5
Al-A'hd Basic School / Ar Ram	Private	348	0	17	12
Ruwwad Al-Ghad School	Private	47	0	4	0
Marah and Farah Basic School	Private	62	0	2	2
Abna' Al-Majd School	Private	19	0	1	1
Bara'em Al-Waha Al-Khadra' School	Private	24	0	5	3
Total		**2,576**	**175**	**112**	**95**

The number of pupils in Ar Ram schools coming from outside the town is 175. The number of teachers in Ar Ram schools who do not live in Ar Ram and Dahiyat Al Bareed is 95 out of 112, or the equivalent of 83% of the total. Most of those teachers live in nearby villages and towns, especially northwest Jerusalem villages, which were no more than eight kilometers away from Ar Ram prior to the wall's construction. Presently, and in the wake of the wall's construction, those teachers have to travel distances as far as twenty kilometers, or for one to one-and-a-half hours, before they arrive at their schools. As travel distances increased, transportation costs increased 10 to 12 NIS. Prior to the wall's construction, transportation costs to Ramallah and Dahiyat Al Bareed ranged from 1.5 to 6 NIS.

University students from Ar Ram and Dahiyat Al Bareed face difficulties in accessing their campuses, especially Al-Quds University in Abu Dis. Such difficulties include waiting for long periods at military checkpoints, facing humiliating treatment at the hands of occupation soldiers manning those checkpoints, and surging transportation costs. Presently, students traveling to Al-Quds University in Abu Dis have to pay 9 NIS. Transportation costs prior to the wall's construction were 5 NIS.

Health and Medical Services

The health sector was adversely affected by the wall construction, because a significant portion of Ar Ram's population used to rely entirely on health and medical services available in East Jerusalem. Until today, there are no hospitals in Ar Ram, not even small, regularly opened medical centers affiliated with the Health Ministry. The few centers that exist operate only a few days a week. Moreover, the town lacks an emergency center **Table IV: 3** summarizes the medical services available to serve the population in Ar Ram and Dahiyat Al Bareed:

Table IV: 3 Medical Facilities in the Ar Ram Enclave

Facilities	Number
Medical Centers (Private)	3
Medical Centers (Governmental)	2
Physicians (Specialized and General)	5
Dentists	25
Pharmacies	6

It should be noted that there are many patients in Ar Ram who need close care and follow-up. The Ar Ram Local Council statistics indicate that there are no fewer than 2,918 diabetes, hypertension, cardiac, cancer, kidney failure and other chronic disease patients. Additionally, there are no fewer than twenty-one loss-of-vision cases that formerly were followed-up at specialized centers in East Jerusalem; and there are a number of handicapped individuals who are in dire need of the medical care available at specialized centers such as the Al-Amal and An-Noor centers in East Jerusalem. All of these cases require follow-up and continuing access to specialized centers and hospitals. Such care is available to persons even of limited income in East Jerusalem. But given the fact that not all of the Ar Ram enclave patients are Jerusalem ID holders, and therefore cannot cross the military checkpoints without permits from Israeli liaison offices, which are extremely difficult to obtain, their suffering in accessing East Jerusalem centers and hospitals is compounded. Added to that, such permits are required each time the patient has to visit the centers and hospitals in East Jerusalem. Furthermore, approximately 8,000 babies and children received periodic vaccinations at the health centers in East Jerusalem, and 95% of birth deliveries were in East Jerusalem hospitals.

The Environment

The construction of the wall destroyed sewage and sanitation networks in some areas such as in the area of the Commercial Bank of Palestine, as well as along the Jerusalem-Ramallah Road. This has led to floods in those areas. The response to several appeals by the Ar Ram Local Council to the occupation authorities was that wall construction was ongoing, and responsibility for the sewage and sanitation network has not yet been handed over to the Palestinian Authority.

Ar Ram residents produce an average of 120 tons of trash every day, which formerly was shipped and dumped in the Al Eizariya Landfill. Presently, only 70 tons are dumped there each day and the remaining 50 tons is withheld until the next day due to the travel restrictions at the checkpoints on the roads leading to Al Eizariya. This leads to a growing inventory of accumulated waste in the community. Moreover, the Ar Ram Local Council has to pay the Israeli Jerusalem Municipality NIS 20 (4.50 USD) per ton per day, or the equivalent of NIS 1,400 (318 USD) daily. Also, some garbage is being incinerated by the residents inside the town, which causes health and environmental damages to the town and its citizens.

II. THE SHU'FAT REFUGEE CAMP/ ANATA ENCLAVE

Standing at approximately three kilometers northeast of the Old City of East Jerusaelem lies a block of interlinked communities with a combined population in excess of 47,000: Shu'fat Refugee Camp (RC), Anata Village, Dahiyat As Salam, Ras Khamis, Ras Shehadeh, and the Bedouin community of Al Fheidat. Well over half of the residents in this cluster hold Jerusalem IDs, the blue card issued by the Israelis to Palestinians who claim East Jerusalem residency, an area designated as J1 by the PA. Some of these clustered communities although adjoined to J1 are considered to be in J2, a Palestinian Jerusalemite suburban area which Israel considers as outside of its Jerusalem Municipal boundaries and part of the West Bank. The Shu'fat Refugee Camp, a J1 community which may be understood as the first link in the group, stands next to and is inseparable from Shu'fat Village. In 2004 the Israelis began building a separation wall which split off the camp from the village. The completed wall will surround the camp and the other communities in the cluster in a single ghetto, the second largest enclave created by the wall, only marginally smaller than the Ar Ram/Dahiyat Al Bareed enclave to the north. For reasons of convenience, we have named the enclave after its two largest communities, styled simply as the Shu'fat Refugee Camp/Anata enclave.

Figure IV: 4 The Shu'fat Refugee Camp, Anata Enclave

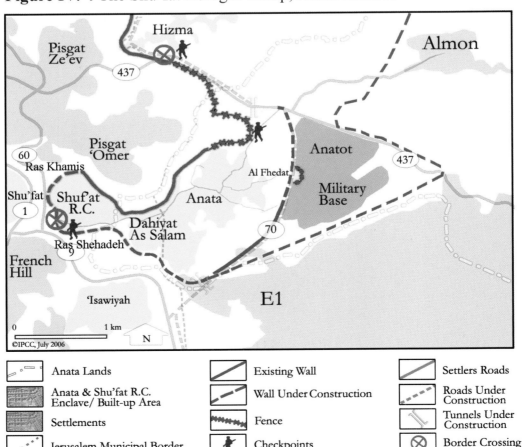

Shu'fat Refugee Camp

Shu'fat Refugee Camp was established in 1966 by the United Nations Relief and Works Agency for Palestine Refugees in the Near East (UNRWA) on 98 dunums (24 acres) of Shu'fat Village lands to provide shelter for 1,500 Palestinians who had been expelled by the Israelis from the Ash-Sharaf neighborhood in the Old City of Jerusalem. The occupation authorities destroyed the Ash-Sharaf and erected on its ruins the so-called "Jewish Quarter." Ash-Sharaf residents who moved to Shu'fat Refugee Camp had been expelled earlier in 1948 from 56 villages surrounding what it presently known as West Jerusalem.

An overview of Shu'fat Refugee Camp. Jan 2007.

Shu'fat Refugee Camp (elsewhere Shu'fat RC) is located three kilometers northeast of the Old City of Jerusalem. It is bordered by Anata and Dahiyat As Salam on the east, Shu'fat Village on the west, Al Issawiya and the French Hill from the south, and the Pisgat Ze'ev and Pisgat 'Omer Israeli settlements in the north. Until the advent of the wall, Shu'fat RC was considered simultaneously part of Arab East Palestine J1 and the Israeli Jerusalem Municipality.

The area of Shu'fat RC expanded gradually to 198 dunums (45 acres) by 1993 and to 347 dunums (87 acres) by 2006, and between these bench mark dates the population increased from 9,000 to 22,000, including 10,612 refugees. The dramatic increase resulted from the natural population increase (births minus deaths) as well as from these additional factors:

- Immigration to the camp in 1996 by thousands of Jerusalem ID card holders who had been living outside of East Jerusalem and the Jerusalem Municipality, especially in Ar Ram and Bir Nabala. They migrated to the camp to avoid the consequnces of a new Israeli policy that would withdraw their Blue ID cards, effectively revoking their right to Jerusalem residency and to government entitlements. (See the discussion of Blue Carders in Chapter Two.)

- Many were drawn to the camp because its residents do not pay Israeli municipal (Arnona) taxes that are the obligation of residents of other East Jerusalem areas.

- The relative ease of proving the place of residence to the occupation authorities.

- Easy access to East Jerusalem for workers coming from the West Bank who worked mostly in the construction sector in East Jerusalem.

- Significant numbers of refugees who were registered in the camp but who in fact lived outside it returned to the camp.

The Israeli occupation government began isolating densely-populated Palestinian areas around Jerusalem and besieging some of those areas with a separation wall as a pre-emptive move to isolate Palestinian East Jerusalem from the West Bank and to ensure a permanent Jewish majority in unilaterally unified Jerusalem. In order to attain this goal, the occupation government began demarcating the borders of target areas and truncating them from East Jerusalem. Shu'fat RC is one of the areas. In 2004 the occupation authorities began erecting a wall around Shu'fat RC and to also annex within the ambit of the wall Ras Khamis and Ras Shehadeh (neighborhoods from Shu'fat Village lands) as well as Anata, Dahiyat As Salam and the Bedouin settlement Al Fheidat. Within the wall, these communities became a block isolated from East Jerusalem and largely disconnected from their West Bank neighbors as well.

The combined area of Shu'fat RC, Ras Khamis and Ras Shehadeh is estimated at approximately 517 dunums (130 acres), all of which were originally Shu'fat Village lands. The 2006 population of this residential block is estimated at 29,500 by the camp's administration. This yields an average population density in this residential ghetto of 57 persons per dunum (or 228 persons per acre). This reality resulted in several problems on many levels that are worsening as progress on the wall's construction continues.

The wall separates Ras Khamis from East Jerusalem. Jan 2007.

Table IV: 4 Area and Estimated Population of the Shu'fat Section of the Enclave

Area	Area (dunums)	Population
Shu'fat RC	3	22,000
Ras Khamis	70	5,000
Ras Shehadeh	100	2,500
Total	517	29,500

The Separation Wall

Construction of the northern segment of the wall is complete. It separates Shu'fat Refugee Camp and Ras Khamis from the Pisgat Ze'ev and Pisgat 'Omer Israeli settlements. The western and southern segments of the wall have not been completed, but the area has been isolated by concrete barriers and barbed wire. This ghetto has two gateways, the first, located at the western entrance of the refugee camp, leads to Shu'fat Village in East Jerusalem and the second, sited in the northwest area of Anata, connects with the route to Ramallah. These two entrances are under the complete control of the Israeli occupation authorities. The separation wall will include upon completion a ghetto composed of Shu'fat Refugee Camp, Ras Khamis, Ras Shehadeh, Anata and Dahiyat As Salam. The area of this ghetto is approximately 1,342 dunums (335 acres), and it will be besieged from all sides by a wall approximately 9.5 kilometers long. At least 47,200 Palestinians will live in this ghetto. The movement and travel of those residents is controlled via two entrances/exits—one in the direction of Ramallah and the other in the direction of Jerusalem. The population will be subject to a 24-hour seven-day surveillance which will monitor all movement and all sectors of this isolated enclave.

East Jerusalem provides, in its capacity as the Palestinian central city for all villages and towns surrounding Jerusalem, vital social, economic, health, educational and religious services to those villages in particular and the rest of the West Bank in general. As the separation wall is being constructed, West Bank residents are barred from entering Jerusalem, and the measures concerning entry of Jerusalem ID holders living outside the city are tightening. Consequently, living anywhere in the Palestinian Jerusalem Governorate has become more complicated and less secure. This wall-created reality has negative implications on all critical aspects of Palestinian life.

The Social Sector

In spite of the successive migrations of Palestinians to Shu'fat RC, residents, particularly following their expulsion from the Old City, continue to maintain strong social ties with East Jerusalem. These social ties, such as marriages, family and relatives, have become difficult to sustain in the face of difficulties associated with the hurdles of entry to Jerusalem. In fact, it has become impossible for West Bank ID card holders to maintain relations with their relatives, especially in the wake of Israeli court support for a law that bars East Jerusalemites from obtaining family reunification for their husbands, wives or relatives. Those laws hold that individuals who carry the Jerusalem ID cards but who are married to Palestinians who do not have the card cannot live with that spouse in East Jerusalem (J1). On the social level, this means tearing apart the natural structure of the Palestinian families and isolating married partners, parents, grandparents, and children from each other. Many people who hold the Blue Card Jerusalem ID bear these conditions in order to preserve the future possibility of uniting with their wife or family in Jerusalem and to not lose the right to Jerusalemite residency. Those who do not have the Jerusalem ID and live in the suburban J2 or West Bank areas and who wish to visit relatives in East Jerusalem (J1) have to apply for permits to enter East Jerusalem at the Israeli Coordination and Liaison offices. The process is usually costly and its results are discouraging as most permit applications are rejected without mentioning the reasons.

In an IPCC interview, Jamal Awad, Director of Shu'fat Refugee Camp, reported that, "The plan to separate the refugee camp from Jerusalem has increased the economic problems, especially for West Bank ID card holders who have become unable, in the wake of the wall, to work in Jerusalem or within the Green Line except with permits from the occupation authorities. This restriction has compounded the social and security problems facing the camp's residents." Such complications include significant increases in early marriages, family violence rates, robbery rates, and the resort to firearms in dealing with disputes.* The absence of security has also lead to surges in drug addiction rates and public drug dealing. These social problems are exacerbated by construction of the wall.

At the Women's Center in the Refugee Camp, In'am Al-Wahidi, an employee at the center, said, "There is no place for children to go and spend their free time. The center receives approximately 300 children daily in an attempt to improve their situation. No place provides those children with educational and sport activities except ours. Moreover, the constant fear of residents carrying West Bank ID cards of taking their children outside the refugee camp has caused psychological pressure for those children. The quality of child care in the refugee camp is constantly deteriorating as a result of several factors, the most important of which is the increase in poverty rates among the camp's population as a result of the wall. Children are the first to suffer from the deterioration of economic and social conditions.

Table IV: 5   Social Centers Operating in Shu'fat Refugee Camp

Center	Beneficiaries (dunums)
The Handicapped Rehabilitation Center	600 handicapped
the Palestinian child Center	100 children
The Women Center	500 women
Shu'fat Refugee Camp Youth Center and Club (destroyed)	0
Shu'fat Refugee Camp Committe Center	10,000

Health and Medical Services

There are no hospitals, specialized medical centers, or even emergency clinics in Shu'fat RC. There is only one medical center affiliated with UNRWA and two medical centers affiliated with the patients' fund (Kopat Holim). There are also two private clinics—one general clinic and one dental clinic.

---

*There are no police in Shu'fat RC or Anata.

Shu'fat RC residents rely primarily on the medical services provided in East Jerusalem, particularly when it comes to hospitals which have specialized medical teams and are equipped with modern equipment. These still serve the poorest in the society, such as the Al-Makassed Hospital. Nowadays they must have a transit permit and negotiate a difficult entry point in order to access those services.

More than 450 Shu'fat RC residents with various kinds of handicaps have serious difficulty accessing rehabilitation facilities in Jerusalem and Ramallah. Having to cross the military checkpoints at the camp's gates compounds their suffering. The problems have become so burdensome that many of them have stopped going to the rehabilitation centers they visited prior to the wall's construction. The suffering is even more egregious for patients with chronic diseases that require frequent treatment at specialized medical centers, such as dialysis and diabetes patients who are exhausted by the long waiting hours at checkpoints as well as by the need to use more than one means of transportation to get to those specialized centers and come back on the same day.

In spite of the existence of a rehabilitation center in the refugee camp, it does not possess the capabilities available at rehabilitation centers in Jerusalem and Ramallah in terms of the staff or equipment. Moreover, clinics in the refugee camp are not equipped to receive emergency cases.

Khader Al-Dibs, Head of the Wall Resistance Committee in Shu'fat RC, reported in an IPCC interview that, "On May 12, 2006, Omar Rasheed (Abu Kamel), 42, a resident of Shu'fat Refugee Camp, was admitted to a medical center in the camp affiliated with Kopat Holim. He had just had a stroke, and because the center had no capabilities for treating him, it was necessary to transfer him to a hospital in Jerusalem. When the ambulance arrived at the checkpoint at the camp gate, the occupation soldiers barred it from entering. The ambulance crew had to enter the camp in a private vehicle and at their risk. A few hours later, an ambulance affiliated with Kopat Holim arrived to transfer the patient to a hospital. He died before arriving there."

The Economy

The refugee camp's economic activities are confined to small shops, blacksmiths, carpenters, and car mechanics. Those activities serve East Jerusalem markets and are dependent on the city for clients and materials. At this writing, and in contrast to other parts of the enclave, none of the camp's enterprises have had to close as a result of the wall.

Main entrance to Shu'fat Refugee Camp. Jan 2007.

The most significant component of the Shu'fat RC economy is its labor force. Camp residents depend on the labor markets in East Jerusalem and within the Green Line. The labor markets have not changed much for camp residents with Jerusalem ID cards, but these markets have become impossible to access for residents with West Bank ID cards. Consequently, poverty rates in the refugee camp have increased.

Education

In Shu'fat RC there are six schools, including four affiliated with UNRWA, and two private schools. Moreover, there are seven kindergartens. The four UNRWA schools have approximately 2,760 pupils in two shifts—a morning and an afternoon shift– in order to accommodate the large student population. Additionally, approximately 1,300 high school students are enrolled in schools outside the camp, especially in Shu'fat Village and East Jerusalem, due to the unavailability of government secondary schools in the refugee camp, as well as the high student density in UNRWA schools. Those students suffer from their inability to get to their East Jerusalem schools on time due to the long waiting periods at the military checkpoint at the gate to the refugee camp, which is also their only exit to Shu'fat Village or East Jerusalem. This problem has caused students to drop out of schools on the other side of the checkpoint. It should be noted also that the camp schools are badly overcrowded, having an average of 43 pupils per class. This is in part due to the inability of many to choose schools outside the refugee camp.

University and college students also suffer from the difficulty of accessing their institutions due to the long waiting periods at checkpoints and the difficulty of transportation since direct bus transportation that was available prior to the wall has been discontinued. Most university students in Shu'fat Refugee Camp study at Al-Quds University in Abu Dis; this used to be no more than a 25minute drive prior to the construction of the wall and erection of the checkpoints. Some students also go to Birzeit University north of Ramallah. Getting there has become a long tedious journey.

Table IV: 6 Schools, Pupils and Teachers in Shu'fat Refugee Camp, Ras Khamis and Ras Shehadeh

School	Type	Pupils		Teachers	
		No. of Pupils	(From outside Shu'fat RC)	No. of Teachers	(From outside Shu'fat RC)
Shu'fat Girl Middle School	UNRWA	1,804	0	57	47
Shu'fat RC Basic School	UNRWA	471	41	18	12
Shu'far Boy Basic School	UNRWA	485	18	15	13
Al-Faqeeh Model School	Private	70	0	5	1
Ahbab Ar-Rahman School	Private	275	0	10	5

Table IV: 6 (continued)

Sawa Rbina School	Private	35	0	2	1
Total		**3,140**	**59**	**107**	**79**

Transportation

In Shu'fat RC, there are 12 buses and minibuses providing transportation from and to Jerusalem. Camp residents normally head to bus stations in East Jerusalem and from there to various areas in the Jerusalem Governorate and to West Bank cities.

The wall's construction harmed the transportation sector and caused hikes in transportation costs and delays in arrivals to Jerusalem and the nearby areas due to the various obstacles at checkpoints and the need to transfer to multiple means of transportation to get to target destinations. These hikes in transportation costs negatively affected the poor community's mobility and its cost of living.

Table IV: 7 Transportation Costs in Shu'fat Refugee Camp, Ras Khamis and Ras Shehadeh Prior to and After the Wall

Destination	Fares prior to the wall (in NIS)	Fares after the wall (in NIS)
Ramallah	4	7 (increase of 75%)
Jerusalem	3	3.5 or 4 (increase of 16 to 33%)
Abu Dis	5	7.2 (increase of 44%)

The Environment

Pollution rates increased in the main streets and the environs of the camp, particularly at its entrances, due to the continuous traffic congestion at the checkpoints. Furthermore, wall construction prevented the refugee camp's garbage trucks from accessing the landfill in Al Eizariya area, the main landfill for the Palestinian Jerusalem area prior to the wall's construction. Presently, garbage is disposed of at the Ramallah District landfill in the Betunia area.

A permanent checkpoint separates Shu'fat Refugee Camp from Shu'fat Village and East Jerusalem. Jan 2007.

The daily average of garbage shipments to Al Eizariya landfill used to be three, but nowadays the refugee camp's administration is unable to get rid of more than one or two truckloads a day. The problem of disposing of garbage was compounded by the Israeli Jerusalem Municipality's refusal to collect garbage from Ras Khamis and Ras Shehadeh areas, which are located within the municipal borders, even though their residents continue to pay property taxes (Arnona) to Jerusalem Municipality.

Anata Village

An overview of Anata from the west. Aug 2006.

Anata village adjoins the refugee camp and is located approximately four kilometers northeast of the Old City of Jerusalem. It is believed that its name is derived from "Anat" – the Canaanites' Goddess of love and war. Anata is the site of the grave of Sheikh Abdul Salam Ar-Rifa'i, an Imam and scholar at Al-Aqsa Mosque in the 19th Century, whom Anata residents consider to be their ancestral grandfather and founder of the present day Anata. Additionally, there are several archeological sites in Anata such as the ruins of the Canaanite town of Almon, which was founded in the second millennium B.C. and is located about 1.6 kilometers from the center of Anata. Ancient mosaics, demolished walls, cemeteries, canals and caves are to be found there as well.

Anata extends from the western borders of the Jericho District in the east to Shu'fat R.C. in the west, and from Hizma and Jaba' in the north to Al Issawiya in the south. The area of Anata is estimated at 30,728 dunums (7,682 acres) classified into Area B and Area C in accordance with the Israeli-Palestinian Oslo Accords. Lands were confiscated from Anata residents before 1992 for establishing Israeli settlements and IDF military camps on them. Upon completion of the separation wall, the area of greater Anata lands that will remain in the possession of Anata residents will be approximately 2,400 dunums (600 acres), or the equivalent of less than 8% of the village's original lands. This entails an area of 1400 dunums (350 acres) of open lands on which the village can possibly build in the future. More than half of this open land, however, is classified as area C, under Israeli control.

By 2006, the total population of Anata had reached 17,964, including 9,764 in Anata and approximately 8,000 in adjoining Dahiyat As Salam; the majority of the residents hold Jerusalem ID cards. The population increase came as a result of Anata's J2 location between East Jerusalem (J1) and the West Bank and the availability of quality inexpensive housing. These factors drew Jerusalemites as well West Bank workers who formerly worked in Jerusalem and within the Green Line. This attractiveness led to enormous economic prosperity and construction activity following 1993. The town's economic prosperity lasted until a permanent checkpoint was erected at the exit/entrance of Shu'fat RC in mid-2002, which consequently led to a tightening of entry measures for West Bank ID card holders into Jerusalem. In addition to this measure, the occupation authorities threatened to withdraw the identity card and revoke the residency right of whoever carries a Jerusalem ID card and resides outside the municipal borders of Jerusalem. This forced many blue card Jerusalemites to leave Anata and return to East Jerusalem.

Anata's strategic location between the Jordan River and Jerusalem made it a target for Israeli expansionist interests. By 1992, a total area of 13,956 dunums (3,489 acres) had been confiscated, including 3,446 dunums (860 acres) for establishing the settlements listed in **Table IV: 8** below.

Table IV: 8 Settlements Established on Anata Lands

Settlement	Area Confiscated (dunums)	Founding Date
Kfar Adumim	934	1979
Almon (Anatot)	1,541	1983
Elon	220	1990
Neve Brath	751	1992
Total	**3,446**	

In addition to these settlements, two military bases were established on Anata lands; one is located directly outside the village, and the other is located at its eastern border with Jericho. This resulted in the loss of 10,500 dunums (2,625 acres).

Furthermore, on March 13, 2005, the occupation authorities approved commencing construction within the framework of the eastward expansionist project which Israelis refer to as the E-1 plan. This project, which will extend Israeli West Jerusalem eastward almost to the Jordan River, will connect the eastern Israeli settlement Ma'aleh Adumim with West Jerusalem and create a territorial contiguity between the Israeli capital and the Jewish settlements north and northeast of Jerusalem. An area of approximately 12,443 dunums (4,110 acres) of land belonging to Anata, Abu Dis, Al Eizariya and Az Za'ayyem have been confiscated to implement the E-1 scheme. This project effectively consumes whatever lands that remained for the Palestinian villages and towns of Anata, Abu Dis, Al Eizariya, Al Issawiya, Az Za'ayyem and Hizma. It denies them any possibility for future expansion and development.

Added to the above Israeli land grabs, Jewish bypass roads were built on Anata's lands to serve the settlements; a 6.9 kilometer extension of Road No. 437 confiscated 1,564 dunums (391 acres) of Anata's lands; a total of 1,070 dunums (267 acres) of Anata, At Tur, and Al Issawiya lands were confiscated for building Road No. 70. The latter project will extend from the north of Az Za'ayyem town, pass through Al Issawiya and Anata, and connect to Road No. 437 in northern Anata.

The Separation Wall

In September 2003, the Israeli inter-cabinet committee for security affairs approved the path of the separation wall in Anata, and by the end of 2004 construction works had begun. Several segments of the wall have been completed, including the segment that extends from the west of Shu'fat Refugee Camp and passes alongside the northern border of Anata until it reaches the north of Hizma village. This segment of the wall, approximately 10 kilometers long within the lands of Anata and Shu'fat, separates the enclave from the Israeli Pisgat Ze'ev settlement.

According to Anata Local Council statistics, between October 27, 2004 and November 21, 2005, 43 houses and structures in Anata were demolished for the sake of building the wall. They included twelve in Anata, two in the Bedouin Al Fheidat community (East of Anata and adjacent to the Anatot Military Camp), and twenty-nine in the Dahiyat As Salam neighborhood (the New Anata).

Road No. 70 (under construction) will run parallel to the wall. Jan 2007.

The wall in the north and east of Anata separates the village from its agricultural and grazing lands which are privately owned by Palestinians. Jan 2007.

Anata: Al Fheidat Neighborhood

This Bedouin community is located at the far west of Anata, adjacent to the Israeli Anatot military camp. Its total area is 30 dunums (7.5 acres) comprising twelve houses originally occupied by thirteen families, four of whom have abandoned the area since the beginning of construction works on the Israelis-only Road No. 70, which passes through the neighborhood.

The wall in the Al Fheidat neighborhood will separate it from its center in Anata. The only ingress or egress for Bedouin community is via the underpass below settlement Road No. 70. Jan 2007.

Nowadays, Al Fheidat is inhabited by nine families comprised of 65 members, including twenty-one children under the age of 10. Six of the children attend elementary schools in Anata. Prior to the army base,the wall, and the highway, the neighborhood residents lead a simple life, depending for their livelihood mainly on agriculture and grazing.

The wall is projected to run along the Anata side of Road 70, and since the beginning of the highway and wall construction, Al Fheidat residents have been living in constant fear that they will be completely besieged by the wall and the highway on one side and the military camp on the other. This prospect, if realized, will deny any chance for natural development and expansion in the Bedouin neighborhood. Al Fheidat will become a prison, having no connection with the outside world except via an underpass below the highway and wall, a virtual tunnel which will be their only access to Anata.

Presently, Al Fheidat neighborhood's residents in general, and children in particular, are facing extremely difficult environmental conditions caused by the construction works and the explosions undertaken in connection with building Road No. 70. Those explosions, the resulting debris, and the noise generated by the heavy machinery operating in the area have turned this neighborhood into a trashed and disordered construction site where no means are made available for protecting the residents. Dust is everywhere, carrying dirt with it, and the noise that accompanies the explosions terrifies the children and damages the foundations and walls of the houses. A lawsuit was filed in this regard, as well as in regard to the negative impact on the health, and the punishing psychological and social conditions.

Ziad Al Fheidat is a 26 year old resident of the Al Fheidat neighborhood. His 100 m² one-story house was demolished in 1998. He said, "In January 2005, my father, who has heart problems, suffered a serious deterioration in his health conditions, which forced me to take him to a Jerusalem hospital (Al Maqased Hospital) at 1:00 a.m. When we arrived at the army checkpoint at the entrance of Shu'fat Refugee Camp, which is our only access to Jerusalem, they allowed my sick father to cross the checkpoint while I was barred from accompanying him. I asked the occupation how my sick father could go to hospital alone in such a critical condition and at such a time past midnight. They did indeed bar me from accompanying him. I had to wait along with my sick father at the checkpoint until I found someone who took him to hospital. Later, I managed to follow my father by walking along an unpaved bypass road through Az Za'ayyem village. I arrived at Al-Makassed Hospital at about 4:30 a.m."

IPCC also interviewed an Al Fheidet family that in many ways typifies the experience of the community. The family is headed by a 54 year-old widow with eight children. The family lost virtually all its land through a series of Israeli confiscations. First, the army confiscated more than half of their agricultural lands; then about a quarter of it was taken by Israel to build a Jews-only highway serving settlements. The remaining plot which adjoins the house supports a small chicken coop. During the years the family was growing, an addition was put on the house without an Israeli permit. Now, years later, the family has been served with a notice that the addition will be demolished. The nature of the structure is such that the entire house is likely to collapse when the addition is bulldozed. None of Mrs. Fheidet's mature children have found employment in the enclave. One is employed outside the area as a taxi driver. He is the sole supporter of the family. One of the widow's sons was imprisoned for a rock throwing incident that occurred in connection with one of the confiscations. He languished in prison for several years until he developed cancer; he was released two weeks before he died of the disease at home.

Social Sector

The wall has had a direct effect on social ties. It deprived many Anata residents from social connections with their relatives who live on the other side of the wall, leading to enormous cracks in the social relations between Jerusalem and Anata West Bank ID card holders. There are no available statistics and data on the number of families comprised of husbands and wives, one carrying the Jerusalem and the other the West Bank ID cards, but the existence of such cases increased the level of tension and fear among those families regarding their future and the future of the fathers, mothers, children and relatives who carry different types of ID cards. It has become impossible for West Bank ID card holders to have any connection with their relatives in Jerusalem without a special permit issued by the occupation forces. Such permits are not easily obtained these days.

Additionally, the wall's construction has violated the freedom of worship and the freedom of visiting religious sites: it deprives Palestinians carrying West Bank ID cards in Anata from entering Jerusalem to visit the holy sites and perform prayers in the Holy City.

Mr. Mahmoud Yousef Khalaf Hamdan (Abu Nasser) is a senior in his sixties. He holds a West Bank ID card and lives in the Dahiyat As Salam neighborhood. One part of his house lies within the Jerusalem J1 borders and he has been paying the Israeli property tax (Arnona) on his entire house. He told us his story:

In April 2005, occupation army soldiers raided the houses of West Bank ID card holders in As Salam Neighborhood, particularly those houses within the Jerusalem Municipality borders [considered by Palestinians to be Anata lands but located within East Jerusalem's J1 borders]. The raid took place at 2:30 a.m. We were rounded up and taken to an area called Az Za'ayyem (south of Anata). We spent that cold dark night without any covers. On the next day, at 10:30 a.m., we were summoned to sign an affidavit in which we confessed that we have violated the Israeli residency laws in Jerusalem. A few hours later, the elderly were released without having to sign such an affidavit. However, younger men who refused to do so were thrown in jail. Although Jerusalem Municipality authorities do not recognize us as Jerusalem residents, we still have to pay them all kinds of taxes.

The Economy

Agriculture formed the main economy in Anata village until the beginning of the nineteen eighties, when it provided approximately 40% of the village's income. The nature of Anata residents' work changed and became diversified, and the village's economy began depending on exporting construction stone and on the labor markets in Jerusalem, within the Green Line, and in the West Bank. But now the entire economy has been devastated. Land confiscations have virtually eliminated the agricultural sector and the quarry industry. Wall related restrictions on movement have ended employment in Jerusalem and stopped any trade with the city for its wood, metal, and aluminum products. The Anata Local Council estimates that the unemployment rate now exceeds 50%.

Table IV: 9 Enterprises Damaged in Anata and Dahiyat As Salam

Enterprises	Number
Stone quarries and marble polishing	6
Blacksmiths' Workshops	7
Carpentries	7
Car Maintenance Workshops	5
Aluminum Workshops	5

Following the separation wall's construction, laborers with West Bank IDs were not allowed to enter Jerusalem markets. Consequently, they were forced to head to markets in Ramallah and the West Bank. This option has been difficult in light of the presence of a huge number of competitors already present in these markets.

The enterprises harmed the most by the wall's construction were on the main street in Anata where business conditions are unstable due to the weakness of the purchasing power in the town. In Dahiyat As Salam, on the other hand, economic damages inflicted on the stores there are limited in comparison with other areas because most of its residents are Jerusalem ID card holders with easier access to labor markets. For them, the nature of their work has not changed much. Nevertheless, of the 348 shops on the main road (from the Shu'fat Refugee Camp checkpoint to the Abu George Checkpoint north of Anata) 100 have been closed as a result of the wall's effect on the area.

A demolished house in Dahiyat As Salam. Jan 2007.

Health and Medical Services

Anata relies almost entirely on the medical services available in East Jerusalem. Anata residents were accustomed to seeking treatment at the hospitals and medical centers in Jerusalem, such as Al-Makassed Hospital which is only five kilometers from the town. After Anata residents carrying West Bank ID cards were prohibited from entering East Jerusalem, they were forced to seek treatment at the hospitals and medical centers of Ramallah and Jericho, eighteen and thirty-three kilometers away, respectively. Moreover, they have to wait, sometimes for long periods, at the military checkpoint north of Anata when they head toward Ramallah or Jericho, and sometimes they are not allowed to cross those checkpoints. The result has been increased suffering for those needing treatment, especially those needing specialized services such the handicapped, heart disease patients, and pregnant women.

There are no government medical centers in Anata. There are just five clinics, three of which are located in Dahiyat As Salam, and there are no doctors or nurses except for a few days each week. The medical center in Shu'fat Refugee Camp sometimes receives cases from Dahiyat As Salam and Anata. There are also two mother and child care centers and two pharmacies in Anata. One of the groups harmed the most from this complicated situation is children, particularly infants in their first months who must be given vaccinations and must receive medical care in specialized technically-competent centers that have the ability to follow up on them.

Education

In Anata, there are three governmental schools, including one coeducational school, and three private schools serving the village and surrounding areas such as Shu'fat Village, Shu'fat Refugee Camp and Hizma.

Table IV: 10 Schools, Pupils and Teachers in Anata

School	Type	Pupils		Teachers	
		No. of Pupils	(From outside Anata)	No. of Teacshers	(From outside Anata)
Anata Secondary Boys School	Government	720	63	29	20
Anata Girls Secondary School	Government	802	78	34	8
Salah Eddin Al-Ayyoubi Basic School	Government	618	78	24	8
Beit Al-Maqdes Basic School	Private	215	0	12	0
Al-Manar Basic School	Private	59	0	5	1
Nour Al-Huda Basic School	Private	97	0	8	3
Total		**2,511**	**219**	**112**	**40**

Furthermore, pupils at Anata Secondary School for Boys suffer from over-crowding after the wall truncated parts of their school grounds and isolated the school from its recreational areas. The remaining area left for the school is approximately 700m^2 for 720 pupils and 29 teachers. The school's staff, as well as the pupils, believe that crowded conditions have led to a significant increase in anti-social behaviors and violence among the pupils. Also, the semi-daily provocations by the occupation soldiers against the pupils at the checkpoints and outside the schools during school hours has led to a state of psychological instability and a constant feeling of fear among the pupils. In fact, Israeli soldiers habitually curse the pupils, photograph them, fire tear gas and stun grenades at them, and intentionally use other provocative methods against them outside the schools and at the road junctions leading to the schools for no apparent reason other than to terrify the students. Not infrequently they also strike the students, chase them, pursue them into the schools, and arrest them on arbitrary grounds.

The educational sector in Anata suffers from various problems, the most significant of which is the difficulty of access to schools for pupils and teachers from outside the town due to the checkpoints and closures. Moreover, university students from Anata have to suffer in order to get to Al-Quds University in Abu Dis and Birzeit University north of Ramallah due to the continuous delays at checkpoints coming and going.

Anata Boys' School. Jan 2007.

The youth in Anata believe that the wall is the cause of the growing frustrations and obvious increase in hostile behaviors in the school, in residential neighborhoods and even inside their own homes. They contend that the wall has deprived them of the simplest recreational facilities and thwarted any hope or vision for a better future.

Hasan, a pupil at Anata Secondary Boys School, told IPCC interviewers that:

Occupation soldiers normally come outside our school at specific times like in the morning and in the afternoon when we finish school, and they create a state of tension and confusion among us and destroy our ability to concentrate on studies. Some pupils come to classes late purposefully so as not to be detained or delayed for long periods. Moreover, the soldiers have raided the school many times on the pretext of searching for wanted pupils. This year they arrested three pupils from the school, one of whom was held for three months. During the physical education class, we are left with just a little playground outside the school since the wall has deprived us of most of the school's playgrounds. When there are soldiers outside the school, the tiny playground becomes an area for provocation by the soldiers. They deprive us of playing even during the physical education class.

Transportation

After 1996, the Anata Bus Company was banned from entering East Jerusalem. This forced its owners to register their vehicles as owned by Jerusalem residents, which allowed them to avoid this restriction. The situation has not changed even after the wall's construction.

Anata residents suffer from long waiting hours at military checkpoints, especially the so-called flying (ad hoc) checkpoints on the road connecting Anata with Ramallah. Sometimes, a journey from Anata to Ramallah takes several hours even though it is merely a distance less than 10 kilometers. The same applies to the checkpoint outside Shu'fat Refugee Camp, which leads to Jerusalem.

Moreover, the security instability and the sharp increase in unemployment levels have led to an increase of unlicensed and stolen vehicles as a means of transportation in Anata.

Furthermore, the separation wall and the military checkpoints have caused excessive hikes in transportation costs to Ramallah, Al Eizariya, Abu Dis and Jerusalem; and the barrier has also forced Anata residents to use two or more transportation means to get to certain areas like Ramallah.

Table IV: 11 Transportation Costs in Anata before and after the Wall

Destination	Fares prior to the wall's construction (in NIS)	Fares after the wall's construction (in NIS)
Ramallah	4	7 (an increase of 75%)
Jerusalem	2	3.5 (an increase of 75%
Al Eizariya and Abu Dis	6	8.5 (an increase of 42%)

Environment

Before the commencement of wall construction, two or three truckloads of garbage were transferred to the landfill in Al Eizariya daily. Nowadays, only one truckload is allowed to be shipped there each day. Consequently, garbage is being incinerated it the village streets in order to prevent the spread of diseases. Moreover, the absence of a police force has led to the operation of autos in miserable condition which cause considerable pollution from their exhaust fumes; waste oil from these vehicles pollutes the ground water and the soil.

The wall also poses an extreme danger to nearby houses, particularly those located in lower areas such as the northern parts of Dahiyat As Salam. These areas are subject to flooding caused by the accumulation of rain and sewage water during winter; the wall blocks water drainage and provides no outlets for run-off. The standing water poses environmental and health risks and even the possible collapse of buildings and facilities. Furthermore, the dust resulting from the wall's construction spreads heavily over the village and causes dirty streets and buildings as well as health hazards. Thewall has also caused the uprooting of trees and the bulldozing of four dunums (an acre) of cultivated lands in the northern area of the village.

Finally, Anata residents' biggest fear is living inside a prison in the future, and the subsequent economic, social, environmental, health and education problems. As Engineer Mohammad Hassan, Head of Anata Local Council, said, "The separation wall has changed people's lives in Anata in a dramatic manner and turned lives upside down."

III. THE ABU DIS, AL EIZARIYA, and AS SAWAHIRA ASH SHARQIYA ENCLAVE

This enclave is considered the eastern gateway of East Jerusalem and a natural extension of the city. The development of the enclaved communities led to a convergence between them and between them and East Jerusalem. Their proximity to Jerusalem and their direct contact through transportation routes and commercial interaction effectively makes them suburbs of East Jerusalem. Moreover, these communities have provided East Jerusalem with many of its needed goods and services.

This geographic reality impacted positively on these communities, generating an expansion of their urbanized territory and increasing investment in them to meet a rising demand in the real estate and construction sectors. The general economy rose significantly, bringing with it higher income levels and improved living standards.

Figure IV: 5 The Abu Dis, Al Eizariya, and As Sawahira Ash Sharqiya Enclave

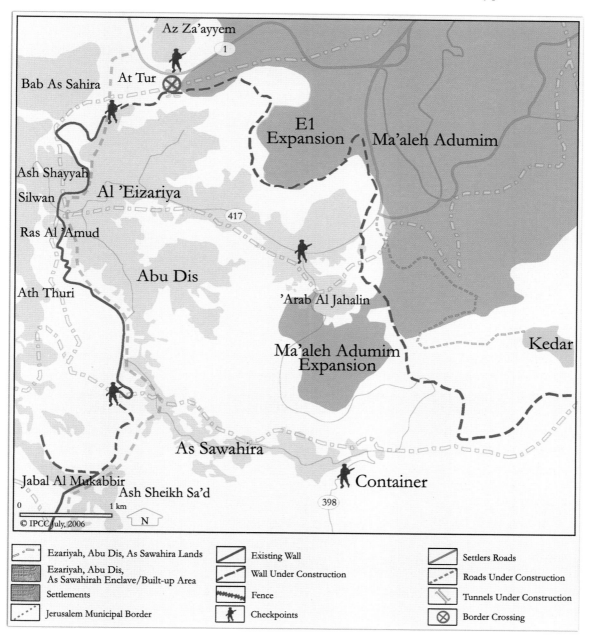

The growth lasted until Israel approved the wall construction in 2002. That decision was accompanied by various arbitrary laws against registered Jerusalemites who lived outside the city's borders. This prompted most Jerusalemites in the enclave to move back into East Jerusalem. Moreover, the restrictions and obstacles placed on entry into the enclave from East Jerusalem led to a rapid deterioration in all of the vital sectors of the communities.

Abu Dis

An overview of Abu Dis from the north. Nov 2006.

Abu Dis village is located about three kilometers southeast of the Old City. It is believed that its name is derived from "Beta Bedouins"—the name of the Roman village on whose ruins the town of Abu Dis is established. Abu Dis is famous for its olive, fig and fruit trees, as well as the abundance of its pastures.

The original area of Abu Dis was 28,232 dunums (7058 acres), most of which was in pasture land. It is surrounded by Al Eizariya on the north, As Sawahira Ash Sharqiya on the south, the Ma'aleh Adumim Israeli settlement and Al-Jahalin Bedouins on the east, and Jabal Al Mukabbir and Ras Al Amud on the west.

The area of Abu Dis shrank following the confiscation of vast parts of the village for the establishment of the large Ma'aleh Adumim and Qedar Israeli settlements, and the separation wall has resulted in an additional confiscation of substantial areas of what was left of the village's lands. The total area of lands classified now as Area B (i.e., land under Palestinian control), which represents essentially only built up lands, is estimated at 2,033 dunums (508 acres)—the equivalent of approximately 7.2% of the original total area of Abu Dis.

At the end of 2005, the official population of Abu Dis was pegged at 11,932. However, this does not include an estimated 5,150 residents (or 30%) who hold the East Jerusalem ID card. Presently, and as an effect of the construction of the western segment of the wall, this percentage has dropped to an estimated 5%. The out-migration resulted from the daily difficulties and harassments at checkpoints, as well as the risks surrounding Jerusalem ID holders who live outside the municipal borders of East Jerusalem. It is predicted that if they maintain residence in Abu Dis they will forfeit their right to enter Jerusalem and to receive Israeli entitlements. This has forced many of them to leave their investments and homes outside the city in East Jerusalem's suburbs and return to live within East Jerusalem.

The importance of Abu Dis surged in the wake of the signing of the Oslo Agreement in 1993; Abu Dis was to have some form of political importance for the Palestinian Authority and East Jerusalem. Accordingly, the PA set up offices in Abu Dis which primarily served residents of the East Jerusalem District and its suburbs. Abu Dis was also selected as the site for the future Palestinian Parliament. Furthermore, the founding of Al-Quds University campus in Abu Dis made it an attractive area for investors.

PA-governmental and international bodies seated in Abu Dis include:

- **Finance and Customs**

- **Civil Affairs and Liaison**

- **The Heritage Center – Ministry of the Waqf**

- **The Red Crescent**

The Separation Wall

Construction of the separation wall in the Abu Dis area began in 2003. A total area of 1,800 dunums (450 acres) from the lands of Abu Dis, Al Eizariya, As Sawahira, Az Za'ayyem, and At Tur was confiscated for wall construction. This demographic enclave will include, once the wall around it is completed, Al Eizariya, Abu Dis and As Sawahira Ash Sharqiya, as well as parts of East Jerusalem.

The wall brings an Israeli settlement in the suburb of Abu Dis into Jerusalem and excludes Abu Dis from the city (11,000). Nov 2006.

The Economy

Prior to the advent of the Palestinian Authority, the economy of Abu Dis depended on close cooperation with East Jerusalem. Abu Dis markets offered many East Jerusalem residents the chance to do shopping without having to go to the crowded and expensive markets of East Jerusalem. Moreover, Abu Dis provided East Jerusalemites with an easily accessible point of contact and exchange with their brethren in the suburbs. These characteristics, added to its proximity to Jerusalem made Abu Dis a preferred place for Jerusalemites to live and invest. Moreover, the ability of workers living in Abu Dis to work in East Jerusalem and within the Green Line increased family income levels to about 5,000 NIS (approximately 1,100 USD) per month, an equivalent level to average family incomes in East Jerusalem.

The economic prosperity of Abu Dis attracted residents from other West Bank areas in addition to East Jerusalem residents. Consequently, demand for housing and commercial space surged, prompting many Abu Dis residents to demolish their small houses and to build housing and residential buildings and complexes. The Abu Dis economy enjoyed this prosperity until the outbreak of the Al-Aqsa Intifada in 2000, when the Israelis began imposing mobility restrictions and checkpoints throughout the West Bank, including in Abu Dis.

The Abu Dis economy began regressing concurrently with the imposition of restrictions on movement to and from East Jerusalem and the Green Line; the reductions led to a deterioration in the income levels of families who depended on the labor market as wall as the investments market. The decision to build the separation wall in 2002, and the commencement of construction works in 2003, marked a critical turning point in the deterioration of the economy. Numerous investors and residents, mostly Jerusalem ID holders, moved out. Furthermore, the inability of East Jerusalemites to enter Abu Dis markets as easily as prior to the wall's construction exacerbated the recession in its markets. For example, there are presently 192 commercial operations on the main road in the town, which links As Sawahira Ash Sharqiya with Al Eizariya, and the number of shuttered businesses on this road has reached 63.

Additionally, the wall, which passes just outside Al-Quds University, isolated vast groves of olive trees on its outer side. The land owners are now unable to harvest the olives or even access them since there are no agricultural gates that would allow ingress and egress, even though that was promised by the Israelis.

Education

There are three public PA-supported schools in Abu Dis, two for males and one for females. Additionally, there are three private schools and one basic coeducational school run by UNRWA. The schools employ 192 instructors, 138 of whom live in Abu Dis while the remaining 62 commute from outside the town on a daily basis. Teachers coming from outside Abu Dis suffer from the daily difficulties of negotiating gates and checkpoints. They and scores of pupils often fail to make it to the first class periods as a result of the daily impediments created by the occupation authorities, which include delaying their access across permanent checkpoints and the imposition of mobile (or "flying") checkpoints on the main road between Abu Dis and Al Eizariya as well as the roads leading to East Jerusalem.

Furthermore, the wall forced scores of residents to register their children with pay-to-ride school buses in spite of the deterioration in their family income levels because the same distance that their children used to walk in 10-15 minutes would now take approximately a full hour.

Table IV:12 Abu Dis Schools

School	Type	Pupils		Teachers	
		No. of Pupils	From outside	No. of Teachers	From outside
Abu Dis Secondary Boys School	Government	389	48	19	12
Abu Dis Secondary Girls School	Government	941	0	42	18
Abu Dis Basic Boys School	Government	171	0	9	1
Abu Dis Basic Co-ed School	UNRWA	570	0	23	11
The Arab Institute	Private	469	309	22	13
The New Generation	Private	179	0	10	4
Jerusalem Children	Private	84	15	4	3
Total		2,803	372	129	62

Most schools in Abu Dis have experienced an increase in drop-out rates, especially during the 2004-2005 school year, as a result of the restrictions imposed on the freedom of movement and the increase in school expenses as a consequence of the separation wall.

The wall passes within the Al Quds University Sports Fields in Abu Dis, splitting the university campus from the city. 2005.

The same situation affects the students and employees of Al-Quds University in Abu Dis, who are no longer able to commit to specific study times, especially those who come from relatively distant places. The number of students and employees of Al-Quds University is approximately 5,000, and East Jerusalem students represent about 40% of the student body. Al-Quds University is one of three universities (all located outside the municipal borders of East Jerusalem), benefiting East Jerusalemites. They are:

- Al-Quds University (Abu Dis)

- Birzeit University (north of Ramallah)

- Bethlehem University (south of Jerusalem)

Since the beginning of the wall's construction, a sharp decline in Jerusalemite enrollments in these universities has been noticed. Moreover, 60% of Al-Quds University students who receive their education in the university's branch colleges in East Jerusalem have been deprived of continuing their education there.

Social Sector

The wall's construction will cause a huge malfunction in the social environment of the Abu Dis community. Al-Jahaleen Bedouins will be expelled from the eastern part of Abu Dis and settled on the outer side of the wall. Moreover, in accordance with a decision passed by the occupation authorities on October 18, 2005, and endorsed by the Knesset on May 30, 2006, Bedouins living between the Israeli settlements, particularly in the area referred to as E-1, will be expelled and re-settled on lands confiscated from Abu Dis within the wall. (Each Arab family will receive a 500 m^2 parcel as compensation for its expulsion.) Hence, Al-Jahaleen Bedouins will be uprooted from their environment and faced with enormous challenges to maintain their way of life and continue grazing livestock, which represents the main pillar of their economy.

The population "transfer" of the Al-Jahaleen Bedouins has its own negative social ramifications and consequences on Abu Dis, since it is impossible for the town—with its present capabilities—to provide infrastructure, planning and organizational services to meet the needs of this huge population, let alone cope with the social, economic and psychological problems resulting from such compulsory displacement.

Furthermore, the wall made family visits for citizens separated by the wall between Abu Dis and East Jerusalem extremely difficult. In fact, it is no longer possible for Abu Dis residents carrying West Bank ID cards to enter East Jerusalem freely.

Health and Medical Services

There are no governmental medical centers in Abu Dis. There is only one center affiliated with UNRWA and two private centers. Due to the inability of many citizens to access East Jerusalem hospitals or to afford treatment in private Abu Dis centers, they presently resort to governmental hospitals and medical centers in Ramallah and Jericho. This entails forcing citizens to travel and wait for several hours at checkpoints on the roads leading to Jericho and Ramallah and frequently to suffer from mistreatment at the hands of unsympathetic Israeli soldiers at checkpoints.

Attorney Bassam Bahar, Member of the Abu Dis Local Council has stated in an IPCC interview that "In late April, 2006, citizen Shehadeh Mohammad Muhsen, 60, was severely beaten at Al-Abbarah Checkpoint (between Ash-Sawahreh Ash-Sharqieh and Al Mukabbir), and died immediately afterwards. Mr. Muhsen was a West Bank ID holder and a resident of Abu Dis who tried to enter East Jerusalem via the Al-Abbarah Checkpoint to receive medical treatment. He carried a document stating that he had an appointment at Al-Makassed Hospital, but he did not have a permit from the occupation authorities to enter Jerusalem. Occupation soldiers barred him from crossing the checkpoint, and after a verbal exchange, an altercation occurred during which occupation soldiers beat him to death."

It should be noted that entry to hospitals and medical centers in Jerusalem formerly required Abu Dis residents to travel no more than ten minutes, but today, if they possess permits to enter the city, it then takes them no less than an hour under normal conditions, depending on the mood of the soldiers manning the checkpoints.

Transportation

Abu Dis is located on the road linking East Jerusalem with the southern part of the West Bank. Formerly, approximately 25 buses connected Abu Dis with nearby areas. This provided sufficient transportation to handle the demand and at a reasonable cost. However, the construction of the western segment of the wall along the Jerusalem-Jericho road, which links Abu Dis with East Jerusalem, disrupted the transportation system. Detours and checkpoints created by the wall have increased travel time in many cases from ten minutes to forty-five, and fares have nearly doubled. Commuters now have to travel first to the entrance of Al Eizariya (at the Ma'aleh Adumim settlement roundabout) and then head to East Jerusalem.

Table IV: 13 Transportation Costs in Abu Dis

Destination	Fares prior to wall construction (in NIS)	Fares after the wall's construction (in NIS)
Jerusalem	2.5	6 (an increase of 140%)
Ramallah	5	11.5 (an increase of 130 %)
Bethlehem	5	8 (an increase of 60%)
Ar Ram	5	8 (an increase of 60%)

These hikes in transportation costs impacted negatively on personal mobility in Abu Dis and on the resident's disposable income.

Figure IV: 6 Transport Routes in Abu Dis, Al Eizariya and As Sawahira Ash Sharqiya Enclave Before and After The Wall

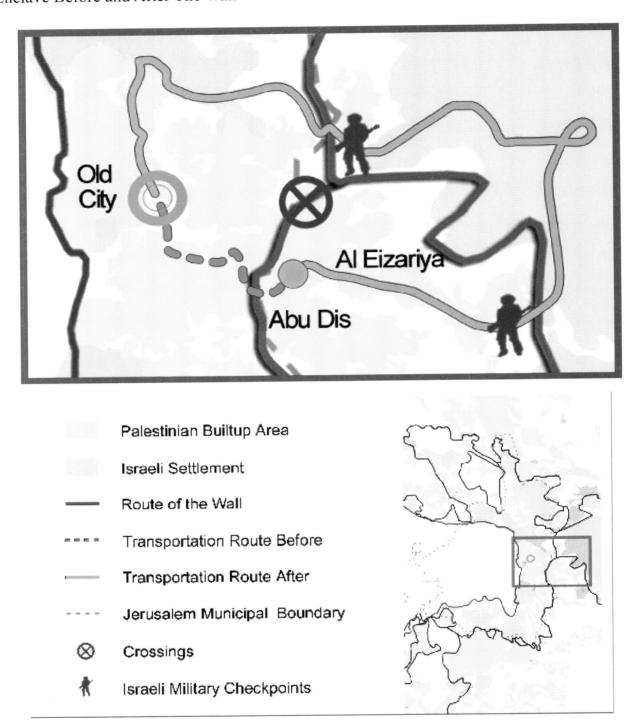

- Palestinian Builtup Area
- Israeli Settlement
- — Route of the Wall
- - - - - Transportation Route Before
- — Transportation Route After
- - - - - Jerusalem Municipal Boundary
- ⊗ Crossings
- 🖊 Israeli Military Checkpoints

The broken green line in this map shows the route taken by Palestinians from Abu Dis and Al Eizariya to reach the center of the city, through the Ras Al Amud community, before the construction of the wall, and which represents a distance 4 km and a travel time of 5 minutes. The solid yellow line shows the current route that should be used in order to enter the city – for those who are lucky enough to obtain permits - which covers a distance of 18 km and requires 40 minutes of travel. This road will be interrupted by the wall soon and will not be accessible to Palestinians; they will travel by a tunnel to Az Za'ayyem and then to Hizma, and from there, via Ramallah. Pedestrians only will enter the city through Az Zaitoon crossing, in At Tur.

Al Eizariya

A general view of Al Eizariya from Ash Shayyah. The built up area is surrounded by the wall from the west, and the settlement of Ma'aleh Adumim from the east. Nov 2006.

Al Eizariya is located approximately two kilometers southeast of the Old City. It is mentioned in the Bible under the name Bet Ania. It was associated with the life of Jesus Christ in the incident of his restoration of the life of a dead man called Eliazer. It is also the birth place of many Muslim religious scholars.

The area of Al Eizariya is 11,179 dunums (2,795 acres). Nowadays, it is surrounded by At Tur and Az Z'ayyem on the north, the Israeli settlement Ma'aleh Adumim on the east, At Tur and Ash-Shayyah on the west, and Abu Dis on the south. The Al Eizariya Local Council estimates its population at approximately 23,000, including 7,000 who carry Jerusalem ID cards.

In 1975, vast areas of Al Eizariya were confiscated to establish the Ma'aleh Adumim Israeli settlement. And in 2005, the Israeli authorities approved confiscation of vast areas for the eastern expansionist settlement project known as E-1.

The infrastructure of Al Eizariya is outdated and incomplete. It has water and power supplies, but it lacks a proper sewage network.

Governmental and international organizations sited in Al Eizariya include a Ministry of Interior office and a rehabilitation center for drug addicts.

The Separation Wall

Construction of the separation wall in Al Eizariya began in 2003; it separates the town from East Jerusalem in the west. This course of the wall in the Jerusalem area extends from the north of Beit Jala, passing through northern Bethlehem and northern Beit Sahour, then Sheikh Sa'ad, As Sawahira Ash Sharqiya and Abu Dis, then Al Eizariya and the southern area of Az Za'ayyem north of Al Eizariya.

According to the Al Eizariya Local Council statistics, two houses located in the path of the separation wall were demolished, and 477 dunums (119 acres) were confiscated for its construction.

Al Eizariya's proximity to East Jerusalem had a positive impact on its economy. Al Eizariya's markets were a favorite place for East Jerusalem residents to do their shopping. This attracted large investments by Jerusalemites in the service sector. Moreover, the availability of open lands mobilized the housing sector in response to an increase in demand for apartments, particularly by Jerusalemites, but also by students and employees of Al-Quds University in Abu Dis, just south of Al Eizariya. The housing sector began flourishing in the wake of the Oslo Accord in 1993, which opened up opportunities for investment even from outside Palestine. The economic prosperity lasted until Israel decided to build the separation wall, which bars entry of Al Eizariya residents to East Jerusalem. The wall's construction prompted most Jerusalemite residents of Al Eizariya, whose number is estimated at approximately 7,000, to return to East Jerusalem. This measure also made it difficult for East Jerusalem residents to access Al Eizariya markets. Those markets used to be no more than five minutes away from Jerusalem prior to the wall's construction, but nowadays Jerusalem residents have to travel for about half an hour and cross an Israeli military checkpoint (Az Za'ayyem) in order to get to Al Eizariya.

The wall separates Al Eizariya from East Jerusalem. Nov 2006.

Additionally, harassments by the Israeli income tax authorities against Jerusalemite shop owners in Al Eizariya generated deep concern among Jerusalemite investors and led to the closure of several commercial establishments. The number of commercial enterprises on the main road (from the end of Jerusalem-Jericho Road to Ma'aleh Adumim Settlement Roundabout) is 608, 108 of which are closed. As a result, Al Eizariya markets were weakened significantly. Moreover, the labor force in Al Eizariya is estimated at approximately 7,200 workers, about half of whom rely on employment in East Jerusalem and within the Green Line. The wall's construction and the closure of roads has led to increased unemployment rates among Al Eizariya laborers to more than 50% and to a general deterioration in the living conditions.

Furthermore, numerous factories in Al Eizariya have either closed or are operating in extremely difficult conditions. They include:

- **The Cigarettes Company**
- **Al-Hayat Company for Food Products**
- **Jawad Abdeen Plastic Factory (This factory has closed, causing a lay-off of 180 workers.)**

Tourism formerly represented a significant source of income for Al Eizariya. An average of 35 buses entered Al Eizariya each day to visit the Eliazer Tomb and the churches in the town. Following the wall's construction, and in light of the occupation practices that include warning tourists against entering PA areas, the number of tourists and tourist buses entering Al Eizariya plummeted to an average of four buses a day.

In an IPCC interview with the head of Al Eizariya Local Council, he said, "Before the wall's construction, operators catering for tourists entering Eliazer Tomb and the holy places collectively paid 45,000 Jordanian Dinars (approximately 63,450 USD) in annual fees. In 2005, no contractor was willing to register, and in the beginning of 2006 a single contractor paid 1,500 JD (2,115 USD). This is a significant indicator of the extent of recession in this key segment of the town's economy."

Education

There are five public government supported schools and six private schools in Al Eizariya. Those schools formerly served a significant number of East Jerusalemite pupils. Nowadays, the number of pupils in those schools from East Jerusalem and neighboring villages is dwindling due to the difficulty of accessing their schools.

Table IV: 14 Al Eizariya Schools

School	Type	Pupils		Teachers	
		No. of Pupils	From outside	No. of Teachers	From outside
Al Eizariya Secondary School	Government	528	13	25	7
Al Eizariya Project Basic Boys School	Government	189	0	9	8
Al Eizariya Project Basic Girls School	Government	246	0	15	11
Yousef Al-Khateeb Girls Secondary School	Government	528	0	26	13
Al Eizariya Boys Basic School	Government	200	0	8	7
The Islamic Orphanage Vocational Training School	Private	208	0	19	15
Al Eizariya Orthodox Secondary School	Private	260	61	17	10
Al-Amal Generation Basic School	Private	230	16	13	6
Al Eizariya Ideal Basic School	Private	257	0	11	6
Al-Awdah Basic Co-ed School	Private	116	0	7	2
Al-Anwar Basic School	Private	27	0	2	1
Total		**2,789**	**90**	**152**	**86**

Transportation

Transportation from Al Eizariya to other areas, including East Jerusalem, remained active until the wall's construction. Until then, an average of 15,000 people traveled to Al Eizariya every day, as it is on the main transportation route between Jerusalem's southern suburbs and East Jerusalem. This location contributed to reliable, convenient, and affordable transportation in Al Eizariya. Presently, and in the wake of the wall's construction, whoever seeks to enter Al Eizariya from East Jerusalem must travel through Az Za'ayyem and then travel along the road adjacent to the Ma'aleh Adumim Israeli settlement before entering Al Eizariya. This circuitous and lengthy route has caused transportation costs to rise sharply.

The occupation authorities are presently digging a tunnel linking Al Eizariya, Abu Dis and As Sawahira Ash Sharqiya, as well as the southern parts of the West Bank such as Bethlehem and Hebron districts, with the northern parts of the West Bank without having to go through East Jerusalem. This tunnel is being dug in Az Za'ayyem area north of Al Eizariya (see **Figure IV: 5**).

Table IV:15 Transportation Costs (see **Figure IV: 6**)

Destination	Rates prior to wall construction (in NIS)	Rates after the wall's construction (in NIS)
Jerusalem	1.5	5 (an increase of 233%)
Ramallah	6	10 (an increase of 66%)
Ar Ram	5	9 (an increase of 80%)

These hikes in transportation costs came amidst economic recession in Al Eizariya, and they contributed to social discontinuity among families isolated from each other by the wall. Presently, whoever seeks to make a family visit across the wall has to travel for a long time—possibly for hours. The rate hikes added economic burdens that are difficult to bear and have decreased the frequency of family visits, which were formerly made on an almost daily basis, to no more than one or two visits a month.

"Jabal Az Zaitoon" Border Crossing. Pedestrian permit holders can enter the city from Al Eizariya/ Abu Dis enclave; vehicles are not allowed to transit the crossing. Nov 2006.

A road tunnel under construction northeast of Al Eizariya will connect Al Eizariya/ Abu Dis enclave with the Shu'fat RC/ Anata enclave replacing the territorial contiguity between south and north West Bank with a transportation link. Jan 2007.

Health Services

Prior to the wall's construction, Al Eizariya residents relied primarily on medical services provided at East Jerusalem's medical centers and hospitals, especially Al-Makassed and Augusta Victoria hospitals. Access to these hospitals was easy—by public transportation vehicles within no more than 15 minutes. Due to Al Eizariya's proximity to Jerusalem, there was no reason for establishing hospitals or specialized medical centers in the town itself. Presently, there is only one hospital in Al Eizariya. In the wake of the wall's construction, every patient seeking treatment at a hospital or medical center in East Jerusalem must obtain an Israeli entry permit from the Coordination and Liaison Office in Bet El. Obtaining such a permit is subject to regulations imposed by the occupation authority's medical coordinator. These impediments have forced patients to seek treatment in the hospitals of Ramallah, Jericho and even Nablus. Consequently, they have to travel for long distances and times and cope with the multitude of military checkpoints on the roads leading to these cities.

As Sawahira Ash Sharqiya

As Sawahira Ash Sharqiya is located about five kilometers southeast of the Old City. It derived its name from its inhabitants—Arab As Sawahira. Arab As Sawahira are divided into two groups—one living within Jerusalem's municipal borders, known as As Sawahira Al Gharbiya, and another living in the West Bank, known as As Sawahira Ash Sharqiya. The area of As Sawahira Ash Sharqiya and Al Gharbiya is approximately 73,100 dunums (18,000 acres). As of April 2006, 2,480 dunums (620 acres) have been confiscated for building the eastern and western segments of the wall in As Sawahira Ash Sharqiya. Nearly 3,500 Arab As Sawahira live in the Sheikh Sa'ad village south of As Sawahira Ash Sharqiya. The total population of the three localities is approximately 36,000.

The Israeli settlements established on the lands of As Sawahira are:

- **Armon Hanatsiv Settlement on the western side of As Sawahira**

- **Talpiyot Settlement on the western side of As Sawahira**

- **Qedar Settlement on the eastern side of As Sawahira**

Occupation authorities are also building a road on the eastern side of As Sawahira as part of the road that will link the southern West Bank (Bethlehem and Hebron districts) with the northern districts parallel to the eastern segment of the wall in As Sawahira.

The Social Impact

The communities of the eastern and western parts of As Sawahira enjoy strong ties; customs and traditions play a significant role in organizing their lives. The separation wall's construction between As Sawahira Ash Sharqiya and As Sawahira Al Gharbiya has virtually separated families from each other and severed ties between residents of AS Sawahira Ash Sharqiya on one side and As Sawahira Al Gharbiya and Jabal Al Mukabbir on the other.

Anyone carrying a West Bank ID card in As Sawahira Ash Sharqiya is effectively barred from visiting family and relatives in As Sawahira Al Gharbiya; anyone holding a West Bank ID card in As Sawahira Al Gharbiya is denied freedom of movement. West Bank ID holders are subject to expulsion from As Sawahira Al Gharbiya although they have been living there, married to relatives carrying Jerusalem ID cards, and have owned houses in As Sawahira Al Gharbiya for many years.

This was the fate of a resident of Jabal Al Mukabbir who carried a West Bank ID card and was married to a woman who carried a Jerusalem ID card. Mr. Mousa As-Sahouri carries a West Bank ID card and is married to a women who carries a Jerusalem ID card. They have several children. Their house was raided by a police patrol during Al-Fitr Feast last year. He was arrested, but his wife and children were released.

Residents of As Sawahira also mentioned in interviews that the only cemetery for Ash-Shawahreh Ash-Sharqieh and As Sawahira Al Gharbiya is located in the western part of As Sawahira. After the death of a resident of As Sawahira Ash Sharqiya, his relatives headed to the cemetery in the western part of the town to bury him. The coffin and the participants in the burial procession were detained at Ash-Shayyah Checkpoint for several hours until the identity of the deceased man was checked to determine if he was a West Bank or a Jerusalem ID holder. After three hours of delay, only the dead man's children were allowed to cross the checkpoint. Their ID cards were held at the checkpoint until they returned after completing the burial.

The eastern area, located on the outer side of the wall (2,400 dunums or 600 acres), is inhabited by approximately 75 families working in agriculture and grazing livestock. They are now threatened under security pretexts to be expelled from their houses and "transferred" to As Sawahira Ash Sharqiya. In the meantime, the occupation authorities confiscated forty-three wells used by those families for irrigation.

The Economy

The economy of As Sawahira Ash Sharqiya relies on the incomes of an urban labor force as well as on livestock and agriculture workers and owners. The number of laborers in As Sawahira Ash Sharqiya is estimated at 3,000; most of them work in East Jerusalem and within the Green Line. After closure of the labor market and their inability to reach their work places, unemployment rates in As Sawahira Ash Sharqiya surged to approximately 64% of the total Work Force, based on the local council's estimates.

The village's economy also relies on agriculture and raising livestock. Due to its abundant milk production, one of the major dairy products companies (Hamouda Company) settled in the village and contributed to the village economy. However, the approval of construction of the eastern segment of the wall and the isolation of grazing and cultivated lands on the outer side of the wall has created instability in milk and dairy production, which naturally has had a negative effect on the economy as a result of a downsizing of the factory work force. The same pattern of decline occurred in a detergents plant (The Brothers Factory). Furthermore, on the main road in As Sawahira Ash Sharqiya (from the beginning of the Container Checkpoint until the entrance of Abu Dis) 103 of the 152 commercial establishments are closed.

Education

There are two governmental schools in As Sawahira Ash Sharqiya enrolling 859 students. An additional 850 pupils are enrolled in the schools of Abu Dis and Al Eizariya, as well as the schools of Jabal Al Mukabbir in East Jerusalem. Also, there is a basic school serving around 150 pupils in the residential area of the Al-Hathaleen Tribe. This school is located in the confiscated area on the outer side of the eastern segment of the wall in As Sawahira Ash Sharqiya. It is uncertain what will happen to the school if the residents are "transferred".

Table IV: 16 As Sawahira Ash Sharqiya Schools

School	Type	Pupils		Teachers	
		No. of Pupils	From outside	No. of Teachers	From outside
As Sawahira Ash Sharqiya Secondary Boys School	Government	337	0	17	12
As Sawahira Ash Sharqiya Basic Girls School	Government	522	2	25	11
Total		859	2	42	23

Health and Medical Services

Similar to other enclaved areas, before the wall As Sawahira Ash Sharqiya relied on the medical services in Jerusalem; therefore there was no need for hospitals or specialized medical centers in it. Hence, the town nowadays lacks the simplest medical services, and there are no government medical centers in it. Therefore, most patients travel in emergency cases to Jericho Hospital or hospitals and medical centers in Ramallah. In such cases, they have to travel about 40 kilometers to get to Jericho or 35 kilometers to get to Ramallah. The distance to the hospitals and medical centers in Jerusalem did not exceed 10 kilometers. This hike in transportation rates has coincided with a decline in family incomes, leading to a significant decline in the resident's movement and travel.

Transportation

Public transportation is available in As Sawahira, although citizens have to travel longer distances to get to East Jerusalem and the western and northern neighborhoods of the city in the wake of the wall's construction. This has impacted negatively on the costs of travel between As Sawahira Ash Sharqiya and other areas.

Table IV:17 Transportation Costs before and after Construction of the Wall

Destination	Cost prior to the wall construction (in NIS)	Cost after to the wall's construction (in NIS/increase)
East Jerusalem	3	6.5 (116% increase)
Ramallah	7	10 (43% increase)

IV. THE BIR NABALA, Al JUDEIRA, AL JIB, BEIT HANINA AL BALAD ENCLAVE

The four villages of this enclave are located north of the Old City of Jerusalem. The combined population of the enclave is approximately 15,000 (not including 2000 Jerusalem ID holders who are not registered in that area), and the total area of the villages is 28,780 dunums (7195 acres). Like the rest of the Palestinian territories, the lands of these villages are classified into Area B and Area C (see the footnote earlier in this chapter). At this writing, 1,012 dunums (250 acres) of the villages' lands have been confiscated for the construction of the separation wall. The total remaining area for the four villages on the wall's outer side is approximately 10,500 dunums (2,625 acres), a large portion of which is classified as Area C and is managed by the occupation authorities only.

These villages were very dependent on East Jerusalem in many respects, particularly the economy of the four villages which was tied entirely to East Jerusalem markets. Moreover, these villages formed, alongside other villages and towns surrounding Jerusalem, an appropriate residential area for Jerusalemites to escape from the crowded conditions of the city but without losing access to the social services and facilities enjoyed by Jerusalem ID card holders. This encouraged a significant number of Jerusalem ID card holders to live in the villages and suburbs outside East Jerusalem borders, and that had a positive impact on those villages and suburbs. Furthermore, those villages were attractive residential areas to many West Bank residents who sought employment in East Jerusalem or within the Green Line. These factors increased these villages' importance and strengthened their economies significantly. The economic prosperity lasted until 2002, when Israel decided to build the wall and isolate many such communities from East Jerusalem. Since then, the occupation authorities have imposed laws that make it difficult for Palestinian citizens carrying Jerusalem ID cards to live outside East Jerusalem borders, which consequently has caused many of them to return to the city, and this has led to the collapse of the vital sectors of many of the towns and villages surrounding Jerusalem.

The separation wall, whose length around this enclave upon completion will reach approximately 17 kilometers, encloses these villages from all sides, isolating them from Jerusalem and other surrounding areas, and severing any outside contact with them except through military checkpoints and gates. At this time, the residents of these villages who carry West Bank ID cards have only one exit and entrance. That is the road from Bir Nabala to Rafat, Al-Manarah, Samiramis, and Qalandiya, and from there through the Qalandiya Crossing to East Jerusalem-- if one has the permits from the occupation authorities to enter the city. This circuitous route presents enormous difficulties in the access of students to their schools and universities, and workers to their work places.

Once the occupation authorities complete construction of the wall, the villages will become an ethnic demographic ghetto completely isolated from its surroundings. It will also isolate the villages from significant portions of their agricultural lands which are only accessible through four agricultural gates which, according to the Israelis, are planned to be opened in the following areas:

- West of Al Jib   **- West of Al Judeira.**   **- West of Beit Hanina Al Balad**

- East of Beit Hanina Al Balad through the tunnel under Road No. 404

Figure IV: 7 The Bir Nabala, Al Judeira, Al Jib, and Beit Hanina Al Balad Enclave

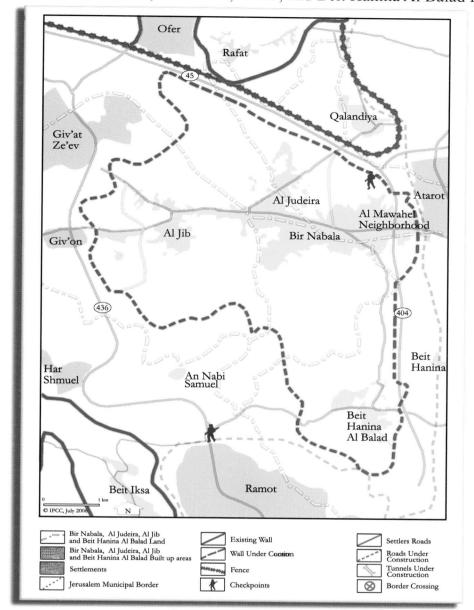

Agricultural land owners in the ghetto will not be able to access their lands via the gates except by obtaining special permits which allow access during special time windows, which are determined by the occupation authorities in accordance with alleged security considerations.

Furthermore, the path of the wall that will surround these villages will run inside and parallel to Road No. 45 from the north, Road No. 436 from the west, and Road No. 404 from the east and south, making those villages completely closed-in and inaccessible except via Bir Nabala. The occupation authorities claim that this ghetto will be connected in the future with northwest Jerusalem villages through a road or a tunnel connecting Al Jib with Biddu.

In short, West Bank ID card holders in these villages are unable to leave or travel outside the ghetto except toward Rafat in the north and then toward Ramallah, and the only entrance to East Jerusalem is via the Qalandiya Crossing which requires permits issued by the occupation authorities.

As we noted earlier, the economy of these villages has depended entirely on East Jerusalem and the nearby villages. More than 360 factories and workshops in these villages relied entirely in their imports and exports on East Jerusalem and its suburbs. Nowadays, those factories and workshops are on the verge of economic collapse since it has become impossible to conduct trade with East Jerusalem and difficult to access nearby villages.

Economic conditions in these villages have deteriorated and unemployment rates have soared. Moreover, the rising transportation costs are adding a huge burden on the residents. In fact, transportation costs have increased several-fold since construction of the wall.

Moreover, the wall will sever social ties between these villages and nearby areas, including East Jerusalem.

Table IV: 18 Schools and Teachers in Bir Nabala, Al Jib, Al Judeira and Beit Hanina Al Balad

Schools	Pupils	Pupils from outside the villages	Teachers	Teachers from outside the villages
14	2,970	176	116	73

The schools provide employment for 116 teachers, only 43 of whom live in the village. Seventy-three teachers come from outside the area. They have considerable difficulty in accessing their schools in a punctual and reliable manner. Further, thirty-eight teachers who live in the village are employed in schools on the other side of the wall. They too experience severe problems in commuting to work. Eighty-one teachers live in these villages, including thirty-six who work in schools outside them. In addition to teacher mobility problems, the schools will also experience in the coming years a sharp decline in students due to the difficulty of accessing these areas.

The residents of these areas have relied on the health and medical services available in East Jerusalem. Now they must go to Ramallah, travel long distances and cross checkpoints. Moreover, the Ramallah Public Hospital is barely able to provide services to the residents of all the areas that formerly relied on Jerusalem hospitals.

Obviously, those who planned the separation wall's construction have not taken into account the simplest economic, humanitarian, or psychological considerations. This wall was built in accordance with one criterion only, which is to place Palestinian villages in enclaves and deprive them of their livelihoods and any possibility for future natural expansion.

Bir Nabala

The village of Bir Nabala is located nine kilometers north of the Old City of Jerusalem. It is bordered by Ar Ram and the Atarot Industrial Zone from the east, Al Judeira village from the north, Al Jib village from the west, and Beit Hanina Al Balad from the south. The area of Bir Nabala is approximately 2,692 dunums (673 acres), utilized in planting produce. In 2006, the population of Bir Nabala was approximately 6,180, the majority of whom worked in the commercial sector.

Parts of Bir Nabala lands were confiscated for establishing the Israeli Atarot Industrial Zone Settlement northeast of the village. Additionally, approximately 1,500 dunums (375 acres)– the equivalent of 55.7% of Bir Nabala lands – were confiscated for building the separation wall, leaving the village with approximately 1,100 dunums (275 acres)– the equivalent of 40% of its original area. This area is classified almost entirely as Area B, under shared Israeli/Palestinian control.

In Bir Nabala, there are branch offices for the Ministry of Agriculture, the Environmental Affairs Ministry, the Meteorology Department, the Magistrates Court, and the Local Governance Council. Moreover, good infrastructure and public services are available in Bir Nabala, including water and electricity supplies, and sewage and sanitation networks.

The wall's path passes through Bir Nabala's eastern and northern lands, isolating it almost entirely from Ar Ram on the east, northwest Jerusalem villages on the west and south, and Rafat and Ramallah on the north. The wall's path parallels Road No. 404, which connects West Jerusalem with the Atarot Industrial Zone, and Road No. 45, which besieges Bir Nabala lands on the north. A two-story building in the northeastern area of Bir Nabala was demolished while Road No. 45 was being built. Road No. 404 passes through the village's lands from the northeastern side in the form of a bridge that bisects it into two areas. The wall's path was supposed to parallel the bridge in Bir Nabala, but it was modified and displaced about 150 meters eastwards. This displacement led to the annexation of parts of the Al-Mawahel neighborhood, which is considered part of Beit Hanina lands, on the outer side of the wall. This measure will transform the neighborhood into a closed ghetto from all sides, with its only entrance and exit toward Bir Nabala via a bridge under Road No. 404.

The occupation authorities built a road connecting the northern part of the village with Road No. 45. This road enables the residents of Bir Nabala and other isolated areas (Al Jib, Al Judeira and Beit Hanina Al Balad) to travel to Ramallah, Qalandiya and Ar Ram without entering the Jerusalem.

Bir Nabala residents depend in all aspects of their lives on connections with East Jerusalem and nearby areas such as Ramallah and Ar Ram. In fact, Bir Nabala formerly represented a bridge, along with Ar Ram, connecting East Jerusalem with Ramallah, and a link leading to west and northwest Jerusalem villages. The village was also favored as a residential area for Jerusalem ID holders due to its proximity to East Jerusalem and an abundance of housing, as well as for West Bank residents who worked in Bir Nabala, East Jerusalem and within the Green Line. As a result, Bir Nabala attracted investors from inside the village as well as from outside, particularly expatriates from Bir Nabala and many East Jerusalemites. Investments in Bir Nabala supported the housing sector as well as the commercial sector in the form of shops and small factories.

The vital commercial strip in Bir Nabala is now defunct after the construction of the wall. Most businesses and workshops have moved to Ramallah or Jerusalem. Jan 2007.

The Bir Nabala Local Council estimates the number of commercial outlets in the village at 300 factories, workshops and retail shops, most of which relied almost entirely on East Jerusalem markets and clientele. A significant portion of those commercial activities are now closed, and the rest are threatened with closure due to the economic recession caused by the separation wall's construction. Moreover, there are presently approximately 1,000 vacant apartments, and there are many apartments currently rented by East Jerusalemite families whose tenants may leave anytime due to their concern at the possibility of losing their permanent residency rights in East Jerusalem. These factors also apply to the residents of the Al-Mawahel neighborhood, which was annexed to the outer side of the wall, although the overwhelming majority of its residents are Jerusalem ID card holders. This situation is expected to increase the number of vacant apartments and closed workshops and stores in the village, leading to a rapid collapse of the construction sector and the village's economy as a whole.

Education

There are three government schools, two private school and four kindergartens in Bir Nabala. Those educational institutions formerly served all nearby towns and villages like Al Jib, Al Judeira, Beit Hanina and Ar Ram. The wall construction in the Bir Nabala area has led to the relocation of a significant number of Bir Nabala residents outside the village; they have enrolled their children in schools close to their areas of residence; therefore, the number of pupils coming from outside the village dropped significantly. Furthermore, the 40 teachers coming from outside the village are facing enormous difficulties in arriving at their work places due to delays at the checkpoints on their way to Bir Nabala. This also applies to university and college students in Bir Nabala, particularly students of Al-Quds University in Abu Dis.

Table IV:19 Governmental and Public Schools in Bir Nabala

School's Name	Type	Pupils		Teachers	
		No. of Pupils	(From outside Beer Nabala)	No. of Teachers	(From outside the village)
Bir Nabala Girls Secondary School	Governmental	238	0	16	12
Bir Nabala Boys Basic School	Governmental	285	0	11	11
Bir Nabala Girls Basic School	Governmental	248	0	17	7
Bir Nabala Expatriates' Basic School	Private	309	0	17	7
Shatha Al-Wurood School	Private	148	0	9	3
Total		**1,228**	**0**	**70**	**40**

Medical Facilities

There are four pharmacies, two resident doctors and one medical center in Bir Nabala where a doctor and nurse work two days a week. Bir Nabala residents formerly relied almost entirely on the medical services available in and close to East Jerusalem. Nowadays, Bir Nabala residents have to seek treatment in the hospitals and medical centers in Ramallah.

Transportation

The transportation sector was adversely impacted by the wall's construction, which is reflected in hikes in transportation costs and the time needed to get from one place to another.

Figure IV: 8 Transport Routes in Bir Nabala, Al Judeira, Al Jib and Beit Hanina Al Balad Enclave Before and After The Wall

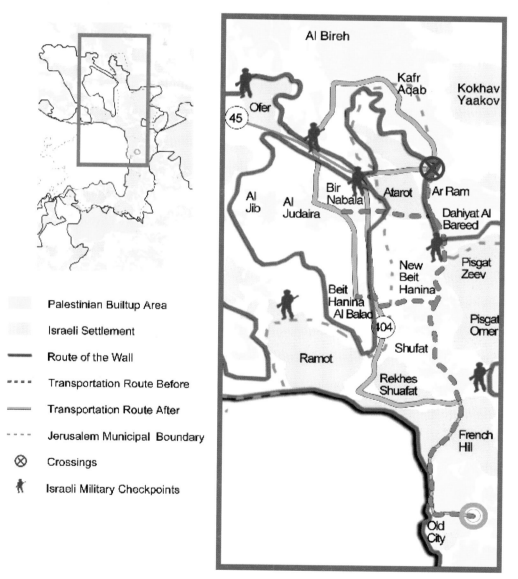

Before the construction of the wall, Palestinians from the Bir Nabala enclave simply took the broken-line routes a maximum distance of 9 km to reach the main north-south axis of Ramallah-Jerusalem road. After the construction of the wall, they are not allowed to enter the city. The few who have permits can take the solid yellow route traveling in parallel roads and opposite directions as indicated on the map. They have to cross the Qalandiya checkpoint in addition to the Atarot checkpoint on Road No. 4/404. This involves a distance of not less than 28 km.

Table IV: 20 Transportation Costs from Bir Nabala prior to and after Construction of the Wall

Destination	Cost prior to the wall construction (in NIS)	Cost after to the wall's construction (in NIS/increase)
East Jerusalem	3	9 (200% increase)
Ramallah	2	5 (150% increase)
Abu Dis	5	12 (140% increase)

Prior to the wall's construction, the road leading from Bir Nabala to East Jerusalem went through Ar Ram Junction, then Dahiyat Al Bareed and from there toward East Jerusalem. The time required was approximately 15 minutes. Nowadays, one must travel via Rafat, then Al-Manarah, then Samiramis, then Qalandiya, and then cross Qalandiya Crossing to East Jerusalem. The time required to complete such journey is one to one-and-a half hours, depending on the conditions at Qalandiya Crossing.

Al Judeira

Al Judeira village is located 10.5 kilometers northwest of the Old City of Jerusalem, approximately 775 meters above sea level. The area of Al Judeira is 2,044 dunums (510 acres). It is known for its olive, grape and almond crops, as well as for vegetable farming. Two-hundred-eighty-eight dunums of the village's lands are classified as Area B, and the rest have been classified as area C. No Israeli settlements are established on the village territory, but its lands have shrunk to approximately 1,368 dunums as a result of wall construction.

The population of Al Judeira is 2,153. Most of the residents work in farming and raising livestock, and fewer work in East Jerusalem and within the Green Line. Presently, Al Judeira is surrounded by Rafat village on the north, the Giv'at Ze'ev settlement on the west, Bir Nabala and the Atarot Industrial Zone on the east, and Bir Nabala on the south. Al Judeira possesses a reasonably good infrastructure; it has a sewage and sanitation network, as well as power and water supplies.

The separation wall passes through the northern parts of Al Judeira. One-hundred-seventy-six dunums of the village lands have been confiscated for the wall's construction. Moreover, the wall isolated approximately 500 dunums (125 acres) of the village's northern lands between the wall and Road No. 45 north of the village, on the pretext that they constituted a security zone parallel to the road. Those agricultural and grazing lands will not be accessible without obtaining permits from the occupation authorities. Such permits, if issued, are limited by specific time windows, and allow access through agricultural gates that the occupation authorities have promised to establish in the wall.

The wall northeast of Al Judeira separates it from Qalandiya Al Balad and Ramallah in the north. Jan 2007.

The Impact of the Wall

The village economy relied on agriculture and grazing livestock. There are no industrial or institutional establishments in the village, except for a juice factory, which is a joint Palestinian-Swedish project employing 12 people and exporting its products to the West Bank and the Gaza Strip. This enterprise was harmed by the difficulties of bringing raw materials into the village and exporting final products to the West Bank and Gaza Strip. None of the factory's workers have been laid-off, but it is presently not operating at its maximum capacity.

There is one basic public government school in Al Judeira and one private school with enrollments of 138 and 108 respectively. Almost half of the teachers in Al Judeira come from outside the village, and this led to problems in completing the curricula last year as a result of either the inability of the teachers to get to the school or the long delays they experienced at the checkpoints en route to school.

There are no medical centers or pharmacies in Al Judeira. The village has two doctors who provide basic treatment to the residents. The village formerly relied entirely on the medical services available in East Jerusalem, but nowadays the residents have to seek treatments at the hospitals and medical centers in Ramallah.

There are no government institutions or civil societies in Al Judeira, except for the Al-Thawrah Sports Club whose activities have been frozen as a result of difficulties and problems caused by the wall's construction.

The number of unemployed laborers is estimated at 20, and the number of farmers harmed by the wall's construction is estimated at 150. Prior to the wall's construction, no laborers were registered with the village council as unemployed.

Ten mixed-identity families (West Bank and Jerusalem ID cards) continue to live in Al-Judeira. But family members carrying Jerusalem ID cards are threatened to lose their residency rights in Jerusalem if they continue to live in Al Judeira or the West Bank. Consequently, those family members must either lose their residency rights in Jerusalem or become separated from each other in order to preserve their Jerusalem ID cards.

Moreover, the wall has caused a transportation crisis and a large hike in transportation costs since distances to Jerusalem, Ar Ram and Ramallah were much shorter prior to the wall's construction.

Table IV: 21 Transportation Costs in Al Judeira (see **Figure IV: 8**)

Destination	Fares prior to the wall's construction (in NIS)	Fares after the wall's construction (in NIS)	Increase (NIS and %)
Jerusalem	4	10	6 (150% increase)
Ramallah	2	7	5 (250 % increase)
Abu Dis	6	14	8 (133% increase)

Prior to the wall's construction, there was direct transportation to Jerusalem, but nowadays passengers have to travel through Bir Nabala, Samiramis, Kafr Aqab, Qalandiya, and then cross the Qalandiya Checkpoint in order to get to Jerusalem. Traveling to Jerusalem formerly required 15 minutes prior to the wall's construction, but nowadays it takes about an hour and a half or longer if there are mobile (flying) checkpoints.

Finally, residents of Al Judeira suffer from health hazards due to the leakage of sewage from Ramallah and the Ofer Prison. A complaint has been made, but the difficulty of coordinating between the offices of the Ramallah District and the Ofer Prison Administration makes finding a solution for this problem very challenging.

Al Jib

Al Jib village is located nine kilometers northwest of the Old City of Jerusalem. It stands on the ruins of the historic Canaanite village of Gabaot, whose name meant "The Hill." It was mentioned by the Romans as Gabaon, and was known for its olive, vine and almond crops.

A panorama of Al Jib from the west. Jan 2007.

The area of Al Jib is 8,205 dunums (2,051 acres) of which 475 dunums (119 acres) are classified as Area B, and the rest are classified as area C. The occupation authorities established several Israeli settlements on some of the village's lands:

- **Giv'on Settlement in 1977**
- **Giv'at Hadashah (Mitspe Giv'on) in 1979**
- **Jerusalem Airport – Expansion of Jerusalem (Qalandiya) Airport**
- **Giv'at Ze'ev Settlement in 1981**
- **Neve Samuel Settlement in 1993, which was later renamed as Har Shmuel.**

Building the settlements involved the confiscation of approximately 5,205 dunums of the village's lands, leaving it with no more than 3,000 dunums (1301 acres). Additionally, 262 dunums (45 acres) were confiscated for the separation wall, and an additional 1,226 dunums (306 acres) of the village's agricultural lands were isolated on the outer side of the wall. Those farming lands are planted with approximately 12,000 olive and almond trees and with vine stock. The establishment of settlements and construction of the wall left Al Jib with 1,512 dunums (378 acres), half of which are classified as Area C. Thus, only 18.4% of the total area of Al Jib remains on the inner side of the wall.

Al Jib is surrounded by the Giv'at Ze'ev settlement on the north, Giv'on Hadashah settlement on the west, Al Judeira and Bir Nabala on the east, and Nabi Samuel village on the south. In 2006, the population of Al Jib was 4,711. The overwhelming majority of the population is West Bank ID card holders. In the wake of the wall, most of the town's Jerusalem ID holders returned to East Jerusalem. Today only 3% of the population holds the Jerusalem ID. The village infrastructure is modern. It is supplied with power and water; it has a decent road network and about 70% of its buildings are connected to a sewage and sanitation network.

There are two health centers in Al Jib; one supported by the Al-Islah Benevolent Society and the other is private. Formerly, Al Jib residents sought treatment in East Jerusalem. Nowadays, they go to the Ramallah Governmental Hospital because of the closure of all means of access to the medical services in East Jerusalem.

The village economy relies on agriculture and raising livestock, as well as on labor in East Jerusalem and within the Green Line. Presently, and after the wall besieged a significant portion of the village's agricultural lands on the outer side of the wall, access to agricultural lands has become difficult; access is allowed through agricultural gates during specific time periods (cultivation and harvesting seasons), and only after obtaining special permits from the occupation authorities. Moreover, the wall's construction has blocked access to pastures and grazing lands in the area. Furthermore, the inability of the labor force in Al Jib to access East Jerusalem and the labor market within the Green Line has caused a dramatic and tragic deterioration of the village's economy.

No houses in Al Jib have been demolished for the sake of the wall construction or building and expanding the roads surrounding the village. However, the occupation authorities plan to build a road that passes through Al Jib lands on the interior side of the wall to connect Al Jib with Al Judeira and then Ramallah. Also, expansion projects are underway on Road No. 436, which connects the Giv'at Ze'ev Israeli settlement with Ramot settlement and borders Al Jib lands on the west. According to Israeli claims, a road connecting Al Jib with Biddu town will be built. It will be dug as a trench and surrounded by walls on both sides. There is another scenario for this road whereby it would be a tunnel connecting those two areas with each other, just as the tunnel presently under construction to connect southern Az Za'ayyem with southern Anata. This tunnel makes up a segment of a road referred to as "the structure of life road" which will connect northwest Jerusalem villages with Ramallah through Al Jib and Rafat villages.

A road under construction west of Al Jib will be the only link between the Bir Nabala enclave and the Biddu enclave northwest of Jerusalem. Here, it runs beneath a settlement road. Jan 2007.

There are four governmental schools in Al Jib: a basic school, two secondary schools, and Fatima Az-Zahra' School. These schools provide educational services to residents of the surrounding villages. There is also a private school.

Table IV: 22 Al Jib Schools

School	Type	Pupils		Teachers	
		No. of Pupils	(From outside the village)	No. of Teachers	(From outside the village)
Iben Khuldoun Boys Basic School	Government	303	0	12	12
Fatima Az-Zahra' Girls Secondary School	Government	415	134	22	22
Al Jib Basic Co-ed School	Government	288	6	13	9
Al Jib Boys Secondary School	Government	365	34	13	12
Nuzhat Al-Muttaqeen School	Private	37	0	2	0
Total		**1,408**	**174**	**62**	**55**

The 174 pupils coming from outside Al Jib suffer enormously in accessing their schools due to the checkpoints and the delay periods at them, as well as from the hikes in transportation costs. Nowadays, pupils coming from Ar Ram have to pay 7 NIS in order to get to school, while prior to the wall's construction they paid only 2 NIS. The same applies to 55 teachers, approximately 89% of the total number of teachers in Al Jib schools, who commute daily from outside the village.

Moreover, the transportation route connecting Al Jib with the adjacent western villages became extremely complicated in the wake of the wall's construction. For example, whoever wants to travel from Al Jib to Biddu or Nabi Samuel village has to travel to Bir Nabala first, then to Rafat village, then to Ramallah, and from there to Biddu or Nabi Samuel. The extended route directly impacts transportation costs. Indeed, transportation costs nowadays represent a source of real suffering for Al Jib residents.

Table IV: 23 Transportation Costs in Al Jib (see **Figure IV: 8**)

Destination	Fares prior to the wall's construction (in NIS)	Fares after the wall's construction (in NIS & % increase)
Jerusalem	4	12 (200% increase)
Ramallah	3	7 (133% increase)
Ar Ram	2	7 (250% increase)

As income levels in Al Jib deteriorated, distances increased and transportation costs rose, and together became major impediments to mobility. Another impediment is the long waiting periods to obtain permits from the Israeli Liaison offices. Travel has become a real burden to those who have social ties with East Jerusalem.

Beit Hanina Al Balad

The village of Beit Hanina Al Balad is located eight kilometers north of the Old City of Jerusalem. It is believed that its name is derived from "Beit Hana" in the Assyrian Language, which means the house of the fighters. Beit Hanina Al Balad's original area was 15,839 dunums (approximately 4,000 acres). It is known for grain, olive, fig and vine crops.

The Israeli occupation authorities annexed approximately two thirds of Beit Hanina Al Balad lands to East Jerusalem when the West Bank and East Jerusalem were occupied in 1967. The annexed area commonly is now called simply Beit Hanina or, sometimes, New Beit Hanina, to distinguish it from Beit Hanina Al Balad. The original community was left with approximately 5,000 dunums (1250 acres) and remained part of the West Bank. The area within East Jerusalem has expanded since 1967; its area became larger and its economy stronger than even that of the Old City of East Jerusalem.

An overview of Beit Hanina Al Balad from New Beit Hanina. The 1.5 km direct road that connected both neighborhoods, and above which Road 404/4 passes, is blocked by the wall. Jan 2007.

The area of Beit Hanina Al Balad lands classified as Area B is approximately 393 dunums (not quite 100 acres). Presently, the population of Beit Hanina Al Balad is 1,406, most of whom are West Bank ID card holders. The local council estimates the percentage of residents holding Jerusalem ID cards and still living in the village at approximately 5%. Most of the expatriates who returned to Beit Hanina Al Balad in the 1990s in the wake of the Oslo Agreement have left, many immigrating to the United States of America at the onset of the Second Intifada. Several Israeli settlements have been established on parts of the village land, including:

- **Ramot Alon and Neve Ya'akov in 1970;**
- **Pisgat Ze'ev and Pisgat 'Omer in 1985;**
- **Rekhes Shu'fat in 1994.**

Creating the settlements involved confiscation of vast areas of Beit Hanina Al Balad's lands. And the construction of the separation wall has consumed additional land (over 300 dunums), hrinking the village's area in 2006 to approximately 1,000 dunums (250 acres). These confiscations have collapsed the village's agricultural economy and reduced open areas that were supposed to ensure the village's natural expansion. Additionally, more than nine hundred orders have been issued for the confiscation of absentee owner properties in Beit Hanina Al Balad. A surveillance tower will be erected atop a high hill on the interior side of the wall in order to monitor the highway (Road No. 404), which has isolated Beit Hanina Al Balad from New Beit Hanina.

The Separation Wall

The former entrance into Beit Hanina Al Balad is blocked with an earthen barricade and concrete blocks to prevent access from the village to new Beit Hanina. Above the former entrance is the regional Road 404 which is the main axis connecting Jerusalem to Tel Aviv. August 2006.

The separation wall negatively impacts the lands and citizens of both segments of Beit Hanina. In fact, its effects cover all aspects of life, particularly in Beit Hanina Al Balad, due to the original town's economic dependence on New Beit Hanina. The isolation of both segments of Beit Hanina has meant severing the close ties between them, including the family and social ties, the shared educational facilities and the once common economy. The result has been the emigration of most Jerusalem ID card holders from Beit Hanina Al Balad to New Beit Hanina.

The two segments of Beit Hanina represent the best example of the distribution of families in East Jerusalem and its suburbs, and the extent of the social ties among them. Such ties are nowadays threatened with disintegration due to the impediments and difficulties facing individuals in both localities. Formerly, a short, one kilometer stretch of road connected the two localities, allowing people to visit their relatives on a daily basis. In 2002, the occupation authorities closed this road as well as the tunnel under Road No. 404 through which people traveled to visit the two communities. This road and tunnel was the only route connecting Beit Hanina Al Balad with New Beit Hanina directly. Nowadays, residents of both segments of Beit Hanina have to travel approximately 25 kilometers to visit each other, if they are indeed given permits. The new route extends from Beit Hanina Al Balad to Bir Nabala, Al Judeira, Rafat, Kafr Aqab, Qalandiya, then through the Qalandiya Crossing to New Beit Hanina. This burdensome inconvenience applies particularly to people who are seeking treatment in East Jerusalem hospitals or the medical centers in Beit Hanina, which were before the wall no more than a few minutes away from their homes.

The case of Mahmoud is instructive. Mahmoud is 34 years old. He is married and lives with his wife in Beit Hanina Al Balad. His parents, in their sixties, and his brothers live in New Beit Hanina. He said in an interview with IPCC that "Prior to the wall's construction, I used to visit my family on a daily basis. The distance between my house and theirs was less than a kilometer. Now, I can hardly visit them twice a month because I have to travel 35 kilometers to get to their home, although I can see them from the rooftop of my house."

The economy of Beit Hanina Al Balad relied on agriculture and the investments of its expatriate citizens. The investments were especially crucial to the housing sector in order to absorb an influx of newcomers from East Jerusalem seeking cheaper housing and those from the West Bank who sought to live nearer to East Jerusalem. And in the wake of the Oslo Agreements many expatriates returned to the community. The village economy began regressing however in 2002, following the closure of the road that connected the two segments of Beit Hanina with each other and Beit Hanina Al Balad with East Jerusalem. Prior to the wall's construction, the overwhelming majority of laborers from Beit Hanina Al Balad worked in New Beit Hanina. The closure made it impossible for those who held West Bank ID cards to travel to employment in New Beit Hanina or elsewhere in East Jerusalem or across the Green Line to Israeli jobs. Poverty rates naturally have increased with the rise in unemployment. Moreover, erection of the separation wall put an end to the investments in the village. Presently, there is a housing surplus of at least 120 vacant apartments. More than 100 tenants have left due to the difficulty of travel to East Jerusalem and the surrounding areas, particularly to New Beit Hanina.

Table IV: 24 Selected Transportation Costs from Beit Hanina Al Balad (see **Figure IV: 8**)

Destination	Fares prior to the wall's construction (in NIS)	Fares after the wall's construction (in NIS & ٪ increase)
Jerusalem	3	10 (233% increase)
Ramallah	4	5 (25% increase)
New Beit Hanina	1	8.5 (750% increase)

Buses from East Jerusalem (including those from new Beit Hanina) are banned from entry to Beit Hanina Al Balad. Citizens are often times forced to walk from Beit Hanina Al Balad to Bir Nabala. Beit Hanina residents formerly entirely relied on the transportation means available in New Beit Hanina and the nearby villages, which used the roads and streets of Beit Hanina Al Balad to access East Jerusalem. Transportation was provided abundantly prior to the isolation of Beit Hanina Al Balad from New Beit Hanina at the hands of the occupation authorities.

This alternative road constructed west of Road No. 404/4 will connect Beit Hanina Al Balad to Ramallah and end its link with Jerusalem. Jan 2007.

The educational sector in Beit Hanina Al Balad has been directly affected by the wall. Beit Hanina secondary school for girls had been located in Beit Hanina Al Balad while the boys' school was located in New Beit Hanina. Construction of the wall made access to either school extremely complicated, especially for West Bank ID card holders.

Table IV: 25 Beit Hanina Al Balad Schools

School	Type	Pupils		Teachers	
		No. of Pupils	(From outside the village)	No. of Teachers	(From outside the village)
Beit Hanina Girls Secondary School	Government	88	2	11	7
Al-Adhamieh Basic Co-Ed School	Government	119	0	7	4
Total		**207**	**2**	**18**	**11**

The schools of Beit Hanina Al Balad formerly served numerous pupils from New Beit Hanina, and vice versa. After checkpoints and barriers were erected between Beit Hanina Al Balad and New Beit Hanina in 2002, the number of pupils coming to Beit Hanina Al Balad from East Jerusalem, specifically from New Beit Hanina, regressed dramatically until the number of pupils from outside Beit Hanina Al Balad in the village's schools reached almost zero.

The only cemetery for the two villages is located in Beit Hanina Al Balad, and burial permits are required in order to bury dead residents of New Beit Hanina or from East Jerusalem. Also, Sidi Ibrahim Mosque in Beit Hanina Al Balad is the traditional place of prayer for residents of both segments of Beit Hanina. Nowadays, it is impossible for many worshipers, particularly the elderly from New Beit Hanina, to get to this mosque because the travel distance, time, and expense have become a real burden.

An IPCC Survey of Jerusalemite Perceptions of the Impact of the Wall on Everyday Life

Robert D. Brooks, Rassem Khamaisi, Sari Hanafi, Amer Hidmi, and Shahd Wa'ary

Methodology

During the period of November 2004 and February 2005, a team of IPCC field researchers interviewed 1223 adult Palestinians in the Jerusalem Governorate. The purposes of the survey were to document the effect of the wall on life in the city and its hinterland and to assess the perceptions of the wall's effect among Jerusalemites. The survey was conducted in the Old City and in thirty-nine communities and neighborhoods in Jerusalem and its suburbs. An effort was made to include a range of communities as comparatively affluent as Ard As Samar and Sheikh Jarrah and as poverty ridden as Ath Thuri and the Shu'fat Refugee Camp. The communities represented commercial centers as large as Ar Ram/Dahiyat Al Bareed (55,000+) and as small as the village of Beit Ijza (680). Communities were selected that are as close to the wall as Abu Dis, which lies adjacent to the barrier, and as distant as the Old City. Care was taken to also include communities that were: a) "inside the wall" on the East Jerusalem and Israeli side of the barrier; b) communities that are "enclaved" or surrounded on three or four sides by the wall on either side of the barrier; c) as well of course as communities on the outside of the barrier, cut off from East Jerusalem. In all, 658 respondents were outside the wall and 550 were inside the barrier. **Attachment One** provides information on the location of the communities.

In a trial study, 100 interviews were conducted with a trial questionnaire. The responses of the trial project were used to refine the questionnaire. The refined questionnaire that was used for the data in this study was administered to 1223 subjects or households. In addition to certain demographic information (such as income level, size of dwelling, size of family), several items were posed in *before-the-wall/after-the-wall* format; others questions sought to rank order various life-difficulties resulting from the wall; others were so-called "choose one" responses among a short list of alternatives; others were in the agree/disagree format; and two open-ended questions concerning feelings about the wall and the future of Jerusalem were asked as well. A copy of the questionnaire is included as **Attachment Two.**

Of the 1223 questionnaires that were administered 1208 were judged to be useable for tabulation. Where appropriate, the data were analyzed by SPSS procedures. Tables of selected results are presented in **Attachment Three**. A summary of the main findings follows immediately below.

Summary of Results and Interpretation

1. *The wall and daily Palestinian life.* Our researchers were interested in the direct effects of the wall on daily life. When this question was addressed generically, we were surprised to see that slightly over one-third (35.6%) of the respondents opined that the wall did not affect them directly. This may be the result of their particular circumstances, but it may well be the result of two not unrelated factors: the official announcement on the route of the wall has not been made (for legal and strategic purposes) and there is wide spread ignorance and parochialism

---

*The field staff who administered the survey included: Noor Dkeidek, Hayam Hushiya, Yusra Hussein, Safa' Jamil, Suhad Jumhour, Mirvat Mansour, Rawan Muwakket, Shatha Owais, Noor Shkeir, Khalil Sinnawi, Ra'fat Sinnawi, and shadi Za'atara.

139

among the residents of Jerusalem communities regarding wall details. But we may risk over-explaining the minority result. The main pattern of response is to be found in the 64% who feel directly affected by the wall. When that general finding is plumbed for detail, the following specific items emerge: 34.5% remarked of negative economic effects; 13.5% were concerned about the loss of personal or community land; 5.7% felt that population density and general living conditions were deteriorating; 88% experienced or expected difficulty (some, medium, or high) in receiving such basic services as health and education; 85% experienced or expected difficulties in reaching the work place; 92.4% experienced or expected difficulties in general transportation and increases in the time required for travel; 137 of the survey subjects (11.2%) have had to contend with a change in the location of their work; and 3.9% of the families surveyed have changed their children's schools; 279 (23%) of the respondents have had to change the location where they normally purchase supplies to meet their basic needs. Almost 14% report that land confiscations have given them a sense of having lost living space. In short, daily life in the governorate is undergoing significant and disturbing changes.

2. *The wall and the family.* For some, the most wrenching effects are those which impact the family fabric. Over 46% of the respondents reported that the wall will separate them from their immediate family (father, mother, brother, sister) and 54% noted separation from their extended family (grandparents, uncles, aunts, cousins). There is some duplication among these data: a single respondent may experience separation from both levels of his/her family. But that does not minimize the impact of the data. While it may be said that the family is the core of any society, including the Israeli, the family is notably salient in the Arab culture, especially one that is not far removed from its agricultural roots and clan affiliations. During the "hard times" that have characterized the Palestinian experience essentially since 1948, the family support unit has for many been the means of survival. Shared and transferred incomes; shared food, shared domiciles; and shared transport have reinforced the importance of the immediate and extended family. The wall will seriously disrupt Palestinian society at the level of its most basic social unit, the family.

3. *Mobility and access issues.* Israel has sought to assuage international and Palestinian alarm over the wall by stressing that mobility and access will be assured by a large number of "gates." Do Palestinians accept these assurances? Surprisingly, a substantial minority (17.4%) were optimistic. "Surprising", we say because of the largely strongly negative experience Palestinians have had with gates and crossings since the mid-1990's. But a strong majority (71.6%) thought the gates would not minimize the wall's effect and an additional 9.7% felt the gates would make no difference, and 45% believe that the wall should be stopped or destroyed. In our view, their pessimism is justified. During the years of closure, various obstacles to movement were implemented by the Israeli army in a manner that can be deemed capricious, punitive, inhumane and unpredictable. Moreover, recent experience with the completed wall in the northern West Bank augurs no good: while 21 gates were included, most are permanently closed; others are open only sporadically. Thus the proffering of gates does not in itself vouchsafe movement. The gate policy with respect to hours and permits, the attitude of the Israeli army, and the dynamic of unforeseen events will commingle to determine the functionality of the gates.

4. *The wall and access to healthcare.* Earlier we noted that a significant number of respondents (88%) experienced some level of difficulty in accessing basic services. Here we shall look in greater detail in the area of medical services (doctors, clinics and neighborhood medical centers) and hospitals. We document considerable disruption in accessing this fundamental community service.

The IPCC researchers sought to determine whether the path of the wall had changed access to the respondents' preferred medical services and hospitals. Of the 1208 respondents, 351 (29%) indicated that they have had to change doctors or medical clinics as a result of access or mobility problems brought on by the wall. For example, of the 838 respondents who had previously patronized doctors or clinics in a given East Jerusalem community, 238 (28%) now seek treatment in some other city, suburban or West Bank location. Of the 245 respondents who prior to the wall sought care in the suburbs or in the West Bank, 62 (25%) have had to change medical services as a consequence of the wall. Of the 110 respondents who previously had accessed medical services in Israeli West Jerusalem, 51 (46%) now seek care in East Jerusalem or suburban communities.

A similar pattern of disruption occurs with regards to accessing hospitals. The survey identified 13 hospitals or major medical centers that were frequented by the 1208 respondents. Of that pool of subjects, 339 (28%) report that they now visit a different hospital as a result of the wall. Access to the major East Jerusalem hospitals has been most effected. For example: for respondents who previously sought care at the Al Maqased Hospital, 53% now go elsewhere; of the former patients of Augusta Victoria Hospital, 67% now go elsewhere; and of the smaller number who in the past patronized St. John Hospital, 75% now must seek help elsewhere. While these are general hospitals, each is known for specializations such as coronary, eye and dialysis units. Thus to "go elsewhere" often means to go a facility of lesser rank.

5. *The wall and political environment.* The vast majority of respondents (95.6%) believe that the wall will deteriorate the political environment and will escalate the conflict crisis. The wall does not appear to be, in the Palestinian view, conducive to either peace, security, or a settlement of the final issues. It has significant potential to de-stabilize an already tense relationship between the contending parties. While immediate overt resistance that could lead to violence was not documented in the survey, such wide spread and deep pessimism signals increasing conflict in the future. A large number of wall routing issues are now pending court review; domestic tranquility may well turn on those decisions.

ATTACHMENT ONE: SURVEYED COMMUNITIES

Neighborhoods within the city	**517**
Neighborhoods within the East Jerusalem cut off from the city-by the wall	**129**
Near suburbs outside of East Jerusalem cut off from the city	**312**
Distant villages around Jerusalem within the Jerusalem Governorate	**250**
TOTAL	**1208**

ATTACHMENT TWO: SURVEY QUESTIONNAIRE ITEMS

(English Translation from the Arabic)

Impact of the Wall on Jerusalem and its Surroundings
Survey Questionnaire

(31) Area:

(32)Survey Questionnaire   (33) Building   (34)Unit   (35)Area #   (36)Student

Services

Use 1 to indicate location before 2000
Use 2 to indicate current location
Use 3 to indicate lack of change in location

1. Where do you seek such medical services as clinics, private doctors?

    1-   Jerusalem (East)
    2-   Jerusalem (West)
    3-   West Bank (Jerusalem surroundings)
    4-   Specify

2. What hospital(s) does your family use?

    1. Al Maqased Hospital   5. Hadassah Mount Scopus
    2. French Hospital   6. Eye Hospital (Sheikh Jarrah)
    3. Hadassah Ein Karem   7. Specify
    4. Augusta Victoria

3. Where do you purchase the ordinary daily needs for your family etc.

    1. Salah Eddin Street (Bab As Sahira)   5. Ar Ram/ Bir Nabala
    2. Old City   6. Beit Hanina
    3. My neighborhood   7. Specify
    4. Al Eizariya

4. Does the family own a private car?

    1. Yes   2. No

If the answer in 4 was # 1 please answer questions 5 and 6.

5. How many cars in your family?

6. Where do you receive car maintenance services

    1. Industrial Neighborhood Wad Al Joz
    2. Al Eizariya

3. Ar Ram
4. Ramallah
5. Specify

Impact of wall on daily life

7. Number of near relatives (father/ mother/ brother/ sister/ son/ daughter) that will be separated from you by the wall

8. Number of other relatives (grandparents, uncles/ cousins, etc) that will be separated from you by the wall

9 .What degree of difficulties will you face on a personal level as a result of the wall? (Order these difficulties according to their importance to your life.)

9.1 Receiving services from the city (education, health, etc.)
9.2 Social and family relationships
9.3 Reaching workplace
9.4 General Transportation and time needed to travel

10. Do you own a house outside the wall?

1. Yes   2. No

Information about your residence

11. Your home is:

1. Privately owned
2. Shared property
3. Old rent system (inexpensive)
4. New rent system
5. Under an Islamic Waqf

12. Number of rooms in current place of residence

13. Street name

14. House number

15. The distance from your house to the nearest transportation stop

16. The distance from your house to the nearest trash dumpster

17. In what year was your house built

18. Area of house (square meters)

19. Cost of housing rent (NIS)

Additional Questions about the impact of the wall on your life

20. What will you miss most in the area you live in after the construction of wall?
      1.   Club.
      2.   Bank
      3.   Parks and restaurants
      4.   Fun fair
      5.   Others.

21. In your opinion, what can be done to reduce the impact of the wall?

      1.   Stopping it.
      2.   Destroying it.
      3.   Changing its path.
      4.   Demonstrations against it
      5.   Providing all the necessary services inside the wall.
      6.   It can't be reduced
      7.   Going to courts
      8.   Peace and reconciliation.
      9.   Providing help and support to the victims

22. Will the Wall change the routine of your daily life? If so, What are the changes?
      No change.
      Change your work location.
      Change your children's school.
      Reduce family and social visits.
      Limit the use of your private car.
      Increase travel time.
      No children entertainment places.

23. How would you describe your feelings as the wall construction proceeds?

      _____

      _____

24. Does the construction of the wall impact you directly?
      1.   Confiscation of land
      2.   Blocking the view from your house
      3.   Increase life expenses.
      4.   Change of residence.
      5.   Increase rents in your neighborhood
      6.   Causes crowdedness and bad living conditions.

Income Level

25. Total amount of family earnings:
      (1) Less than 2000 NIS per month
      (2) 2000- 4000
      (3) 4000- 6000
      (4) More than 6000

(5) Depending on government welfare insurance

(6) No earnings

26. Number of employed persons in the family prior to 2000

27. Current number of employed persons in your family

28. In your opinion what is the most important factor/s that will influence the future of Jerusalem?

29. The Israelis say they will provide gates in the wall. Do you think that the proposed gates will minimize the affect of the wall on the people?

(1) Yes   (2) No   (3) No difference

30. Do you think that the wall will worsen the political situation?

(1) Yes   (2) No   (3) No difference.

ATTACHMENT THREE: SELECTED RESULTS

Number of near relatives (father/ mother/ brother/ sister/ son/ daughter) that will be separated from you by the wall?

	Frequency	Percent	Valid Percent	Cumulative Percent
No relative	639	52.3	52.9	52.9
Few relatives(1-5)	498	40.8	41.2	94.1
A lot of Relatives (more than 6)	71	5.8	5.9	100.0
Total	1208	98.9	100.0	

Number of other relatives (grandparents, uncles/ cousins, etc) separated from you by the wall?

	Frequency	Percent	Valid Percent	Cumulative Percent
No relative	541	44.3	44.8	44.8
Few relatives (1-5)	565	46.2	46.8	91.6
A lot of relatives (more than 6)	102	8.3	8.4	100.0
Total	1208	98.9	100.0	

What difficulties will you face on a personal level as a result of wall (Order these difficulties according to their importance?

1. Accessing services from the city (education, health, etc.)

	Frequency	Percent	Valid Percent	Cumulative Percent
No Difficulty	134	11.0	11.1	11.1
Low difficulty	362	29.6	30.0	41.1
Medium difficulty	214	17.5	17.7	58.8
High difficulty	498	40.8	41.2	100.0
Total	1208	98.9	100.0	

2. Difficulties in social and family relationships

	Frequency	Percent	Valid Percent	Cumulative Percent
No Difficulty	75	6.1	6.2	6.2
Low difficulty	269	22.0	22.3	28.5
Medium difficulty	336	27.5	27.8	56.3
High difficulty	527	43.1	43.6	100
Total	1208	98.9	100.0	

3. Difficulties in reaching workplace

	Frequency	Percent	Valid Percent	Cumulative Percent
No Difficulty	170	13.9	14.1	14.1
Low difficulty	414	33.9	34.3	48.3
Medium difficulty	165	13.5	13.7	62.0
High difficulty	459	37.6	38.0	100.0
Total	1208	98.9	100.0	

4. Difficulties in accessing public transportation and time needed to travel

	Frequency	Percent	Valid Percent	Cumulative Percent
No Difficulty	80	6.5	6.6	6.6
Low difficulty	303	24.8	25.1	31.7
Medium difficulty	227	18.6	18.8	50.5
High difficulty	598	48.9	49.5	100.0
Total	1208	98.9	100.0	

What will you miss most in the area you live in after the construction of wall?

	Frequency	Percent	Valid Percent	Cumulative Percent
No relevant response	246	20.1	20.4	20.4
Club	55	4.5	4.6	24.9
Bank	246	20.1	20.4	45.3
Restaurant	86	7.0	7.1	52.4
Fun Fair	23	1.9	1.9	54.3
Other facilities (shops, utility companies, women's center, net café)	549	44.9	45.4	99.8
School	3	.2	.2	100.0
Total	1208	98.8	100.0	

What can be done to reduce the impact of the wall?

	Frequency	Percent	Valid Percent	Cumulative Percent
No relevant response	232	18.9	19.1	19.1
Stopping It	105	8.6	8.7	27.8
Destroying It	447	36.5	37.0	64.9
Changing its route	14	1.1	1.2	66.0
Demonstrations	60	4.9	5.0	71.0
Providing all necessary services inside the wall	40	3.3	3.3	74.3
It can't be reduced	106	8.7	8.8	83.1
Going to courts	33	2.7	2.7	85.8
Peace and reconciliation	115	9.4	9.5	95.4
Providing help and support to victims	56	4.6	4.6	100.0
Total	1208	98.7	100.0	

Will the wall change the routine of your daily life?

	Frequency	Percent	Valid Percent	Cumulative Percent
No relevant response	234	19.1	19.4	19.4
No change	142	11.6	11.8	31.1
Changing work location	137	11.2	11.3	42.5
Changing children's school	48	3.9	4.0	46.4
Limit the use of private cars	52	4.3	4.3	63.9
Reducing family and social visits	211	17.3	17.5	68.2
Increase travel time	366	29.9	30.3	98.5
No children's entertainment places	13	1.1	1.1	99.6
Economic and financial effect	1	.1	.1	99.7
Change of work place	3	.2	.2	99.9
Psychological	1	.1	.1	100.0
Total	1208	98.8	100.0	

Does the construction of the wall impact you directly?

	Frequency	Percent	Valid Percent	Cumulative Percent
No impact	435	35.6	36.0	36.0
Confiscation of personal or community land (sense of a loss of space)	165	13.5	13.7	49.7
Blocking the view from your house	46	3.8	3.8	53.5
Increase life expenses	417	34.1	34.5	88.0
Change of residence	41	3.4	3.4	91.4
Increase rents in your neighborhood	19	1.6	1.6	93.0
Causes crowdedness and bad living conditions	70	5.7	5.8	98.8
Loss of work place	12	1.0	1.0	100.0
Total	1205	98.8	100.0	

Income level: total family earnings.

	Frequency	Percent	Valid Percent	Cumulative Percent
No relevant response	15	1.2	1.2	1.2
Less than 2000 NIS	147	12.0	12.2	13.4
Between 2000 and 4000 NIS	543	44.4	45.0	58.4
Between 4000 and 6000 NIS	319	26.1	26.4	84.8
More than 6000	167	13.7	13.8	98.6
Depending on welfare	9	.7	.7	99.3
No Earning	8	.7	.7	100.0
Total	1208	98.8	100.0	

Will gates minimize the effect of the wall?

	Frequency	Percent	Valid Percent	Cumulative Percent
Yes	213	17.4	17.6	36.6
No	876	71.6	72.6	90.1
No difference	119	9.7	9.9	100.0
Total	1208	98.8	100.0	

Will the wall worsen the political situation?

	Frequency	Percent	Valid Percent	Cumulative Percent
Yes	1171	95.7	96.9	96.9
No	12	1.0	1.0	97.9
No difference	25	2.0	2.1	100.0
Total	1208	98.8	100.0	

CHAPTER SIX

A Map Of Palestinian Interests

Rami Nasrallah

The Geopolitical Context of the Jerusalem Wall

Most political proposals for the future of Jerusalem have addressed in some manner the reality imposed on the ground or the so-called settlement realities created by Israel since its occupation of the city in 1967. However, the situation that we witness today proves that the imposed realities represent a live danger to any possibility of reaching a final settlement, not only for the future of Jerusalem, but also they threaten the very feasibility of the two-state solution. Many of the Israeli proposals being made nowadays replace the principle of geographic and demographic contiguity of West Bank territories with a so-called functional continuity, especially in the critical area of Ma'aleh Adumim. Current Israeli plans for the area represents a huge obstacle to the contiguity of the northern and southern areas of the West Bank and undermines the possibility of establishing a geographically and functionally contiguous Palestinian state.

The main axis for contiguity of the West Bank territories passes through Jerusalem. This axis has been eroded gradually since the onset of the peace process more than a decade ago. Recently, the wall has been constructed to end Palestinian contiguity and to define the nature of the final settlement according to the unilateral goals of Israel. Such a settlement evolves around Israeli security and demographic arrangements which disregard the Palestinian demographic existence and besiege it with a wall and fragmenting barriers and a network of settler roads that break up Jerusalem and the Palestinian territories and isolate them from each other and from their uninhabited lands and territories. Those uninhabited Palestinian lands and territories now represent areas for the future expansion of existing and new Israeli settlements. Currently the vacant lands constitute spatial vacuums between the towns and villages surrounding Jerusalem, between the city and the Jordan Valley area, and in uninhabited areas near the north end of the Dead Sea, as well as in those reserves southwest of Jerusalem and those in the Hebron area.

The process of constructing the wall in the West Bank and around Jerusalem represents "the final step" in determining the future of Jerusalem. This process is not expected to continue in accordance with the present projected path of the wall; new paths will be drawn that will isolate more Palestinian neighborhoods from and within the city. It will be a unilateral action that creates more virtually irreversible facts on the ground.

The Israeli Case

The following points are the main justifications used by Israel as a rationale for modifying the geo-political reality of Jerusalem.

- *The Jewish majority in Jerusalem is in danger*. The percentage of Jews in the city has dropped from 75% in 1967 to 65% at the end of 2005. This percentage is expected to continue to decline, reaching 58% in 2020. Israel considers getting rid of the demographic burden a condition for preserving its Jewish nature. The wall can bring more Jews into the city from the suburban settlements and push Arab Palestinian neighborhoods to the outside of the wall.

- *Israel is experiencing negative Jewish migration from Jerusalem*, especially among the youth and the middle and educated classes. During the past two decades more than 100 thousand Jews emigrated from the city, with half of them moving to live in Jerusalem's surroundings. Expanding the municipality's borders can capture or retain this migration for Jewish Jerusalem.

- *Jerusalem is the poorest major city in Israel,* an embarrassment as the capital of the Jewish state. According to 2003 statistics, one third of the families inhabiting the city live under the poverty line. The poorest population group in Jerusalem is the Palestinians; 60% of the Palestinians in the city live under the poverty line. The percentage of poor Palestinian children in the city represents 77% of the percentage of poor children in Jerusalem. By contrast, 29% of the Jews in Jerusalem and 38% of their children live under the poverty line. Maneuvering walls to cynically exclude from the city many of the poor, such as the thousands who reside in the Shu'fat Refugee Camp, artificially lowers the poverty rate and enfolding middle class settlements within the "new" city border will have a positive impact on the city's standard of living statistics.

- *The Palestinian contribution to the city's economy is minimal* due to a lower labor participation rate, a higher dependency ratio between number of workers and number of dependents and a low percentage of working women. This means the Palestinian Jerusalemites have a lower purchasing power, a lower impact on tax revenues, and a higher need for social services from the Israeli state. Israelis consider the Palestinians to be a drag on the economy and a key factor in the low income levels and living standards in the city. The wall, if cleverly routed, can improve all these data from the Israeli perspective.

- *Security considerations, coupled with the economic situation and living standards in Jerusalem, represent a central consideration in forming a negative stereotype about Jerusalem among the Israelis.* They believe that most of the recent bombings inside Israel were executed by Palestinians entering through Jerusalem. According to an opinion poll conducted by the Jerusalem Institute for Israel Studies, 16% of the Israelis expressed fears about visiting Jerusalem, while 27% expressed fears of living in the city (the poll was conducted in the beginning of January 2006).

The Israeli Scenario

Based on these Israeli considerations and ethnocentric perceptions, the following points are advanced by Israel as an axis for "the solution" or "the arrangements" that the Israelis seek to impose in Jerusalem.

- *Jerusalem, as Israel's capital, must have a clear Jewish majority.* Ensuring a perpetual majority will end the "eternal" city's suffering.

- *The solution lies in relinquishing or spinning off Palestinian neighborhoods in the north and east of Jerusalem, i.e situating them in enclaves outside of the city's wall/boundary.* According to the opinion poll conducted by the Jerusalem Institute for Israel Studies (January 2006), 54.5% of the Israelis are willing to part with the Palestinian neighborhoods in Jerusalem and to modify the city's municipal borders for the sake of ensuring a Jewish majority. The present Israeli mode of thinking, based on the euphemistically titled "convergence" or "realignment" plan declared by Israeli Prime Minister Ehud Olmert, is to unilaterally trim the Palestinian neighborhoods from the city while keeping security authorities in them in Israel's hands. According to the conceptions proposed by academic groups, Israel seeks to maintain control over the Old City and its surroundings even though the Palestinian population within these areas ranges from 40 to 80 thousand people. In return, the neighborhoods of Beit Hanina, Shu'fat, Al Issawiya, As Sawahira Al Gharbiya, Sur Bahir and Um Tuba are to be relinquished and trimmed off the city through the wall's path, which will separate them completely from the city. This is the same strategy that effectively moved the neighborhoods of Kafr Aqab, Samiramis, Ras Khamis, Dahiyat As Salam and Shu'fat Refugee Camp outside the present path of the wall.

● *Trimming the Palestinian neighborhoods is paralleled by a process of annexing into the city Jewish settlements from Jerusalem's surroundings to transform Jewish Jerusalem into a spatially contiguous and administratively and functionally integrated metropolitan center.* The concept of the Greater Jewish Jerusalem is vital to the city's image as a metropolitan center and as a would-be national capital.

● *Developing the Old City area and its surroundings within the so-called holy basin,* which includes an area of more than 2,210 dunums (500+ acres), extending from the Mount of Olives to parts of Ras Al Amud and Silwan. (The latter is considered by Jews to be the ancient City of David). This entire area will be red-lined and is not to be given up in any international arrangements or negotiations with Palestinians. According to Israeli strategic planning concepts, this area is considered the nucleus and the heart of Jerusalem's development since it is a political, religious and tourism center and a cultural inheritance forming the basis for the economy of Jerusalem and the development of services associated with its historical and spiritual status.

● *Enforcing control over the Haram Ash-Sharif area.* Israel considers its sovereignty over the Haram Ash-Sharif a historical and societal pillar that must be guaranteed in any political arrangements or settlement; therefore, Israeli control must be enforced through Israeli security control, imposing construction laws, barring the Muslim Waqf (endowments) administration from undertaking any renovation works, and imposing the control of the Israeli Antiquities Authority over the Haram Ash-Sharif area. Enforcing the Israeli control aims at eliminating the possibility of reaching an undesirable settlement for Israel. During the past few years, the issue of the Haram Ash-Sharif underwent transformation from an issue of controlling entrance to the Haram Ash-Sharif area and allowing prayer in it to a "national symbol" issue emphasizing Israel's determination to keep Jerusalem. This transformation occurred in a speedy manner after the second Camp David Summit in 2000 and intensified after the collapse of the religious consensus which forbade "pilgrimage and prayer" in the Haram area. This consensus was based on cleanliness and purity laws, but a significant number of Jewish religious leaders, especially from national religious movements, viewed the courtyards surrounding Al-Aqsa Mosque and the Dome of the Rock as places where prayer will be allowed until the Third Temple is built in place of the Second Temple, which was destroyed in the year 70 AD, according to the Israeli faith. In the Israeli view, the "Jewish linkage" with the Haram Ash-Sharif and its holiness for Jews is a status that must be guaranteed in any future political arrangements and settlements, and the issue is seen as nonnegotiable. That scenario rests on the Israeli presumption that Palestinians misjudge the salience of this issue and lack understanding of its centrality for Israel. In that regard, we should note that only 9% of the Israelis would agree to relinquish the Haram Ash-Sharif while 51% of the Israelis insist on the Haram Ash-Sharif remaining under Israeli sovereignty under any future for Jerusalem [Jerusalem Institute report to Herzeliya Conference, 21-25 January 2006].

The scenario which Israel is imposing on the ground today encompasses a number of strategies that combine to ensure a Jewish hegeonomy in Jerusalem. Some we have already mentioned: trimming-off Palestinian neighborhoods and isolating them from the city; replacing the concept of a unified Jerusalem ("indivisible") with that of a sprawling Greater (Metropolitan) Jewish Jerusalem that annexes to the city outlying settlements and vast spaces in their surroundings; placing the Old City and its adjacent neighborhoods under Israeli control. Parallel to these strategies has been a strengthening of the Ultra Orthodox Haredi settlements in East Jerusalem and a boosting of extremist Jewish religious movements which seek to impose control over the areas surrounding the Haram Ash-Sharif mosque area, including those areas which overlook the gardens of this holy site. This scenario may achieve its goals in the short run, but it marks a major transformation in the conflict by raising the significance of the Jerusalem issue to the level of a comprehensive Pan-Arab/Islam clash with Israel—this, after a four decade diminution of the issue to the point that it had become a national Palestine-Israel issue.

This scenario cannot stand in the long run, notwithstanding imposed Israeli realities. Its chances for success remain marginal on the following grounds.

- There is a contradiction between this arbitrary, confiscatory, and inhuman reality imposed on the ground and the international law and conventions respecting occupation and human rights.

- The unilaterally imposed reality virtually cancels the Palestinian demand for East Jerusalem to become the capital of the Palestinian state, a matter the international community insists be negotiated.

- A demographic solution in isolation from a political settlement serves the Israeli interests only in the short and immediate term. However, its ramifications on the possibility of resolving the conflict and achieving security (including for Israel itself) are dangerous, and the results of this "solution" are unpredictable in terms of the deterioration and exacerbation of the conflict. Clearly, the scenario that Israel wants to impose, especially in the Old City and its surroundings, intensifies the conflict and transforms it into a conflict over Jerusalem's religious identity, which brings in external parties, principally other Arab states and Muslim countries, which have remained rather passive until today.

- Israel seeks, under the best circumstances and on the basis of its definition of its interests, to transform the Palestinian-Israeli conflict into a dispute over borders with a Palestinian entity enjoying only limited authority. It believes that such a transformation will allow it to push the issue of Jerusalem off the negotiations agenda. This approach will be rejected by the Palestinians, and it will also be difficult to gather support for that shift from the international community.

- International recognition of Jerusalem as Israel's capital cannot be achieved without a political settlement.

- The pluralistic nature of Jerusalem is impossible to preserve under Israel's plan to Judaize the entire city and subject it to its sovereignty and control. The Jerusalem urban fabric lies at the heart of its identity and at the center of its external image. Colonial images that the Israeli imposed realities scenario would create are also alien to the world at large. Jerusalem cannot be a city, a center and a capital unless a political settlement is reached with international intervention; and without international participation the city cannot maximize the international role and status the city has heretofore enjoyed. Strengthening Jerusalem and transforming it into an Israeli center has failed until today and has no chance except through a political settlement and partnership in peace with the Palestinian side and through establishing a viable Palestinian state.

Mapping a Palestinian Response to the Israeli Scenario

It follows from the preceding discussion that the Palestinian side has to develop a reconciliation map for Jerusalem, in a manner based not only on the Palestinian general demands of sovereignty and the national right, but also based on merging these demands with a plan that determines the means of responding to the functional conditions that must be achieved in the settlement establishing a viable Palestinian state. The settlement must provide for Jerusalem to become a capital capable of responding to the demands and aspirations of the Palestinian people, a state that applies international law and enjoys legitimacy, and one that achieves a centrality for the city as an economic and administrative capital. Thus, it is not possible to accept the geo-political reality imposed on the ground by Israel in Jerusalem as a given fact.

The following points represent the broad lines of a map of Palestinian interests that should be protected in future negotiations or advanced to international parties in the event of an Israeli refusal to negotiate with the Palestinian side and to continue in its implementation of unilateral measures. These guidelines are general suggestions that will require elaboration and further detail. They are subject to the considerations of decision-makers, and to conditions that will evolve when the issue of Jerusalem is raised in the frame of any future negotiations between the two parties.

Legal, administrative, theoretical and practical international terms of reference must be set that form principles for evaluating the reality created by the wall and the settlements and their negative effect on the establishment of a Palestinian state and a capital capable of meeting its people's needs and performing its functions.

It must be possible to implement any negotiated solution effectively, and the solution must positively impact the economic, social and political transformation processes for the sake of achieving sustainable development. Otherwise, it will be impossible to reach stability and security in the city and between the Palestinians and Israelis.

In order to achieve Palestinian-Israeli peace and security in Jerusalem, there must be a proposal that responds to the Palestinian national rights and contributes to building a viable Palestinian state and a vibrant capital alongside Israel. In the following we propose axis points that must be taken into consideration in any proposition for a future settlement:

1. Rejection of any geo-demographic Israeli territorial and demographic domination facts or formula as a starting basis for the solution.

2. Not starting from the present political and administrative borders as a basis for the solution. Such "facts on the ground" are not to be accorded automatic legitimacy.

3. Negotiations should proceed from an acceptance of international legitimacy principles with only minor modifications at the implementation phase.

4. The national borders are to be agreed in accordance with the truce of 1949; municipal borders should be based on those that prevailed during the Jordanian era, reflecting Jerusalem's role as the heart and center of the future Palestinian state.

5. Rejection of any proposal for a new re-definition of the Palestinian Jerusalem that excludes the Old City and the neighborhoods surrounding it. The Old City represents the nucleus of the historical Jerusalem and the center of Palestinian culture.

6. Are-parceling of the East Jerusalem space must take place based on planning it as a Palestinian center with contiguity with the cities and areas surrounding.

7. The Palestinian definition of Jerusalem's municipal and the metropolis borders is an administrative and service issue subject to Palestinian considerations linked to the Palestinian urban functions and the strong relationship of Jerusalem with all of the West Bank territories.

8. There must be a geographic contiguity of the neighborhoods with each other and with the city center, and a connectedness with the cities and neighborhoods of the Palestinian Jerusalem metropolis, especially Ramallah and Bethlehem. Therefore, intensive efforts must be launched to stop the Ma'aleh Adumim expansion scheme and its annexation to Jerusalem within the so called El Area where construction has recently begun.

9. The future absorptive capacity and expansion and development trends and the various functions performed by Jerusalem must be on the basis of discussion of any geo-political proposals concerning the future of Jerusalem.

10. Any settlement must provide for the realization of developmental/economic/structural conditions for the city to perform its functions as a Palestinian center and a capital. There must be the possibility of establishing new neighborhoods to absorb the natural population growth and immigration into the capital, taking into consideration such factors as the distribution of the population densities and their relationship to the historical and religious nature of the city, the climatic nature, and the preservation of the environment (including the outskirts of the desert, natural reserves areas in the east, and green areas).

11. An agreement must define the relationship with West Jerusalem and develop clear mechanisms for the daily relations on the strategic and functional levels, as well as determining areas and functions that require cooperation and partnership.

12. Determining the city's international functions and the nature of the international parties and actors involved in the city and how their interests relate to the city's future. (This includes preparing scenarios for the roles of the international parties in reaching a settlement acceptable to both parties in any conflict over Jerusalem).

13. Developing functional zones, for especially higher education, light industries, tourism, information technology, state institutions, embassies and international organizations.

Israel may seek to impose a unilateral plan that would cancel the scenario implicit in the conditions detailed above and cancel the Palestinian national demand for Jerusalem to be a capital for two states. They may proceed with the establishment of the wall in spite of its negative effects and may attempt to impose the path of the wall as a border. But experience has shown that it is nevertheless possible to reconsider any imposed reality which was considered in the past as irreversible. Thus, Israeli actions notwithstanding, a different geo-political map could be drawn that takes into consideration the Palestinian needs and demands. "Facts on the ground", past or future, need not be eternal.

Other Publications by the International Peace and Cooperation Center:

"Conflict Over Housing: The Housing Sector in Jerusalem: Existing Situation, Barriers, Needs and Future Policies". (2006). (in Arabic).

"Discrimination in the Heart of the Holy City". (2006).

"Divided Cities in Transition". (2003).

"Divided Cities in Transition II". (2005).

"Envisioning the Future of Jerusalem". (2003).

"Jerusalem in the Future: Scenarios and a Shared Vision". (2006).

"Jerusalem in the Future: Scenarios and a Shared Vision". (2006). (in Arabic).

"The Jerusalem Urban Fabric: Demography, Infrastructure, and Institutions". (2003).

"Jerusalem on the Map". (2003).

"Jerusalem on the Map II". (2005).

"Jerusalem: The City of Lost Peace: The Geo-Political Proposals from the Beginning of the 20th Century until the Unilateral Convergence Plan 2006". (2006). (in Arabic).

"The Wall of Annexation and Expansion in the Jerusalem Area". (2005).